Praise for *Presto: The Definitive Guide*

This book provides a great introduction to Presto and teaches you everything you need to know to start your successful usage of Presto.

—*Dain Sundstrom and David Phillips, Creators of the Presto Projects and Founders of the Presto Software Foundation*

Presto plays a key role in enabling analysis at Pinterest. This book covers the Presto essentials, from use cases through how to run Presto at massive scale.

—*Ashish Kumar Singh, Tech Lead, Bigdata Query Processing Platform, Pinterest*

Presto has set the bar in both community-building and technical excellence for lightning-fast analytical processing on stored data in modern cloud architectures. This book is a must-read for companies looking to modernize their analytics stack.

—*Jay Kreps, Cocreator of Apache Kafka, Cofounder and CEO of Confluent*

Presto has saved us all—both in academia and industry—countless hours of work, allowing us all to avoid having to write code to manage distributed query processing. We're so grateful to have a high-quality open source distributed SQL engine to start from, enabling us to focus on innovating in new areas instead of reinventing the wheel for each new distributed data system project.

—*Daniel Abadi, Professor of Computer Science, University of Maryland, College Park*

Presto: The Definitive Guide

SQL at Any Scale, on Any Storage,
in Any Environment

Matt Fuller, Manfred Moser, and Martin Traverso

Beijing · Boston · Farnham · Sebastopol · Tokyo

Presto: The Definitive Guide

by Matt Fuller, Manfred Moser, and Martin Traverso

Published by O'Reilly Media, Inc., 1005 Gravenstein Highway North, Sebastopol, CA 95472.

O'Reilly books may be purchased for educational, business, or sales promotional use. Online editions are also available for most titles (*http://oreilly.com*). For more information, contact our corporate/institutional sales department: 800-998-9938 or *corporate@oreilly.com*.

Acquisition Editor: Jonathan Hassell	**Indexer:** Potomac Indexing, LLC
Development Editor: Michele Cronin	**Interior Designer:** David Futato
Production Editor: Elizabeth Kelly	**Cover Designer:** Karen Montgomery
Copyeditor: Sharon Wilkey	**Illustrator:** Rebecca Demarest
Proofreader: Piper Editorial	

April 2020:   First Edition

Revision History for the First Edition
2020-04-03:   First release

See *http://oreilly.com/catalog/errata.csp?isbn=9781492044277* for release details.

978-1-492-04427-7

[LSI]

Table of Contents

Part I.   Getting Started with Presto

Part II. Diving Deeper into Presto

Foreword

What a tremendous ride it has been so far! Looking back at the time when we started the Presto project at Facebook in 2012, we certainly thought that we were going to create something useful. We always planned to have a successful open source project and community, and we released Presto in 2013 under the Apache License.

How far Presto has come since then, however, is beyond what we imagined. We are proud of the project community's accomplishments, but, more importantly, we are very humbled by all the positive feedback and help we have received.

Presto has grown tremendously and provided a lot of value to its large community of users. You can find fellow Presto community members across the globe, and developers in Brazil, Canada, China, Germany, India, Israel, Japan, Poland, Singapore, the United States, the United Kingdom, and other countries.

Launching the Presto Software Foundation in early 2019 was another major milestone. The not-for-profit organization is dedicated to the advancement of the Presto open source distributed SQL engine. The foundation is committed to ensuring that the project remains open, collaborative, and independent for decades to come.

Now, about one year after the launch of the foundation, we can look back at an accelerated rate of impressive contributions from a larger community.

We are pleased that Matt, Manfred, and Martin created this book about Presto with the help of O'Reilly. It provides a great introduction to Presto and teaches you everything you need to know to start using it successfully.

Enjoy the journey into the depths of Presto and the related world of business intelligence, reporting, dashboard creation, data warehousing, data mining, machine learning, and beyond.

Of course, make sure to dive into the additional resources and help we offer on the Presto website at *https://prestosql.io*, the community chat, the source repository, and beyond.

Welcome to the Presto community!

— Dain Sundstrom and David Phillips
Creators of the Presto Projects and Founders of the
Presto Software Foundation

Preface

About the Book

Presto: The Definitive Guide is the first and foremost book about the Presto distributed query engine. The book is aimed at beginners and existing users of Presto alike. Ideally, you have some understanding of databases and SQL, but if not, you can divert from reading and look things up while working your way through this book. No matter your level of expertise, we are sure that you'll learn something new from this book.

The first part of the book introduces you to Presto and then helps you get up and running quickly so you can start learning how to use it. This includes installation and first use of the command-line interface as well as many client- and web-based applications, such as SQL database management or dashboard and reporting tools, using the JDBC driver.

The second part of the book advances your knowledge and includes details about the Presto architecture, cluster deployment, many connectors to data sources, and a lot of information about the main power of Presto—querying any data source with SQL.

The third part of the book rounds out the content with further aspects you need to know when running and using a production Presto deployment. This includes Web UI usage, security configuration, and some discussion of real-world uses of Presto in other organizations.

Conventions Used in This Book

The following typographical conventions are used in this book:

Italic
Indicates new terms, URLs, email addresses, filenames, and file extensions.

`Constant width`
Used for program listings, as well as within paragraphs to refer to program elements such as variable or function names, databases, data types, environment variables, statements, and keywords.

`Constant width bold`
Shows commands or other text that should be typed literally by the user.

`Constant width italic`
Shows text that should be replaced with user-supplied values or by values determined by context.

 This element signifies a tip or suggestion.

 This element signifies a general note.

 This element indicates a warning or caution.

Code Examples, Permissions, and Attribution

Supplemental material for the book is documented in greater detail in "Book Repository" on page 15.

If you have a technical question, or a problem using the code examples, please contact us on the community chat—see "Community Chat" on page 13—or file issues on the book repository.

This book is here to help you get your job done. In general, if example code is offered with this book, you may use it in your programs and documentation. You do not need to contact us for permission unless you're reproducing a significant portion of the code. For example, writing a program that uses several chunks of code from this book does not require permission. Selling or distributing examples from O'Reilly books does require permission. Answering a question by citing this book and quoting example code does not require permission. Incorporating a significant amount of example code from this book into your product's documentation does require permission.

We appreciate, but generally do not require, attribution. An attribution usually includes the title, author, publisher, and ISBN. For example: *"Presto: The Definitive Guide* by Matt Fuller, Manfred Moser, and Martin Traverso (O'Reilly). Copyright 2020 Matt Fuller, Martin Traverso, and Simpligility Technologies Inc., 978-1-492-04427-7.

If you feel your use of code examples falls outside fair use or the permission given above, feel free to contact us *permissions@oreilly.com*.

O'Reilly Online Learning

 For more than 40 years, O'Reilly Media (*http://oreilly.com*) has provided technology and business training, knowledge, and insight to help companies succeed.

Our unique network of experts and innovators share their knowledge and expertise through books, articles, and our online learning platform. O'Reilly's online learning platform gives you on-demand access to live training courses, in-depth learning paths, interactive coding environments, and a vast collection of text and video from O'Reilly and 200+ other publishers. For more information, visit *http://oreilly.com*.

How to Contact Us

Please address comments and questions concerning this book to the publisher:

O'Reilly Media, Inc.
1005 Gravenstein Highway North
Sebastopol, CA 95472
800-998-9938 (in the United States or Canada)
707-829-0515 (international or local)
707-829-0104 (fax)

We have a web page for this book, where we list errata, examples, and any additional information. You can access this page at *https://oreil.ly/PrestoTDG*.

Email *bookquestions@oreilly.com* to comment or ask technical questions about this book.

to learn more about our books, courses, and news, visit *http://www.oreilly.com*.

Find us on Facebook: *http://facebook.com/oreilly*

Follow us on Twitter: *http://twitter.com/oreillymedia*

Watch us on YouTube: *http://www.youtube.com/oreillymedia*

Acknowledgments

We would like to thank everyone in the larger Presto community for using Presto, spreading the word, helping other users, contributing to the project, and even committing to the code or documentation. We are excited to be part of the community and look forward to many shared successes in the future.

A critical part of the Presto community is Starburst. We want to thank everyone at Starburst for their help and really appreciate the work, resources, stability, and support Starburst provides to the project, its customers using Presto, and the authors, who are part of the Starburst team.

Specifically related to the book, we would like to thank everyone who helped us with idea, input, and reviews, including the following, probably incomplete list of people:

Anu Sundarsan, Dain Sundstrom, David Phillips, Grzegorz Kokosiński, Jeffrey Breen, Jess Iandiorio, Justin Borgman, Kamil Bajda-Pawlikowski, Karol Sobczak, Kevin Kline, Megan Sifferlen, Neeraj Soparawala, Piotr Findeisen, Raghav Sethi, Thomas Nield, Tom Nats, Will Morrison, and Wojciech Biela.

In addition, the authors want to express their personal gratitude:

Matt would like to thank his wife, Meghan, and his three children, Emily, Hannah, and Liam, for their patience and encouragement while Matt worked on the book. The kids' excitement about their dad becoming an "author" helped Matt through many long weekends and late nights.

Manfred would like to thank his wife, Yen, and his three sons, Lukas, Nikolas, and Tobias, not only for putting up with the tech-mumbo-jumbo but also for genuinely sharing an interest and passion for technology, writing, learning, and teaching.

Martin would like to thank his wife, Melina, and his four children, Marcos, Victoria, Joaquin, and Martina, for their support and enthusiasm over the past seven years of working on Presto.

PART I

Getting Started with Presto

Presto is a SQL query engine enabling SQL access to any data source. You can use Presto to query very large data sets by horizontally scaling the query processing.

In this first part, you learn about Presto and its use cases. Then you move on to get a simple Presto installation up and running. And finally, you learn about the tools you can use to connect to Presto and query the data. You get to concentrate on a minimal setup so you can start using Presto successfully as quickly as possible.

CHAPTER 1

Introducing Presto

So you heard of Presto and found this book. Or maybe you are just browsing this first section and wondering whether you should dive in. In this introductory chapter, we discuss the problems you may be encountering with the massive growth of data creation, and the value locked away within that data. Presto is a key enabler to working with all the data and providing access to it with proven successful tools around Structured Query Language (SQL).

The design and features of Presto enable you to get better insights, beyond those accessible to you now. You can gain these insights faster, as well as get information that you could not get in the past because it cost too much or took too long to obtain. And for all that, you end up using fewer resources and therefore spending less of your budget, which you can then use to learn even more!

We also point you to more resources beyond this book but, of course, we hope you join us here first.

The Problems with Big Data

Everybody is capturing more and more data from device metrics, user behavior tracking, business transactions, location data, software and system testing procedures and workflows, and much more. The insights gained from understanding that data and working with it can make or break the success of any initiative, or even a company.

At the same time, the diversity of storage mechanisms available for data has exploded: relational databases, NoSQL databases, document databases, key-value stores, object storage systems, and so on. Many of them are necessary in today's organizations, and it is no longer possible to use just one of them. As you can see in Figure 1-1, dealing with this can be a daunting task that feels overwhelming.

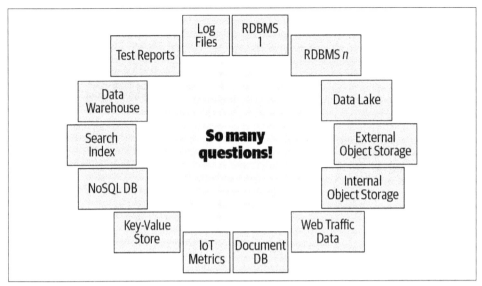

Figure 1-1. Big data can be overwhelming

In addition, all these different systems do not allow you to query and inspect the data with standard tools. Different query languages and analysis tools for niche systems are everywhere. Meanwhile, your business analysts are used to the industry standard, SQL. A myriad of powerful tools rely on SQL for analytics, dashboard creation, rich reporting, and other business intelligence work.

The data is distributed across various silos, and some of them can not even be queried at the necessary performance for your analytics needs. Other systems, unlike modern cloud applications, store data in monolithic systems that cannot scale horizontally. Without these capabilities, you are narrowing the number of potential use cases and users, and therefore the usefulness of the data.

The traditional approach of creating and maintaining large, dedicated data warehouses has proven to be very expensive in organizations across the globe. Most often, this approach is also found to be too slow and cumbersome for many users and usage patterns.

You can see the tremendous opportunity for a system to unlock all this value.

Presto to the Rescue

Presto is capable of solving all these problems, and of unlocking new opportunities with federated queries to disparate systems, parallel queries, horizontal cluster scaling, and much more. You can see the Presto project logo in Figure 1-2.

Figure 1-2. Presto logo

Presto is an open source, distributed SQL query engine. It was designed and written from the ground up to efficiently query data against disparate data sources of all sizes, ranging from gigabytes to petabytes. Presto breaks the false choice between having fast analytics using an expensive commercial solution, or using a slow "free" solution that requires excessive hardware.

Designed for Performance and Scale

Presto is a tool designed to efficiently query vast amounts of data by using distributed execution. If you have terabytes or even petabytes of data to query, you are likely using tools such as Apache Hive that interact with Hadoop and its Hadoop Distributed File System (HDFS). Presto is designed as an alternative to these tools to more efficiently query that data.

Analysts, who expect SQL response times from milliseconds for real-time analysis to seconds and minutes, should use Presto. Presto supports SQL, commonly used in data warehousing and analytics for analyzing data, aggregating large amounts of data, and producing reports. These workloads are often classified as *online analytical processing (OLAP)*.

Even though Presto understands and can efficiently execute SQL, Presto is *not* a database, as it does not include its own data storage system. It is not meant to be a general-purpose relational database that serves to replace Microsoft SQL Server, Oracle Database, MySQL, or PostgreSQL. Further, Presto is not designed to handle online transaction processing (OLTP). This is also true of other databases designed and optimized for data warehousing or analytics, such as Teradata, Netezza, Vertica, and Amazon Redshift.

Presto leverages both well-known and novel techniques for distributed query processing. These techniques include in-memory parallel processing, pipelined execution across nodes in the cluster, a multithreaded execution model to keep all the CPU cores busy, efficient flat-memory data structures to minimize Java garbage collection, and Java bytecode generation. A detailed description of these complex Presto internals is beyond the scope of this book. For Presto users, these techniques translate into faster insights into your data at a fraction of the cost of other solutions.

SQL-on-Anything

Presto was initially designed to query data from HDFS. And it can do that very effi-ciently, as you learn later. But that is not where it ends. On the contrary, Presto is a query engine that can query data from object storage, relational database manage-ment systems (RDBMSs), NoSQL databases, and other systems, as shown in Figure 1-3.

Presto queries data where it lives and does not require a migration of data to a single location. So Presto allows you to query data in HDFS and other distributed object storage systems. It allows you to query RDBMSs and other data sources. As such, it can really query data wherever it lives and therefore be a replacement to the tradi-tional, expensive, and heavy extract, transform, and load (ETL) processes. Or at a minimum, it can help you with them and lighten the load. So Presto is clearly not just another SQL-on-Hadoop solution.

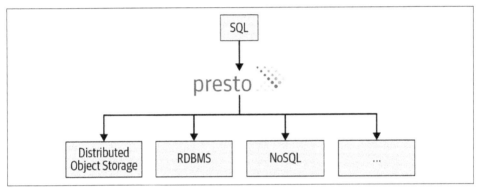

Figure 1-3. SQL support for a variety of data sources with Presto

Object storage systems include Amazon Web Services (AWS) Simple Storage Service (S3), Microsoft Azure Blob Storage, Google Cloud Storage, and S3-compatible stor-age such as MinIO and Ceph. Presto can query traditional RDBMSs such as Micro-soft SQL Server, PostgreSQL, MySQL, Oracle, Teradata, and Amazon Redshift. Presto can also query NoSQL systems such as Apache Cassandra, Apache Kafka, MongoDB, or Elasticsearch. Presto can query virtually anything and is truly a SQL-on-Anything system.

For users, this means that suddenly they no longer have to rely on specific query lan-guages or tools to interact with the data in those specific systems. They can simply leverage Presto and their existing SQL skills and their well-understood analytics, dashboarding, and reporting tools. These tools, built on top of using SQL, allow analysis of those additional data sets, which are otherwise locked in separate systems. Users can even use Presto to query across different systems with the SQL they know.

Separation of Data Storage and Query Compute Resources

Presto is not a database with storage; rather, it simply queries data where it lives. When using Presto, storage and compute are decoupled and can be scaled independently. Presto represents the compute layer, whereas the underlying data sources represent the storage layer.

This allows Presto to scale up and down its compute resources for query processing, based on analytics demand to access this data. There is no need to move your data, and provision compute and storage to the exact needs of the current queries, or change that regularly, based on your changing query needs.

Presto can scale the query power by scaling the compute cluster dynamically, and the data can be queried right where it lives in the data source. This characteristic allows you to greatly optimize your hardware resource needs and therefore reduce cost.

Presto Use Cases

The flexibility and powerful features of Presto allow you to decide for yourself how exactly you are using Presto, and what benefits you value and want to take advantage of. You can start with only one small use for a particular problem. Most Presto users start like that.

Once you and other Presto users in your organization have gotten used to the benefits and features, you'll discover new situations. Word spreads, and soon you see a myriad of needs being satisfied by Presto accessing a variety of data sources.

In the following section, we discuss several of these use cases. Keep in mind that you can expand your use to cover them all. On the other hand, it is also perfectly fine to solve one particular problem with Presto. Just be prepared to like Presto and increase its use after all.

One SQL Analytics Access Point

RDBMSs and the use of SQL have been around a long time and have proven to be very useful. No organization runs without them. In fact, most companies run multiple systems. Large commercial databases like Oracle Database or IBM DB2 are probably backing your enterprise software. Open source systems like MariaDB or PostgreSQL may be used for other solutions and a couple of in-house applications.

As a consumer and analyst, you likely run into numerous problems:

- Sometimes you do not know where data is even available for you to use, and only tribal knowledge in the company, or years of experience with internal setups, can help you find the right data.

- Querying the various source databases requires you to use different connections, as well as different queries running different SQL dialects. They are similar enough to look the same, but they behave just differently enough to cause confusion and the need to learn the details.

- You cannot combine the data from different systems in a query without using the data warehouse.

Presto allows you to get around these problems. You can expose all these databases in one location: Presto.

You can use one SQL standard to query all systems—standardized SQL, functions, and operators supported by Presto.

All your dashboarding and analytics tools, and other systems for your business intelligence needs, can point to one system, Presto, and have access to all data in your organization.

Access Point to Data Warehouse and Source Systems

When organizations find the need to better understand and analyze data in their numerous RDBMSs, the creation and maintenance of data warehouse systems comes into play. Select data from various systems is then going through complex ETL processes and, often via long-running batch jobs, ends up in a tightly controlled, massive data warehouse.

While this helps you a lot in many cases, as a data analyst, you now encounter new problems:

- Now you have another entry point, in addition to all the databases themselves, for your tools and queries.

- The data you specifically need today is not in the data warehouse. Getting the data added is a painful, expensive process full of hurdles.

Presto allows you to add any data warehouse database as a data source, just like any other relational database.

If you want to dive deeper into a data warehouse query, you can do it right there in the same system. You can access the data warehouse *and* the source database system in the same place and even write queries that combine them. Presto allows you to query any database in the same system, data warehouse, source database, and any other database.

Provide SQL-Based Access to Anything

The days of using only RDBMSs are long gone. Data is now stored in many disparate systems optimized for relevant use cases. Object-based storage, key-value stores, document databases, graph databases, event-streaming systems, and other so-called NoSQL systems all provide unique features and advantages.

At least some of these systems are in use in your organization, holding data that's crucial for understanding and improving your business.

Of course, all of these systems also require you to use different tools and technologies to query and work with the data.

At a minimum, this is a complex task with a huge learning curve. More likely, however, you end up only scratching the surface of your data and not really gaining a complete understanding. You lack a good way to query the data. Tools to visualize and analyze in more detail are hard to find or simply don't exist.

Presto, on the other hand, allows you to connect to all these systems as a data source. It exposes the data to query with standard American National Standards Institute (ANSI) SQL and all the tooling using SQL, as shown in Figure 1-4.

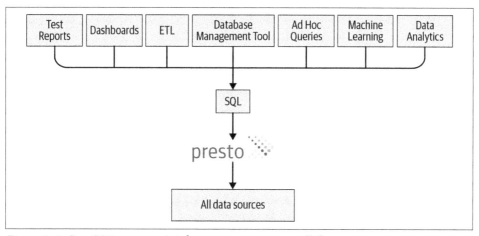

Figure 1-4. One SQL access point for many use cases to all data sources

So with Presto, understanding the data in all these vastly different systems becomes much simpler, or even possible, for the first time.

Federated Queries

Exposing all the data silos in Presto is a large step toward understanding your data. You can use SQL and standard tools to query them all. However, often the questions you want answered require you to reach into the data silos, pull aspects out of them, and then combine them in a local manner.

Presto allows you to do that by using federated queries. A *federated query* is a SQL query that references and uses different databases and schemas from entirely different systems in the same statement. All the data sources in Presto are available for you to query at the same time, with the same SQL in the same query.

You can define the relationships between the user-tracking information from your object storage with the customer data in your RDBMS. If your key-value store contains more related information, you can hook it into your query as well.

Using federated queries with Presto allows you to gain insights that you could not learn about otherwise.

Semantic Layer for a Virtual Data Warehouse

Data warehouse systems have created not only huge benefits for users but also a burden on organizations:

- Running and maintaining the data warehouse is a large, expensive project.
- Dedicated teams run and manage the data warehouse and the associated ETL processes.
- Getting the data into the warehouse requires users to break through red tape and typically takes too much time.

Presto, on the other hand, can be used as a virtual data warehouse. It can be used to define your semantic layer by using one tool and standard ANSI SQL. Once all the databases are configured as data sources in Presto, you can query them. Presto provides the necessary compute power to query the storage in the databases. Using SQL and the supported functions and operators, Presto can provide you the desired data straight from the source. There is no need to copy, move, or transform the data before you can use it for your analysis.

Thanks to the standard SQL support against all connected data sources, you can create the desired semantic layer for querying from tools and end users in a simpler fashion. And that layer can encompass all underlying data sources without the need to migrate any data. Presto can query the data at the source and storage level.

Using Presto as this "on-the-fly data warehouse" provides organizations the potential to enhance their existing data warehouse with additional capabilities, or even to avoid building and maintaining a warehouse altogether.

Data Lake Query Engine

The term *data lake* is often used for a large HDFS or similar distributed object storage system into which all sorts of data is dumped without much thought about accessing it. Presto unlocks this to become a useful data warehouse. In fact, Presto emerged from Facebook as a way to tackle faster and more powerful querying of a very large Hadoop data warehouse than what Hive and other tools could provide. This led to the Presto Hive connector, discussed in "Hive Connector for Distributed Storage Data Sources" on page 93.

Modern data lakes now often use other object storage systems beyond HDFS from cloud providers or other open source projects. Presto is able to use the Hive connector against any of them and hence enable SQL-based analytics on your data lake, wherever it is located and however it stores the data.

SQL Conversions and ETL

With support for RDBMSs and other data storage systems alike, Presto can be used to move data. SQL, and the rich set of SQL functions available, allow you to query data, transform it, and then write it to the same data source or any other data source.

In practice, this means that you can copy data out of your object storage system or key-value store and into a RDBMS, and use it for your analytics going forward. Of course, you can also transform and aggregate the data to gain new understanding.

On the other hand, it is also common to take data from an operational RDBMS, or maybe an event-streaming system like Kafka, and move it into a data lake to ease the burden on the RDBMS in terms of querying by many analysts. ETL processes, now often also called data preparation, can be an important part of this process to improve the data and create a data model better suited for querying and analysis.

In this scenario, Presto is a critical part of an overall data management solution.

Better Insights Due to Faster Response Times

Asking complex questions and using massive data sets always runs into limitations. It might end up being too expensive to copy the data and load it into your data warehouse and analyze it there. The computations require too much compute power to be able to run them at all, or it takes numerous days to get an answer.

Presto avoids data copying by design. Parallel processing and heavy optimizations regularly lead to performance improvements for your analysis with Presto.

If a query that used to take three days can now run in 15 minutes, it might be worth running it after all. And the knowledge gained from the results gives you an advantage and the capacity to run yet more queries.

These faster processing times of Presto enable better analytics and results.

Big Data, Machine Learning, and Artificial Intelligence

The fact that Presto exposes more and more data to standard tooling around SQL, and scales querying to massive data sets, makes it a prime tool for big data processing. Now this often includes statistical analysis and grows in complexity toward machine learning and artificial intelligence systems. With the support for R and other tools, Presto definitely has a role to play in these use cases.

Other Use Cases

In the prior sections, we provided a high-level overview of Presto use cases. New use cases and combinations are emerging regularly.

In Chapter 13, you can learn details about the use of Presto by some well-known companies and organizations. We present that information toward the end of the book so you can first gain the knowledge required to understand the data at hand by reading the following chapters.

Presto Resources

Beyond this book, many more resources are available that allow you to expand your knowledge about Presto. In this section, we enumerate the important starting points. Most of them contain a lot of information and include pointers to further resources.

Website

The *Presto Software Foundation* governs the community of the open source Presto project and maintains the project website. You can see the home page in Figure 1-5. The website contains documentation, contact details, community blog posts with the latest news and events, and other information at *https://prestosql.io*.

Figure 1-5. Home page of Presto website at prestosql.io

Documentation

The detailed documentation for Presto is maintained as part of the code base and is available on the website. It includes high-level overviews as well as detailed reference information about the SQL support, functions and operators, connectors, configuration, and much more. You also find release notes with details of latest changes there. Get started at *https://prestosql.io/docs*.

Community Chat

The community of beginner, advanced, and expert users, as well as the contributors and maintainers of Presto, is very supportive and actively collaborates every day on the community chat available at *https://prestosql.slack.com*.

Join the *general* channel, and then check out the numerous channels focusing on various topics such as bug triage, releases, and development.

You can find Matt, Manfred, and Martin on the community chat nearly every day, and we would love to hear from you there.

Source Code, License, and Version

Presto is an open source project distributed under the Apache License, v2 with the source code managed and available in the Git repository at *https://github.com/prestosql/presto*.

The `prestosql` organization at *https://github.com/prestosql* contains numerous other repositories related to the project, such as the source code of the website, clients, other components, or the contributor license management repository.

Presto is an active open source project with frequent releases. By using the most recent version, you are able to take advantage of the latest features, bug fixes, and performance improvements. This book refers to, and uses, the latest Presto version 330 at the time of writing. If you choose a different and more recent version of Presto, it should work the same as described in this book. While it's unlikely you'll run into issues, it is important to refer to the release notes and documentation for any changes.

Contributing

As we've mentioned, Presto is a community-driven, open source project, and your contributions are welcome and encouraged. The project is very active on the community chat, and committers and other developers are available to help there.

Here are a few tasks to get started with contributing:

- Check out the Developer Guide section of the documentation.
- Learn to build the project from source with instructions in the *README* file.
- Read the research papers linked on the Community page of the website.
- Read the Code of Conduct from the same page.
- Find an issue with the label *good first issue*.
- Sign the contributor license agreement (CLA).

The project continues to receive contributions with a wide range of complexity—from small documentation improvements, to new connectors or other plug-ins, all the way to improvements deep in the internals of Presto.

Of course, any work you do with and around Presto is welcome in the community. This certainly includes seemingly unrelated work such as writing blog posts, presenting at user group meetings or conferences, or writing and managing a plug-in on your own, maybe to a database system you use.

Overall, we encourage you to work with the team and get involved. The project grows and thrives with contributions from everyone. We are ready to help. You can do it!

Book Repository

We provide resources related to this book—such as configuration file examples, SQL queries, data sets and more—in a Git repository for your convenience.

Find it at *https://github.com/prestosql/presto-the-definitive-guide*, and download the content as an archive file or clone the repository with git.

Feel free to create a pull request for any corrections, desired additions, or file issues if you encounter any problems.

Iris Data Set

In later sections of this book, you are going to encounter example queries and use cases that talk about iris flowers (*https://en.wikipedia.org/wiki/Iris_(plant)*) and the iris data set. The reason is a famous data set, commonly used in data science classification examples, which is all about iris flowers.

The data set consists of one simple table of 150 records and columns with values for sepal length, sepal width, petal length, petal width, and species.

The small size allows users to test and run queries easily and perform a wide range of analyses. This makes the data set suitable for learning, including for use with Presto. You can find out more about the data set on the Wikipedia page about it (*https://en.wikipedia.org/wiki/Iris_flower_data_set*).

Our book repository contains the directory *iris-data-set* with the data in comma-separated values (CSV) format, as well as a SQL file to create a table and insert it. After reading Chapter 2 and "Presto Command-Line Interface" on page 25, the following instructions are easy to follow.

You can use the data set by first copying the *etc/catalog/memory.properties* file into the same location as your Presto installation and restarting Presto.

Now you can use the Presto CLI to get the data set into the iris table in the default schema of the memory catalog:

```
$ presto -f iris-data-set/iris-data-set.sql
USE
CREATE TABLE
INSERT: 150 rows
```

Confirm that the data can be queried:

```
$ presto --execute 'SELECT * FROM memory.default.iris;'
"5.1","3.5","1.4","0.2","setosa"
"4.9","3.0","1.4","0.2","setosa"
"4.7","3.2","1.3","0.2","setosa"
...
```

Alternatively, you can run the queries in any SQL management tool connected to Presto; for example, with the Java Database Connectivity (JDBC) driver described in "Presto JDBC Driver" on page 30.

Later sections include example queries to run with this data set in Chapter 8 and Chapter 9, as well as information about the memory connector in "Memory Connector" on page 107.

Flight Data Set

Similar to the iris data set, the flight data set is used later in this book for example queries and usage. The data set is a bit more complex than the iris data set, consisting of lookup tables for carriers, airports, and other information, as well as transactional data about specific flights. This makes the data set suitable for more complex queries using joins and for use in federated queries, where different tables are located in different data sources.

The data is collected from the Federal Aviation Administration (FAA) and curated for analysis. The `flights` table schema is fairly large, with a subset of the available columns shown in Table 1-1.

Table 1-1. Subset of available columns

flightdate	airlineid	origin	dest	arrtime	deptime

Each row in the data set represents either a departure or an arrival of a flight at an airport in the United States.

The book repository—see "Book Repository" on page 15—contains a separate folder, *flight-data-set*. It contains instructions on how to import the data into different database systems, so that you can hook them up to Presto and run the example queries.

A Brief History of Presto

In 2008, Facebook open sourced Hive, later to become Apache Hive. Hive became widely used within Facebook for running analytics against data in HDFS on its very large Apache Hadoop cluster.

Data analysts at Facebook used Hive to run interactive queries on its large data warehouse. Before Presto existed at Facebook, all data analysis relied on Hive, which was not suitable for interactive queries at Facebook's scale. In 2012, its Hive data warehouse was 250 petabytes in size and needed to handle hundreds of users issuing tens of thousands of queries each day. Hive started to hit its limit within Facebook and did not provide the ability to query other data sources within Facebook.

Presto was designed from the ground up to run fast queries at Facebook scale. Rather than create a new system to move the data to, Presto was designed to read the data from where it is stored via its pluggable connector system. One of the first connectors developed for Presto was the Hive connector; see "Hive Connector for Distributed Storage Data Sources" on page 93. This connector queries data stored in a Hive data warehouse directly.

In 2012, four Facebook engineers started Presto development to address the performance, scalability, and extensibility needs for analytics at Facebook. From the beginning, the intent was to build Presto as an open source project. At the beginning of 2013, the initial version of Presto was rolled out in production at Facebook. By the fall of 2013, Presto was officially open sourced by Facebook. Seeing the success at Facebook, other large web-scale companies started to adopt Presto, including Netflix, LinkedIn, Treasure Data, and others. Many companies continued to follow.

In 2015, Teradata announced a large commitment of 20 engineers contributing to Presto, focused on adding enterprise features such as security enhancements and ecosystem tool integration. Later in 2015, Amazon added Presto to its AWS Elastic MapReduce (EMR) offering. In 2016, Amazon announced Athena, in which Presto serves as a major foundational piece. And 2017 saw the creation of Starburst, a company dedicated to driving the success of Presto everywhere.

At the end of 2018, the original creators of Presto left Facebook and founded the Presto Software Foundation to ensure that the project remains collaborative and independent. Since then, the innovation and growth of the project has accelerated even more.

Today, the Presto community thrives and grows, and Presto continues to be used at large scale by many well-known companies. The project is maintained by a flourishing community of developers and contributors from many companies across the world, including Alibaba Group, Amazon, Appian, Gett, Google, Facebook, Hulu, Line, LinkedIn, Lyft, Motorola, Qubole, Red Hat, Salesforce, Starburst, Twitter, Uber, Varada, Walmart, and Zoho.

Conclusion

In this chapter, we introduced you to Presto. You learned more about some of its features, and we explored possible use cases together.

In Chapter 2, you get Presto up and running, connect a data source, and see how you can query the data.

Installing and Configuring Presto

In Chapter 1, you learned about Presto and its possible use cases. Now you are ready to try it out. In this chapter, you learn how to install Presto, configure a data source, and query the data.

Trying Presto with the Docker Container

The Presto project provides a Docker container. It allows you to easily start up a configured demo environment of Presto for a first glimpse and exploration.

To run Presto in Docker, you must have Docker installed on your machine. You can download Docker from the Docker website (*https://www.docker.com*), or use the packaging system of your operating systems.

Use docker to download the container image, save it with the name **presto-trial**, and start it to run in the background:

```
docker run -d --name presto-trial prestosql/presto
```

Now let's connect to the container and run the Presto command-line interface (CLI), presto, on it. It connects to the Presto server running on the same container. In the prompt, you then execute a query on a table of the tpch benchmark data:

```
$ docker exec -it presto-trial presto
presto> select count(*) from tpch.sf1.nation;
 _col0
-------
    25
(1 row)

Query 20181105_001601_00002_e6r6y, FINISHED, 1 node
Splits: 21 total, 21 done (100.00%)
0:06 [25 rows, 0B] [4 rows/s, 0B/s]
```

If you try to run Docker and see an error message resembling `Query 20181217_115041_00000_i6juj failed: Presto server is still initializing`, try waiting a bit and then retry your last command.

You can continue to explore the data set with your SQL knowledge, and use the `help` command to learn about the Presto CLI. More information about using the CLI can be found in "Presto Command-Line Interface" on page 25.

Once you are done with your exploration, just type the command **quit**.

To stop and remove the container, simply execute the following:

```
$ docker stop presto-trial
presto-trial
$ docker rm presto-trial
presto-trial
```

Now you can run it again if you want to experiment further. If you have learned enough and do not need the Docker images anymore, you can delete all related Docker resources:

```
$ docker rmi prestosql/presto
Untagged: prestosql/presto:latest
...
Deleted: sha256:877b494a9f...
```

Installing from Archive File

After trying Presto with Docker, or even as a first step, you can install Presto on your local workstation or a server of your choice.

Presto works on most modern Linux distributions and macOS. It requires a Java Virtual Machine (JVM) and a Python installation.

Java Virtual Machine

Presto is written in Java and requires a JVM to be installed on your system. Presto requires the long-term support version Java 11. Presto does not support older versions of Java. Newer releases might work, but Presto is not well tested on these.

Confirm that `java` is installed and available on the PATH:

```
$ java --version
openjdk 11.0.4 2019-07-16
OpenJDK Runtime Environment (build 11.0.4+11)
OpenJDK 64-Bit Server VM (build 11.0.4+11, mixed mode, sharing)
```

If you do not have Java 11 installed, Presto fails to start.

Python

Python version 2.6 or higher is required by the launcher script included with Presto.

Confirm that `python` is installed and available on the `PATH`:

```
$ python --version
Python 2.7.15+
```

Installation

The Presto release binaries are distributed on the Maven Central Repository. The server is available as a *tar.gz* archive file.

You can see the list of available versions at *https://repo.maven.apache.org/maven2/io/ prestosql/presto-server*.

Determine the largest number, which represents the latest release, and navigate into the folder and download the *tar.gz* file. You can also download the archive on the command line; for example, with `wget` for version 330:

```
$ wget https://repo.maven.apache.org/maven2/\
    io/prestosql/presto-server/330/presto-server-330.tar.gz
```

As a next step, extract the archive:

```
$ tar xvzf presto-server-*.tar.gz
```

The extraction creates a single top-level directory, named identical to the base file-name without an extension. This directory is referred to as the *installation* directory.

The installation directory contains these directories:

lib

Contains the Java archives (JARs) that make up the Presto server and all required dependencies.

plugins

Contains the Presto plug-ins and their dependencies, in separate directories for each plug-in. Presto includes many plug-ins by default, and third-party plug-ins can be added as well. Presto allows for pluggable components to integrate with Presto, such as connectors, functions, and security access controls.

bin

Contains launch scripts for Presto. These scripts are used to start, stop, restart, kill, and get the status of a running Presto process. Learn more about the use of these scripts in "Launcher" on page 77.

etc

This is the configuration directory. It is created by the user and provides the necessary configuration files needed by Presto. You can find out more about the configuration in "Configuration Details" on page 73.

var

Finally, this is a data directory, the place where logs are stored. It is created the first time the Presto server is launched. By default, it is located in the installation directory. We recommend configuring it outside the installation directory to allow for the data to be preserved across upgrades.

Configuration

Before you can start Presto, you need to provide a set of configuration files:

- Presto logging configuration
- Presto node configuration
- JVM configuration

By default, the configuration files are expected in the *etc* directory inside the installation directory.

With the exception of the JVM configuration, the configurations follow the Java properties standards. As a general description for Java properties, each configuration parameter is stored as a pair of strings in the format key=value per line.

Inside the Presto installation directory you created in the previous section, you need to create the basic set of Presto configuration files. You can find ready-to-go configuration files in the Git repository for the book detailed in "Book Repository" on page 15. Here is the content of the three configuration files:

etc/config.properties:

```
coordinator=true
node-scheduler.include-coordinator=true
http-server.http.port=8080
query.max-memory=5GB
query.max-memory-per-node=1GB
query.max-total-memory-per-node=2GB
discovery-server.enabled=true
discovery.uri=http://localhost:8080
```

etc/node.properties:

```
node.environment=demo
```

etc/jvm.config:

```
-server
-Xmx4G
-XX:+UseG1GC
-XX:G1HeapRegionSize=32M
-XX:+UseGCOverheadLimit
-XX:+ExplicitGCInvokesConcurrent
-XX:+HeapDumpOnOutOfMemoryError
-XX:+ExitOnOutOfMemoryError
-Djdk.nio.maxCachedBufferSize=2000000
-Djdk.attach.allowAttachSelf=true
```

With the preceding configuration files in place, Presto is ready to be started. You can find a more detailed description of these files in Chapter 5.

Adding a Data Source

Although our Presto installation is ready, you are not going to start it just yet. After all, you want to be able to query some sort of external data in Presto. That requires you to add a data source configured as a catalog.

Presto *catalogs* define the data sources available to users. The data access is performed by a Presto connector configured in the catalog with the connector.name property. Catalogs expose all the schemas and tables inside the data source to Presto.

For example, the Hive connector maps each Hive database to a schema. If a Hive database web contains a table clicks and the catalog is named sitehive, the Hive connector exposes that table. The Hive connector has to be specified in the catalog file. You can access the catalog with the fully qualified name syntax cata log.schema.table; so in this example, sitehive.web.clicks.

Catalogs are registered by creating a catalog properties file in the *etc/catalog* directory. The name of the file sets the name of the catalog. For example, let's say you create catalog properties files *etc/cdh-hadoop.properties*, *etc/sales.properties*, *etc/web-traffic.properties*, and *etc/mysql-dev.properties*. Then the catalogs exposed in Presto are cdh-hadoop, sales, web-traffic, and mysql-dev.

You can use the TPC-H connector for your first exploration of a Presto example. The TPC-H connector is built into Presto and provides a set of schemas to support the TPC Benchmark H (TPC-H). You can learn more about it in "Presto TPC-H and TPC-DS Connectors" on page 92.

To configure the TPC-H connector, create a catalog properties file, *etc/catalog/tpch.properties* with the tpch connector configured:

```
connector.name=tpch
```

Every catalog file requires the `connector.name` property. Additional properties are determined by the Presto connector implementations. These are documented in the Presto documentation, and you can start to learn more in Chapter 6 and Chapter 7.

Our book repository contains a collection of other catalog files that can be very useful for your learning with Presto.

Running Presto

Now you are truly ready to go, and we can proceed to start Presto. The installation directory contains the launcher scripts. You can use them to start Presto:

```
$ bin/launcher run
```

The `run` command starts Presto as a foreground process. Logs and other output of Presto are written to `stdout` and `stderr`. A successful start is logged, and you should see the following line after a while:

```
INFO          main io.prestosql.server.PrestoServer ======== SERVER STARTED
```

Running Presto in the foreground can be useful for first testing and quickly verifying whether the process starts up correctly and that it is using the expected configuration settings. You can stop the server with Ctrl-C.

You can learn more about the launcher script in "Launcher" on page 77, and about logging in "Logging" on page 75.

Conclusion

Now you know how simple it is to get Presto installed and configured. It is up and running and ready to be used.

In Chapter 3, you learn how to interact with Presto and use it to query the data sources with the configured catalogs. You can also jump ahead to Chapter 6 and Chapter 7 to learn more about other connectors and include the additional catalogs in your next steps.

CHAPTER 3

Using Presto

Congratulations! In the prior chapters, you were introduced to Presto and learned how to get it installed, configured, and started. Now you get to use it.

Presto Command-Line Interface

The *Presto command-line interface (CLI)* provides a terminal-based, interactive shell for running queries and for interacting with the Presto server to inspect metadata about it.

Getting Started

Just like the Presto server itself, the Presto CLI release binaries are distributed on the Maven Central Repository. The CLI application is available as an executable JAR file, which allows you to use it like a normal Unix executable.

You can see the list of available versions at *https://repo.maven.apache.org/maven2/io/ prestosql/presto-cli*.

Locate the version of the CLI that is identical to the Presto server version you are running. Download the **-executable.jar* file from the versioned directory, and rename it to **presto**; for example, with wget and version 330:

```
$ wget -O presto \
https://repo.maven.apache.org/maven2/\
io/prestosql/presto-cli/330/presto-cli-330-executable.jar
```

Ensure that the file is set to be executable. For convenience, make it available on the PATH; for example, by copying it to *~/bin* and adding that folder to the PATH:

```
$ chmod +x presto
$ mv presto ~/bin
$ export PATH=~/bin/:$PATH
```

You can now run the Presto CLI and confirm the version:

```
$ presto --version
Presto CLI 330
```

Documentation for all available options and commands is available with the help option:

```
$ presto --help
```

Before you start using the CLI, you need to determine which Presto server you want to interact with. By default, the CLI connects to the Presto server running on *http://localhost:8080*. If your server is running locally for testing or development, or you access the server with SSH, or you're using the Docker container with exec and the CLI is installed there, you are ready to go:

```
$ presto
presto>
```

If Presto is running at a different server, you have to specify the URL:

```
$ presto --server https://presto.example.com:8080
presto>
```

The presto> prompt shows that you are using the interactive console accessing the Presto server. Type **help** to get a list of available commands:

```
presto> help
Supported commands:
QUIT
EXPLAIN [ ( option [, ...] ) ] <query>
    options: FORMAT { TEXT | GRAPHVIZ | JSON }
             TYPE { LOGICAL | DISTRIBUTED | VALIDATE | IO }
DESCRIBE <table>
SHOW COLUMNS FROM <table>
SHOW FUNCTIONS
SHOW CATALOGS [LIKE <pattern>]
SHOW SCHEMAS [FROM <catalog>] [LIKE <pattern>]
SHOW TABLES [FROM <schema>] [LIKE <pattern>]
USE [<catalog>.]<schema>
```

Most commands, and especially all SQL statements, in the CLI need to end with a semicolon. You can find much more information about SQL on Presto in "SQL with Presto" on page 36. For now, you can just explore a few simple things to get started.

First, you can check what data sources are configured as catalogs. At a minimum, you find the internal metadata catalog—system. In our case, you also find the tpch catalog:

```
presto> SHOW CATALOGS;
 Catalog
---------
 system
 tpch
(2 rows)

Query 20191212_185850_00001_etmtk, FINISHED, 1 node
Splits: 19 total, 19 done (100.00%)
0:01 [0 rows, 0B] [0 rows/s, 0B/s]
```

You can easily display available schemas as well as tables in the schemas. Each time you query Presto, query processing statistics are returned, together with the result. You see them just as in the preceding code. We are going to omit them in the following listings:

```
presto> SHOW SCHEMAS FROM tpch;
       Schema
--------------------
 information_schema
 sf1
 sf100
 sf1000
 sf10000
 sf100000
 sf300
 sf3000
 sf30000
 tiny
(10 rows)

presto> SHOW TABLES FROM tpch.sf1;
   Table
----------
 customer
 lineitem
 nation
 orders
 part
 partsupp
 region
 supplier
(8 rows)
```

Now you are ready to query some actual data:

```
presto> SELECT count(name) FROM tpch.sf1.nation;
 _col0
-------
    25
(1 row)
```

Alternatively, you can select a schema to work with, and then omit the qualifier from the query:

```
presto> USE tpch.sf1;
USE
presto:sf1> SELECT count(name) FROM nation:
```

If you know that you are going to work with a specific schema, before you start the CLI, you can specify it at startup:

```
$ presto --catalog tpch --schema sf1
```

Now you are ready to exercise all your SQL knowledge and the power of Presto to query the configured data sources.

To exit out of the CLI, you can simply type **quit** or **exit**, or press Ctrl-D.

Pagination

By default, the results of queries are paginated using the less program, which is configured with a carefully selected set of options. This behavior can be overridden by setting the environment variable PRESTO_PAGER to the name of a different program such as more, or set it to an empty value to completely disable pagination.

History

The Presto CLI keeps a history of the previously used commands. You can use the up and down arrows to scroll through the history as well as Ctrl-S and Ctrl-R to search through the history. If you want to execute a query again, press Enter to execute the query.

By default, the Presto history file is located in ~/.presto_history. You can change the default with the PRESTO_HISTORY_FILE environment variable.

Additional Diagnostics

The Presto CLI provides the --debug option to enable debug information when running queries:

```
$ presto --debug

presto:sf1> SELECT count(*) FROM foo;
```

```
Query 20181103_201856_00022_te3wy failed:
  line 1:22: Table tpch.sf1.foo does not exist
io.prestosql.sql.analyzer.SemanticException:
  line 1:22: Table tpch.sf1.foo does not exist
...
at java.lang.Thread.run(Thread.java:748)
```

Executing Queries

It is possible to execute a query directly with the `presto` command and have the Presto CLI exit after query completion. This is often desirable if you are scripting execution of multiple queries or are automating a more complex workflow with another system. The execution returns the query results from Presto.

To run a query with the Presto CLI, use the `--execute` option. It is also important to fully qualify the table (for example, `catalog.schema.table`):

```
$ presto --execute 'SELECT nationkey, name, regionkey FROM tpch.sf1.nation LIMIT 5'
"0","ALGERIA","0"
"1","ARGENTINA","1"
"2","BRAZIL","1"
"3","CANADA","1"
"4","EGYPT","4"
```

Alternatively, use the `--catalog` and `--schema` options:

```
$ presto --catalog tpch --schema sf1 \
   --execute 'select nationkey, name, regionkey from nation limit 5'
```

You can execute multiple queries by separating the queries with a semicolon.

The Presto CLI also supports executing commands and SQL queries in a file, like *nations.sql*:

```
USE tpch.sf1;
SELECT name FROM nation;
```

When you use the CLI with the `-f` option, it returns the data on the command line and then exits:

```
$ presto -f nations.sql
USE
"ALGERIA"
"ARGENTINA"
"BRAZIL"
"CANADA"
...
```

Output Formats

The Presto CLI provides the option `--output-format` to control how the output is displayed when running in noninteractive mode. The available options are `ALIGNED`, `VERTICAL`, `CSV`, `TSV`, `CSV_HEADER`, `TSV_HEADER`, and `NULL`. The default value is `CSV`.

Ignoring Errors

The Presto CLI provides the option `--ignore-error`, if you want to skip any errors that are encountered while executing the queries in a file. The default behavior is to stop execution of the script upon encountering the first error.

Presto JDBC Driver

Presto can be accessed from any Java application using a Java Database Connectivity (JDBC) driver. JDBC is a standard API that provides the necessary methods such as querying, inserting, deleting, and updating data in a relational database. Many client and server-side applications running on the JVM implement features for database management, reporting, and other aspects and are using JDBC to access the underlying database. All of these applications can use Presto with the JDBC driver.

The Presto JDBC driver allows you to connect to Presto and interact with Presto via SQL statements.

 If you're familiar with the different implementations of JDBC drivers, the Presto JDBC driver is a Type 4 driver. This simply means it talks to the Presto native protocol.

Using the JDBC driver enables you to use powerful SQL client and database administration tools, such as the open source tools DBeaver (*https://dbeaver.io*) or SQuirreL SQL Client (*http://www.squirrelsql.org*) and many others. Report generation, dashboard, and analytics tools using JDBC can also be used with Presto.

The steps to use any of these tools with Presto are similar:

1. Download the JDBC driver.

2. Make the JDBC driver available on the classpath of the application.

3. Configure the JDBC driver.

4. Configure the connection to Presto.

5. Connect to Presto and use it.

For example, the open source database management tool DBeaver makes this process simple. After installing and starting DBeaver, follow these simple steps:

1. From the File menu, select New.

2. From the DBeaver section, select Database Connection and then click Next.

3. Type **prestosql** in the input field, select the icon, and click Next.

4. Configure the connection to Presto and click Finish. Note that a username value is *required*. You can provide a random name on a default installation of Presto without authentication.

Now you see the connection in the Database Navigator on the left and can inspect the schemas and tables, with an example displayed in Figure 3-1. You can also start the SQL Editor and start writing your queries and working with Presto.

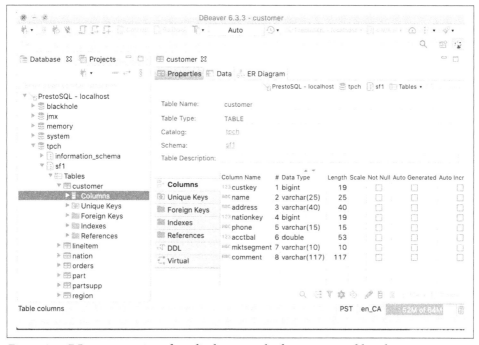

Figure 3-1. DBeaver user interface displaying tpch.sf1.customer table columns

SQuirreL SQL Client (*http://www.squirrelsql.org*) and many other tools use a similar process. Some steps, such as downloading the JDBC driver, and configuring the database driver and connection, are more manual. Let's look at the details.

Downloading and Registering the Driver

The Presto JDBC driver is distributed on the Maven Central Repository. The server is available as a JAR file.

You can see the list of available versions at *https://repo.maven.apache.org/maven2/io/prestosql/presto-jdbc*.

Determine the largest number, which represents the latest release, and navigate into the folder and download the *.jar* file. You can also download the archive on the command line; for example, with `wget` for version 330:

```
$ wget https://repo.maven.apache.org/maven2/\
io/prestosql/presto-jdbc/330/presto-jdbc-330.jar
```

To use the Presto JDBC driver in your application, you add it to the classpath of the Java application. This differs for each application but often uses a folder named *lib*, as is the case for SQuirreL SQL Client. Some applications include a dialog to add libraries to the classpath, which can be used alternatively to copying the file into place manually.

Loading of the driver typically requires a restart of the application.

Now you are ready to register the driver. In SQuirreL SQL Client, you can do that with the + button to create a new driver in the Drivers tab on the left of the user interface.

When configuring the driver, you need to ensure that you configure the following parameters:

- Class name: `io.prestosql.jdbc.PrestoDriver`
- Example JDBC URL: `jdbc:presto://host:port/catalog/schema`
- Name: `Presto`
- Website: `https://prestosql.io`

Only the class name, JDBC URL, and the JAR on the classpath are truly required for the driver to operate. Other parameters are optional and depend on the application.

Establishing a Connection to Presto

With the driver registered and Presto up and running, you can now connect to it from your application.

In SQuirreL SQL Client, this connection configuration is called an *alias*. You can use the Alias tab on the left of the user interface and the + button to create a new alias with the following parameters:

Name

A descriptive name for the Presto connection. The name is more important if you end up connecting to multiple Presto instances, or different schemas and databases.

Driver

Select the Presto driver you created earlier.

URL

The JDBC URL uses the pattern *jdbc:presto://host:port/catalog/schema*, with catalog and schema values optional. You can connect to Presto, installed earlier on your machine and running on *http://localhost:8080*, with the JDBC URL *jdbc:presto://localhost:8080*. The host parameter is the host where the Presto coordinator is running. It is the same hostname you use when connecting via the Presto CLI. This can be in the form of an IP address or DNS hostname. The port parameter is the HTTP port to connect to Presto on the host. The optional catalog and schema parameters are used to establish a connection by using the catalog and schema specified. When you specify these, you do not have to fully qualify the table names in the queries.

Username

A username value is *required*, even when no authentication is configured on Presto. This allows Presto to report the initiator for any queries.

Password

The password is associated with the user and used for authentication. No password is required for a default installation of Presto without configured authentication.

The JDBC driver can receive further parameters as properties. The mechanism for providing these values depends on the application. Both DBeaver and SQuirreL SQL Client include a user interface to specify properties as part of the connection configuration:

SSL

Enable SSL usage of the connection, `true` or `false`.

SSLTrustStorePath

Path to the SSL truststore.

SSLTrustStorePassword

Password for the SSL truststore.

user *and* password

Equivalent to the username and password parameters.

`applicationNamePrefix`

Property used to identify the application to Presto. This is used to set the source name for the Presto query. This name is displayed in the Presto Web UI so that administrators can see where the query originated. Furthermore, it can be used in conjunction with resource groups in which you can use the `ApplicationName` to decide how to assign resources in Presto. This is discussed in "Resource Groups" on page 262.

The full list of available parameters for the JDBC drivers can be found in the Presto documentation; see "Documentation" on page 13.

Once you have configured the connection, you can use it to connect to Presto. This enables you to query Presto itself and all configured schemas and databases. The specific features available for query execution or report generation or any other functionality depend on the application connected to Presto. Figure 3-2 shows a successful connection to Presto in SQuirreL SQL Client with some example queries and a result set.

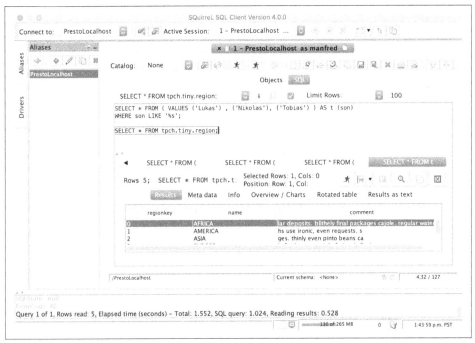

Figure 3-2. SQuirreL SQL Client user interface displaying queries and result set

Presto and ODBC

Similar to the connection to Presto with the JDBC driver—"Presto JDBC Driver" on page 30—Open Database Connectivity (ODBC) allows any application supporting ODBC to use Presto. It provides an API for typically C-based applications.

Currently, no open source ODBC driver for Presto is available. However, commercial drivers can be purchased from Starburst (*https://www.starburstdata.com*) and Simba (*https://www.simba.com*).

This enables several popular applications from the database administration, business intelligence, and reporting and analytics space, such as Microsoft Power BI, Tableau, SAS, Quest Toad, and others. ODBC also enables Microsoft Excel usage.

Client Libraries

Besides the Presto CLI and the JDBC driver, maintained by the Presto team directly, numerous members of the larger Presto community have created client libraries for Presto.

You can find libraries for Python, C, Go, Node.js, R, Ruby, and others. A list is maintained on the Presto website discussed in "Website" on page 12.

These libraries can be used to integrate Presto with applications in these language ecosystems, including your own applications.

Presto Web UI

Every Presto server provides a web interface, commonly referred to as the *Presto Web UI*. The Presto Web UI, shown in Figure 3-3, exposes details about the Presto server and query processing on the server.

The Presto Web UI is accessible at the same address as the Presto server, using the same HTTP port number. By default, this port is 8080; for example, http://presto.example.com:8080. So on your local installation, you can check out the Web UI at http://localhost:8080.

The main dashboard shows details about the Presto utilization and a list of queries. Further details are available in the UI. All this information is of great value for operating Presto and managing the running queries.

Using the Web UI is very useful for monitoring Presto and tuning performance, as explained in more detail in "Monitoring with the Presto Web UI" on page 239. As a beginner user, it is mostly useful to confirm that the server is up and running and is processing your queries.

Figure 3-3. Presto Web UI display of high-level information about the cluster

SQL with Presto

Presto is an ANSI SQL-compliant query engine. It allows you to query and manipulate data in any connected data source with the same SQL statements, functions, and operators.

Presto strives to be compliant with existing SQL standards. One of the main design principles of Presto is to neither invent another SQL-like query language nor deviate too much from the SQL standard. Every new functionality and language feature attempts to comply with the standard.

Extending the SQL feature set is considered only when the standard does not define an equivalent functionality. And even then, great care is taken to design the feature by considering similar features in the standard and other existing SQL implementations as a sign of what can become standard in the future.

> In rare cases, when the standard does not define an equivalent functionality, Presto extends the standard. A prominent example are Lambda expressions; see "Lambda Expressions" on page 192.

Presto does not define any particular SQL standard version it complies with. Instead, the standard is treated as a living document, and the newest standard version is always considered important. On the other hand, Presto does not yet implement all the mandatory features defined in the SQL standard. As a rule, if an existing functionality is found as noncompliant, it is deprecated and later replaced with a standard compliant one.

Querying Presto can be done with the Presto CLI as well as any database management tool connected with JDBC or ODBC, as discussed earlier.

Concepts

Presto enables SQL-based access to external *data sources* such as relational databases, key-value stores, and object storage. The following concepts are important to understand in Presto:

Connector
    Adapts Presto to a data source. Every catalog is associated with a specific connector.

Catalog
    Defines details for accessing a data source; contains schemas and configures a specific connector to use.

Schema
    A way to organize tables. A catalog and schema together define a set of tables that can be queried.

Table
    A set of unordered rows, which are organized into named columns with data types.

First Examples

This section presents a short overview of supported SQL and Presto statements, with much more detail available in Chapter 8 and Chapter 9.

Presto metadata is contained in the `system` catalog. Specific statements can be used to query that data and, in general, find out more about the available catalogs, schemas, information schemas, tables, functions, and more.

Use the following to list all catalogs:

```
SHOW CATALOGS;
 Catalog
---------
 system
 tpch
(2 rows)
```

Show all schemas in the tpch catalog as follows:

```
SHOW SCHEMAS FROM tpch;
       Schema
------------------
 information_schema
 sf1
 sf100
 sf1000
 sf10000
 sf100000
 sf300
 sf3000
 sf30000
 tiny
(10 rows)
```

Here's how to list the tables in the sf1 catalog:

```
SHOW TABLES FROM tpch.sf1;
  Table
---------
 customer
 lineitem
 nation
 orders
 part
 partsupp
 region
 supplier
(8 rows)
```

Find out about the data in the region table as follows:

```
DESCRIBE tpch.sf1.region;
  Column   |     Type     | Extra | Comment
-----------+--------------+-------+---------
 regionkey | bigint       |       |
 name      | varchar(25)  |       |
 comment   | varchar(152) |       |
(3 rows)
```

Other useful statements, such as USE and SHOW FUNCTIONS, are available. More information about the system catalog and Presto statements is available in "Presto Statements" on page 132.

With the knowledge of the available catalogs, schemas, and tables, you can use standard SQL to query the data.

You can check what regions are available:

```
SELECT name FROM tpch.sf1.region;
    name
-----------
 AFRICA
 AMERICA
 ASIA
 EUROPE
 MIDDLE EAST
(5 rows)
```

You can return a subset and order the list:

```
SELECT name
FROM tpch.sf1.region
WHERE name like 'A%'
ORDER BY name DESC;
  name
---------
 ASIA
 AMERICA
 AFRICA
(3 rows)
```

Joining multiple tables and other parts of the SQL standard are supported as well:

```
SELECT nation.name AS nation, region.name AS region
FROM tpch.sf1.region, tpch.sf1.nation
WHERE region.regionkey = nation.regionkey
AND region.name LIKE 'AFRICA';
   nation    | region
-------------+--------
 MOZAMBIQUE | AFRICA
 MOROCCO    | AFRICA
 KENYA      | AFRICA
 ETHIOPIA   | AFRICA
 ALGERIA    | AFRICA
(5 rows)
```

Presto supports operators like || for string concatenation. You can also use mathematical operators such as + and -.

You can change the preceding query to use JOIN and concatenate the result string to one field:

```
SELECT nation.name || ' / ' || region.name AS Location
FROM tpch.sf1.region JOIN tpch.sf1.nation
ON region.regionkey = nation.regionkey
AND region.name LIKE 'AFRICA';
      Location
 -------------------
 MOZAMBIQUE / AFRICA
 MOROCCO / AFRICA
 KENYA / AFRICA
 ETHIOPIA / AFRICA
 ALGERIA / AFRICA
(5 rows)
```

In addition to the operators, Presto supports a large variety of functions. They range from simple use cases to very complex functionality. You can display a list in Presto by using SHOW FUNCTIONS.

A simple example is to calculate the average prices of all orders and display the rounded integer value:

```
SELECT round(avg(totalprice)) AS average_price
FROM tpch.sf1.orders;
 average_price
 --------------
      151220.0
(1 row)
```

More details about SQL usage are available in the Presto documentation and in Chapter 8. Information about functions and operators is also available on the website, and you can find a good overview with more examples in Chapter 9.

Conclusion

Presto is up and running. You connected a data source and used SQL to query it. You can use the Presto CLI, or applications connected to Presto with JDBC.

With this powerful combination in place, you are ready to dive deeper. In the next chapters, we are going to do exactly that: learn how to install Presto for a larger production deployment, understand the architecture of Presto, and get into the details about SQL usage.

PART II
Diving Deeper into Presto

After learning about Presto and various use cases, installing it, and starting to use it, you are now ready to dive deeper and find out more.

In this second part of the book, you learn about the internal workings of Presto in preparation of installing it for production-ready usage, running it, tuning the setup, and more.

We discuss more details about connecting data sources and then querying them with the Presto support for SQL statements, operators, functions, and more.

Presto Architecture

After the introduction to Presto, and an initial installation and usage in the earlier chapters, we now discuss the Presto architecture. We dive deeper into related concepts, so you can learn about the Presto query execution model, query planning, and cost-based optimizations.

In this chapter, we first discuss the Presto high-level architectural components. It is important to have a general understanding of the way Presto works, especially if you intend to install and manage a Presto cluster yourself, as discussed in Chapter 5.

In the later part of the chapter, we dive deeper into those components when we talk about the query execution model of Presto. This is most important if you need to diagnose or tune a slow performance query, all discussed in Chapter 8, or if you plan to contribute to the Presto open source project.

Coordinator and Workers in a Cluster

When you first installed Presto, as discussed in Chapter 2, you used only a single machine to run everything. For the desired scalability and performance, this deployment is not suitable.

Presto is a distributed SQL query engine resembling massively parallel processing (MPP) style databases and query engines. Rather than relying on vertical scaling of the server running Presto, it is able to distribute all processing across a cluster of servers in a horizontal fashion. This means that you can add more nodes to gain more processing power.

Leveraging this architecture, the Presto query engine is able to process SQL queries on large amounts of data in parallel across a cluster of computers, or nodes. Presto runs as a single-server process on each node. Multiple nodes running Presto, which are configured to collaborate with each other, make up a Presto cluster.

Figure 4-1 displays a high-level overview of a Presto cluster composed of one coordinator and multiple worker nodes. A Presto user connects to the coordinator with a client, such as a tool using the JDBC driver or the Presto CLI. The coordinator then collaborates with the workers, which access the data sources.

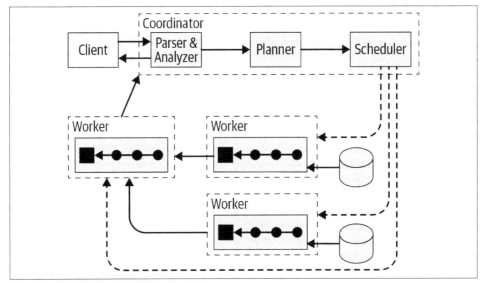

Figure 4-1. Presto architecture overview with coordinator and workers

A *coordinator* is a Presto server that handles incoming queries and manages the *workers* to execute the queries.

A *worker* is a Presto server responsible for executing tasks and processing data.

The *discovery service* typically runs on the coordinator and allows workers to register to participate in the cluster.

All communication and data transfer between clients, coordinator, and workers uses REST-based interactions over HTTP/HTTPS.

Figure 4-2 shows how the communication within the cluster happens between the coordinator and the workers, as well as from one worker to another. The coordinator talks to workers to assign work, update status, and fetch the top-level result set to return to the users. The workers talk to each other to fetch data from upstream tasks, running on other workers. And the workers retrieve result sets from the data source.

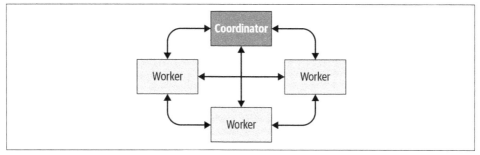

Figure 4-2. Communication between coordinator and workers in a Presto cluster

Coordinator

The Presto *coordinator* is the server responsible for receiving SQL statements from the users, parsing these statements, planning queries, and managing worker nodes. It's the brain of a Presto installation and the node to which a client connects. Users interact with the coordinator via the Presto CLI, applications using the JDBC or ODBC drivers, or any other available client libraries for a variety of languages. The coordinator accepts SQL statements from the client such as SELECT queries for execution.

Every Presto installation must have a coordinator alongside one or more workers. For development or testing purposes, a single instance of Presto can be configured to perform both roles.

The coordinator keeps track of the activity on each worker and coordinates the execution of a query. The coordinator creates a logical model of a query involving a series of stages.

Figure 4-3 displays the communication between client, coordinator, and workers.

Once it receives a SQL statement, the coordinator is responsible for parsing, analyzing, planning, and scheduling the query execution across the Presto worker nodes. The statement is translated into a series of connected tasks running on a cluster of workers. As the workers process the data, the results are retrieved by the coordinator and exposed to the clients on an output buffer. Once an output buffer is completely read by the client, the coordinator requests more data from the workers on behalf of the client. The workers, in turn, interact with the data sources to get the data from them. As a result, data is continuously requested by the client and supplied by the workers from the data source until the query execution is completed.

Coordinators communicate with workers and clients by using an HTTP-based protocol.

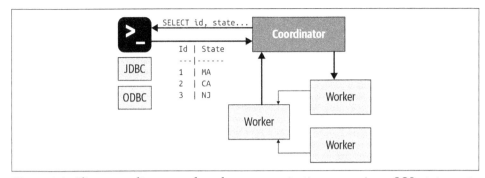

Figure 4-3. Client, coordinator, and worker communication processing a SQL statement

Discovery Service

Presto uses a *discovery service* to find all nodes in the cluster. Every Presto instance registers with the discovery service on startup and periodically sends a heartbeat signal. This allows the coordinator to have an up-to-date list of available workers and use that list for scheduling query execution.

If a worker fails to report heartbeat signals, the discovery service triggers the failure detector, and the worker becomes ineligible for further tasks.

To simplify deployment and avoid running an additional service, the Presto coordinator typically runs an embedded version of the discovery service. It shares the HTTP server with Presto and thus uses the same port.

Worker configuration of the discovery service therefore typically points at the host name and port of the coordinator.

Workers

A Presto *worker* is a server in a Presto installation. It is responsible for executing tasks assigned by the coordinator and for processing data. Worker nodes fetch data from data sources by using connectors and then exchange intermediate data with each other. The final resulting data is passed on to the coordinator. The coordinator is responsible for gathering the results from the workers and providing the final results to the client.

During installation, workers are configured to know the hostname or IP address of the discovery service for the cluster. When a worker starts up, it advertises itself to the discovery service, which makes it available to the coordinator for task execution.

Workers communicate with other workers and the coordinator by using an HTTP-based protocol.

Figure 4-4 shows how multiple workers retrieve data from the data sources and collaborate to process the data, until one worker can provide the data to the coordinator.

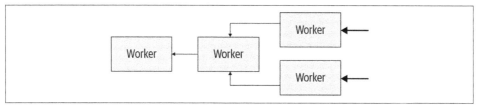

Figure 4-4. Workers in a cluster collaborate to process SQL statements and data

Connector-Based Architecture

At the heart of the separation of storage and compute in Presto is the connector-based architecture. A *connector* provides Presto an interface to access an arbitrary data source.

Each connector provides a table-based abstraction over the underlying data source. As long as data can be expressed in terms of tables, columns, and rows by using the data types available to Presto, a connector can be created and the query engine can use the data for query processing.

Presto provides a *service provider interface (SPI)*, which is a type of API used to implement a connector. By implementing the SPI in a connector, Presto can use standard operations internally to connect to any data source and perform operations on any data source. The connector takes care of the details relevant to the specific data source.

Every connector implements the three parts of the API:

- Operations to fetch table/view/schema metadata
- Operations to produce logical units of data partitioning, so that Presto can parallelize reads and writes
- Data sources and sinks that convert the source data to/from the in-memory format expected by the query engine

Presto provides many connectors to systems such as HDFS/Hive, MySQL, PostgreSQL, MS SQL Server, Kafka, Cassandra, Redis, and many more. In Chapter 6 and Chapter 7, you learn about several of the connectors. The list of available connectors is continuously growing. Refer to the Presto documentation, described in "Documentation" on page 13, for the latest list of supported connectors.

Presto's SPI also gives you the ability to create your own custom connectors. This may be needed if you need to access a data source without a compatible connector. If you end up creating a connector, we strongly encourage you to learn more about the

Presto open source community, use our help, and contribute your connector. Check out "Presto Resources" on page 12 for more information. A custom connector may also be needed if you have a unique or proprietary data source within your organization. This is what allows Presto users to query any data source by using SQL—truly *SQL-on-Anything*.

Figure 4-5 shows how the Presto SPI includes separate interfaces for metadata, data statistics, and data location used by the coordinator, and for data streaming used by the workers.

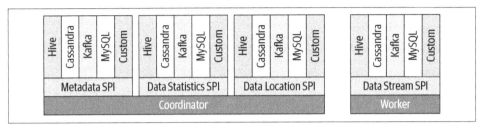

Figure 4-5. Overview of the Presto service provider interface (SPI)

Presto connectors are plug-ins loaded by each server at startup. They are configured by specific parameters in the catalog properties files and loaded from the plug-ins directory. We explore this more in Chapter 6.

Presto uses a plug-in-based architecture for numerous aspects of its functionality. Besides connectors, plug-ins can provide implementations for event listeners, access controls, and function and type providers.

Catalogs, Schemas, and Tables

The Presto cluster processes all queries by using the connector-based architecture described earlier. Each catalog configuration uses a connector to access a specific data source. The data source exposes one or more schemas in the catalog. Each schema contains tables that provide the data in table rows with columns using different data types. You can find out more about catalogs, schemas, tables, and more in Chapter 8, specifically in "Catalogs" on page 136, "Schemas" on page 137, and "Tables" on page 139.

Query Execution Model

Now that you understand how any real-world deployment of Presto involves a cluster with a coordinator and many workers, we can look at how an actual SQL query statement is processed.

Check out Chapters 8 and 9 to learn details about the SQL support of Presto.

Understanding the execution model provides you the foundational knowledge necessary to tune Presto's performance for your particular queries.

Recall that the coordinator accepts SQL statements from the end user, from the CLI software using the ODBC or JDBC driver or other clients' libraries. The coordinator then triggers the workers to get all the data from the data source, creates the result data set, and makes it available to the client.

Let's take a closer look into what happens inside the coordinator first. When a SQL statement is submitted to the coordinator, it is received in textual format. The coordinator takes that text and parses and analyzes it. It then creates a plan for execution by using an internal data structure in Presto called the *query plan*. This flow is displayed in Figure 4-6. The query plan broadly represents the needed steps to process the data and return the results per the SQL statement.

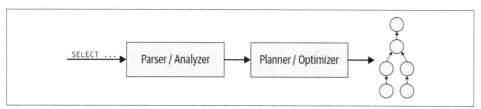

Figure 4-6. Processing a SQL query statement to create a query plan

As you can see in Figure 4-7, the query plan generation uses the metadata SPI and the data statistics SPI to create the query plan. So the coordinator uses the SPI to gather information about tables and other metadata connecting to the data source directly.

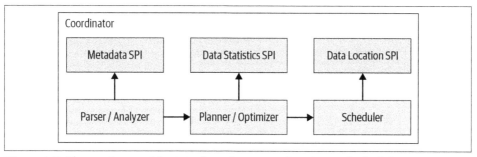

Figure 4-7. The service provider interfaces for query planning and scheduling

The coordinator uses the metadata SPI to get information about tables, columns, and types. These are used to validate that the query is semantically valid, and to perform type checking of expressions in the original query and security checks.

The statistics SPI is used to obtain information about row counts and table sizes to perform cost-based query optimizations during planning.

The data location SPI is then facilitated in the creation of the distributed query plan. It is used to generate logical splits of the table contents. Splits are the smallest unit of work assignment and parallelism.

> The different SPIs are more of a conceptual separation; the actual lower-level Java API is separated by different Java packages in a more fine-grained manner.

The distributed query plan is an extension of the simple query plan consisting of one or more stages. The simple query plan is split into *plan fragments*. A *stage* is the runtime incarnation of a plan fragment, and it encompasses all the tasks of the work described by the stage's plan fragment.

The coordinator breaks up the plan to allow processing on clusters facilitating workers in parallel to speed up the overall query. Having more than one stage results in the creation of a dependency tree of stages. The number of stages depends on the complexity of the query. For example, queried tables, returned columns, JOIN statements, WHERE conditions, GROUP BY operations, and other SQL statements all impact the number of stages created.

Figure 4-8 shows how the *logical query plan* is transformed into a *distributed query plan* on the coordinator in the cluster.

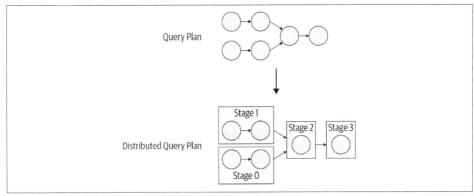

Figure 4-8. Transformation of the query plan to a distributed query plan

The distributed query plan defines the stages and the way the query is to execute on a Presto cluster. It's used by the coordinator to further plan and schedule *tasks* across the workers. A stage consists of one or more tasks. Typically, many tasks are involved, and each task processes a piece of the data.

The coordinator assigns the tasks from a stage out to the workers in the cluster, as displayed in Figure 4-9.

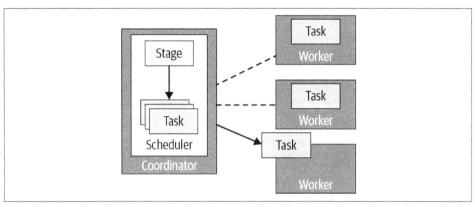

Figure 4-9. Task management performed by the coordinator

The unit of data that a task processes is called a *split*. A split is a descriptor for a segment of the underlying data that can be retrieved and processed by a worker. It is the unit of parallelism and work assignment. The specific operations on the data performed by the connector depend on the underlying data source.

For example, the Hive connector describes splits in the form of a path to a file with offset and length that indicate which part of the file needs to be processed.

Tasks at the source stage produce data in the form of *pages*, which are a collection of rows in columnar format. These pages flow to other intermediate downstream stages. Pages are transferred between stages by exchange operators, which read the data from tasks within an upstream stage.

The *source* tasks use the data source SPI to fetch data from the underlying data source with the help of a connector. This data is presented to Presto and flows through the engine in the form of pages. Operators process and produce pages according to their semantics. For example, filters drop rows, projections produce pages with new derived columns, and so on. The sequence of operators within a task is called a *pipeline*. The last operator of a pipeline typically places its output pages in the task's output buffer. Exchange operators in downstream tasks consume the pages from an upstream task's output buffer. All these operations occur in parallel on different workers, as seen in Figure 4-10.

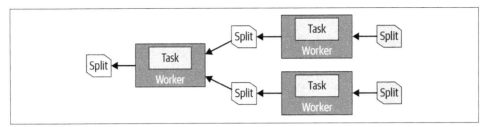

Figure 4-10. Data in splits is transferred between tasks and processed on different workers

So a task is the runtime incarnation of a plan fragment when assigned to a worker. After a task is created, it instantiates a *driver* for each split. Each driver is an instantiation of a pipeline of operators and performs the processing of the data in the split. A task may use one or more drivers, depending on the Presto configuration and environment, as shown in Figure 4-11. Once all drivers are finished, and the data is passed to the next split, the drivers and the task are finished with their work and are destroyed.

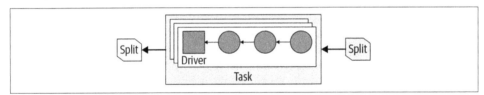

Figure 4-11. Parallel drivers in a task with input and output splits

An *operator* processes input data to produce output data for a downstream operator. Example operators are table scans, filters, joins, and aggregations. A series of these operators form an operator pipeline. For example, you may have a pipeline that first scans and reads the data, and then filters on the data, and finally does a partial aggregation on the data.

To process a query, the coordinator creates the list of splits with the metadata from the connector. Using the list of splits, the coordinator starts scheduling tasks on the workers to gather the data in the splits. During query execution, the coordinator tracks all splits available for processing and the locations where tasks are running on workers and processing splits. As tasks finish processing and are producing more splits for downstream processing, the coordinator continues to schedule tasks until no splits remain for processing.

Once all splits are processed on the workers, all data is available, and the coordinator can make the result available to the client.

Query Planning

Before diving into how the Presto query planner and cost-based optimizations work, let's set up a stage that frames our considerations in a certain context. We present an example query as context for our exploration to help you understand the process of query planning.

Example 4-1 uses the TPC-H data set—see "Presto TPC-H and TPC-DS Connectors" on page 92—to sum up the value of all orders per nation and list the top five nations.

Example 4-1. Example query to explain query planning

```
SELECT
    (SELECT name FROM region r WHERE regionkey = n.regionkey) AS region_name,
    n.name AS nation_name,
    sum(totalprice) orders_sum
FROM nation n, orders o, customer c
WHERE n.nationkey = c.nationkey
  AND c.custkey = o.custkey
GROUP BY n.nationkey, regionkey, n.name
ORDER BY orders_sum DESC
LIMIT 5;
```

Let's try to understand the SQL constructs used in the query and their purpose:

- A SELECT query using three tables in the FROM clause, implicitly defining a CROSS JOIN between the nation, orders, and customer tables

- A WHERE condition to retain the matching rows from the nation, orders and customer tables

- An aggregation using GROUP BY regionkey to aggregate values of orders for each nation

- A subquery, (SELECT name FROM region WHERE regionkey = n.regionkey), to pull the region name from the region table; note that this query is correlated, as if it was supposed to be executed independently for each row of the containing result set

- An ordering definition, ORDER BY orders_sum DESC, to sort the result before returning

- A limit of five rows defined to return only nations with the highest order sums and filter out all others

Parsing and Analysis

Before a query can be planned for execution, it needs to be parsed and analyzed. Details about SQL and the related syntactic rules for building the query can be found in Chapter 8 and Chapter 9. Presto verifies the text for these syntax rules when parsing it. As a next step, Presto analyses the query:

Identifying tables used in a query
> Tables are organized within catalogs and schemas, so multiple tables can have the same name. For example, TPC-H data provides `orders` tables of various sizes in the different schemas as `sf10.orders`, `sf100.orders`, etc.

Identifying columns used in a query
> A qualified column reference `orders.totalprice` unambiguously refers to a `totalprice` column within the `orders` table. Typically, however, a SQL query refers to a column by name only—`totalprice`, as seen in Example 4-1. The Presto analyzer can determine which table a column originates from.

Identifying references to fields within ROW values
> A dereference expression `c.bonus` may refer to a `bonus` column in the table named `c` or aliased with `c`. Or, it may refer to `bonus` field in a `c` column of row type (a struct with named fields). It is the job of the analyzer in Presto to decide which is applicable, with a table-qualified column reference taking precedence in case of ambiguity. Analysis needs to follow SQL language's scoping and visibility rules. The information collected, such as identifier disambiguation, is later used during planning, so that the planner does not need to understand the query language scoping rules again.

As you see, the query analyzer has complex and cross-cutting duties. Its role is very technical, and it remains invisible from the user perspective as long as the queries are correct. The analyzer manifests its existence whenever a query violates SQL language rules, exceeds user's privileges, or is unsound for some other reason.

Once the query is analyzed and all identifiers in the query are processed and resolved, Presto proceeds to the next phase, which is query planning.

Initial Query Planning

A query plan can be viewed as a program that produces query results. Recall that SQL is a declarative language: the user writes a SQL query to specify the data they want from the system. Unlike an imperative program, the user does not specify how to process the data to get the result. This part is left to the query planner and optimizer to determine the sequence of steps to process the data for the desired result.

This sequence of steps is often referred to as the *query plan*. Theoretically, an exponential number of query plans could yield the same query result. The performance of the plans varies dramatically, and this is where the Presto planner and optimizer try to determine the optimal plan. Plans that always produce the same results are called *equivalent plans*.

Let's consider the query shown previously in Example 4-1. The most straightforward query plan for this query is the one that most closely resembles the query's SQL syntactical structure. This plan is shown in Example 4-2. For the purpose of this discussion, the listing should be self-explanatory. You just need to know that the plan is a tree, and its execution starts from leaf nodes and proceeds up along the tree structure.

Example 4-2. Manually condensed, straightforward textual representation of the query plan for example query

```
- Limit[5]
  - Sort[orders_sum DESC]
    - LateralJoin[2]
      - Aggregate[by nationkey...; orders_sum := sum(totalprice)]
      - Filter[c.nationkey = n.nationkey AND c.custkey = o.custkey]
        - CrossJoin
          - CrossJoin
            - TableScan[nation]
            - TableScan[orders]
          - TableScan[customer]
      - EnforceSingleRow[region_name := r.name]
        - Filter[r.regionkey = n.regionkey]
          - TableScan[region]
```

Each element of the query plan can be implemented in a straightforward, imperative fashion. For example, `TableScan` accesses a table in its underlying storage and returns a result set containing all rows within the table. `Filter` receives rows and applies a filtering condition on each, retaining only the rows that satisfy the condition. `Cross Join` operates on two data sets that it receives from its child nodes. It produces all combinations of rows in those data sets, probably storing one of the data sets in memory, so that the underlying storage does not have to be accessed multiple times.

 Latest Presto releases changed naming for the different operations in a query plan. For example, `TableScan` is equivalent to `ScanPro ject` with a table specification. A `Filter` operation is renamed to `FilterProject`. The ideas presented, however, remain the same.

Let's now consider the computational complexity of this query plan. Without knowing all the nitty-gritty details of the actual implementation, we cannot fully reason about the complexity. However, we can assume that the lower bound for the complexity of a query plan node is the size of the data set it produces. Therefore, we describe complexity by using Big Omega notation, which describes the asymptotic lower bound. If N, O, C, and R represent the number of rows in `nation`, `orders`, `customer`, and `region` tables, respectively, we can observe the following:

- `TableScan[orders]` reads the `orders` table, returning O rows, so its complexity is $\Omega(O)$. Similarly, the other two `TableScans` return N and C rows; thus their complexity is $\Omega(N)$ and $\Omega(C)$, respectively.
- `CrossJoin` above `TableScan[nation]` and `TableScan[orders]` combines the data from `nation` and `orders` tables; therefore, its complexity is $\Omega(N \times O)$.
- The `CrossJoin` above combines the earlier `CrossJoin`, which produced $N \times O$ rows, with `TableScan[customer]` so with data from the `customer` table, therefore its complexity is $\Omega(N \times O \times C)$.
- `TableScan[region]` at the bottom has complexity $\Omega(R)$. However, because of the `LateralJoin`, it is invoked N times, with N as the number of rows returned from the aggregation. Thus, in total, this operation incurs $\Omega(R \times N)$ computational cost.
- The `Sort` operation needs to order a set of N rows, so it cannot take less time than proportional to $N \times \log(N)$.

Disregarding other operations for a moment as no more costly than the ones we have analyzed so far, the total cost of the preceding plan is at least $\Omega[N + O + C + (N \times O) + (N \times O \times C) + (R \times N) + (N \times \log(N))]$. Without knowing the relative table sizes, this can be simplified to $\Omega[(N \times O \times C) + (R \times N) + (N \times \log(N))]$. Adding a reasonable assumption that `region` is the smallest table and `nation` is the second smallest, we can neglect the second and third parts of the result and get the simplified result of $\Omega(N \times O \times C)$.

Enough of algebraic formulas. It's time to see what this means in practice! Let's consider an example of a popular shopping site with 100 million customers from 200 nations who placed 1 billion orders in total. The `CrossJoin` of these two tables needs to materialize 20 quintillion (20,000,000,000,000,000,000) rows. For a moderately beefy 100-node cluster, processing 1 million rows a second on each node, it would take over 63 centuries to compute the intermediate data for our query.

Of course, Presto does not even try to execute such a naive plan. A naive plan has its role, though. The initial plan serves as a bridge between two worlds: the world of SQL language and its semantic rules, and the world of query optimizations. The role of query optimization is to transform and evolve the initial plan into an equivalent plan that can be executed as fast as possible, at least in a reasonable amount of time, given finite resources of the Presto cluster. Let's talk about how query optimizations attempt to reach this goal.

Optimization Rules

In this section, you get to take a look at a handful of the many important optimization rules implemented in Presto.

Predicate Pushdown

Predicate pushdown is probably the single most important optimization and easiest to understand. Its role is to move the filtering condition as close to the source of the data as possible. As a result, data reduction happens as early as possible during query execution. In our case, it transforms a `Filter` into a simpler `Filter` and an `InnerJoin` above the same `CrossJoin` condition, leading to a plan shown in Example 4-3. Portions of the plan that didn't change are excluded for readability.

Example 4-3. Transformation of a `CrossJoin` and `Filter` into an `InnerJoin`

```
...
- Aggregate[by nationkey...; orders_sum := sum(totalprice)]
  - Filter[c.nationkey = n.nationkey AND c.custkey = o.custkey]  // original filter
    - CrossJoin
      - CrossJoin
        - TableScan[nation]
        - TableScan[orders]
      - TableScan[customer]
...
...
- Aggregate[by nationkey...; orders_sum := sum(totalprice)]
  - Filter[c.nationkey = n.nationkey]              // transformed simpler filter
    - InnerJoin[o.custkey = c.custkey]             // added inner join
      - CrossJoin
        - TableScan[nation]
        - TableScan[orders]
      - TableScan[customer]
...
```

The "bigger" join that was present is now converted into `InnerJoin` on an equality condition. Without going into details, let's assume for now that such a join can be efficiently implemented in a distributed system, with computational complexity equal to the number of produced rows. This means that predicate pushdown replaced an "at least" $\Omega(N \times O \times C)$ `CrossJoin` with a `Join` that is "exactly" $\Theta(N \times O)$.

However, predicate pushdown could not improve the `CrossJoin` between `nation` and `orders` tables because no immediate condition is joining these tables. This is where cross join elimination comes into play.

Cross Join Elimination

In the absence of the cost-based optimizer, Presto joins the tables contained in the SELECT query in the order of their appearance in the query text. The one important exception to this occurs when the tables to be joined have no joining condition, which results in a *cross join*. In almost all practical cases, a cross join is unwanted, and all the multiplied rows are later filtered out, but the cross join itself has so much work to do that it may never complete.

Cross join elimination reorders the tables being joined to minimize the number of cross joins, ideally reducing it to zero. In the absence of information about relative table sizes, other than the cross join elimination, table join ordering is preserved, so the user remains in control. The effect of cross join elimination on our example query can be seen in Example 4-4. Now both joins are inner joins, bringing overall computational cost of joins to $\Theta(C + O) = \Theta(O)$. Other parts of the query plan did not change since the initial plan, so the overall query computation cost is at least $\Omega[O + (R \times N) + (N \times \log(N))]$—of course, the O component representing the number of rows in the orders table is the dominant factor.

Example 4-4. Reordering the joins such that the cross join is eliminated

```
...[i]
  - Aggregate[by nationkey...; orders_sum := sum(totalprice)]
    - Filter[c.nationkey = n.nationkey]        // filter on nationkey first
      - InnerJoin[o.custkey = c.custkey]       // then inner join cutkey
        - CrossJoin
          - TableScan[nation]
          - TableScan[orders]
        - TableScan[customer]
...
...
  - Aggregate[by nationkey...; orders_sum := sum(totalprice)]
    - InnerJoin[c.custkey = o.custkey]         // reordered to custkey first
      - InnerJoin[n.nationkey = c.nationkey]   // then nationkey
        - TableScan[nation]
        - TableScan[customer]
      - TableScan[orders]
...
```

TopN

Typically, when a query has a LIMIT clause, it is preceded by an ORDER BY clause. Without the ordering, SQL does not guarantee which result rows are returned. The combination of ORDER BY followed by LIMIT is also present in our query.

When executing such a query, Presto could sort all the rows produced and then retain just the first few of them. This approach would have $\Theta(row\_count \times$

log(row_count)) computational complexity and $\Theta(row\_count)$ memory footprint. However, it is not optimal and is wasteful to sort the entire results only to keep a much smaller subset of the sorted results. Therefore, an optimization rule rolls ORDER BY followed by LIMIT into a *TopN* plan node. During query execution, TopN keeps the desired number of rows in a heap data structure, updating the heap while reading input data in a streaming fashion. This brings computational complexity down to $\Theta(row\_count \times \log(limit))$ and memory footprint to $\Theta(limit)$. Overall query computation cost is now $\Omega[O + (R \times N) + N]$.

Partial Aggregations

Presto does not need to pass all rows from the orders table to the join because we are not interested in individual orders. Our example query computes an aggregate, the sum over totalprice for each nation, so it is possible to pre-aggregate the rows as shown in Example 4-5. We reduce the amount of data flowing into the downstream join by aggregating the data. The results are not complete, which is why this is referred to as a *pre-aggregation*. But the amount of data is potentially reduced, significantly improving query performance.

Example 4-5. Partial pre-aggregation can significantly improve performance

```
...
- Aggregate[by nationkey...; orders_sum := sum(totalprice)]
  - InnerJoin[c.custkey = o.custkey]
    - InnerJoin[n.nationkey = c.nationkey]
      - TableScan[nation]
      - TableScan[customer]
    - Aggregate[by custkey; totalprice := sum(totalprice)]
      - TableScan[orders]
...
```

For improved parallelism, this kind of pre-aggregation is implemented differently, as a so-called *partial aggregation*. Here, we are presenting simplified plans, but in an actual EXPLAIN plan, this is represented differently than the final aggregation.

This kind of pre-aggregation as shown in Example 4-5 is not always an improvement. It is detrimental to query performance when partial aggregation does not reduce the amount of data. For this reason, the optimization is currently disabled by default and can be enabled with the push_partial_aggregation_through_join session toggle. By default, Presto uses partial aggregations and places them above the join to reduce the amount of data transmitted over the network between Presto nodes. To fully appreciate the role of these partial aggregations, we would need to consider nonsimplified query plans.

Implementation Rules

The rules we have covered so far are optimization rules—rules with a goal to reduce query processing time, a query's memory footprint, or the amount of data exchanged over the network. However, even in the case of our example query, the initial plan contained an operation that is not implemented at all: the lateral join. In the next section, we have a look at how Presto handles these kind of operations.

Lateral Join Decorrelation

The *lateral join* could be implemented as a for-each loop that traverses all rows from a data set and executes another query for each of them. Such an implementation is possible, but this is not how Presto handles the cases like our example. Instead, Presto *decorrelates* the subquery, pulling up all the correlated conditions and forming a regular left join. In SQL terms, this corresponds to transformation of a query:

```
SELECT
    (SELECT name FROM region r WHERE regionkey = n.regionkey)
        AS region_name,
    n.name AS nation_name
FROM nation n
```

into

```
SELECT
    r.name AS region_name,
    n.name AS nation_name
FROM nation n LEFT OUTER JOIN region r ON r.regionkey = n.regionkey
```

Even though we may use such constructs interchangeably, a cautious reader familiar with SQL semantics immediately realizes that they are not fully equivalent. The first query fails when they are duplicate entries in the region table with the same region key, whereas the second query does not fail. Instead, it produces more result rows. For this reason, lateral join decorrelation uses two additional components besides the join. First, it "numbers" all the source rows so that they can be distinguished. Second, after the join, it checks whether any row was duplicated, as shown in Example 4-6. If duplication is detected, the query processing is failed, to preserve the original query semantics.

Example 4-6. Lateral join decompositions require additional checks

```
- TopN[5; orders_sum DESC]
  - MarkDistinct & Check
    - LeftJoin[n.regionkey = r.regionkey]
      - AssignUniqueId
        - Aggregate[by nationkey...; orders_sum := sum(totalprice)]
          - ...
      - TableScan[region]
```

Semi-Join (IN) Decorrelation

A subquery can be used within a query not only to pull information, as we just saw in the lateral join example, but also to filter rows by using the IN predicate. In fact, an IN predicate can be used in a filter (the WHERE clause), or in a projection (the SELECT clause). When you use IN in a projection, it becomes apparent that it is not a simple Boolean-valued operator like EXISTS. Instead, the IN predicate can evaluate to true, false, or null.

Let's consider a query designed to find orders for which the customer and item suppliers are from the same country, as shown in Example 4-7. Such orders may be interesting. For example, we may want to save shipping costs, or reduce shipping environmental impact, by shipping directly from the supplier to the customer, bypassing our own distribution centers.

Example 4-7. Semi-join (IN) example query

```
SELECT DISTINCT o.orderkey
FROM lineitem l
  JOIN orders o ON o.orderkey = l.orderkey
  JOIN customer c ON o.custkey = c.custkey
WHERE c.nationkey IN (
    -- subquery invoked multiple times
    SELECT s.nationkey
    FROM part p
      JOIN partsupp ps ON p.partkey = ps.partkey
      JOIN supplier s ON ps.suppkey = s.suppkey
    WHERE p.partkey = l.partkey
);
```

As with a lateral join, this could be implemented with a loop over rows from the outer query, where the subquery to retrieve all nations for all suppliers of an item gets invoked multiple times.

Instead of doing this, Presto decorrelates the subquery—the subquery is evaluated once, with the correlation condition removed, and then is joined back with the outer query by using the correlation condition. The tricky part is ensuring that the join does not multiply result rows (so a deduplicating aggregation is used) and that the transformation correctly retains the IN predicate's three-valued logic.

In this case, the deduplicating aggregation uses the same partitioning as the join, so it can be executed in a streaming fashion, without data exchange over the network and with minimal memory footprint.

Cost-Based Optimizer

In "Query Planning" on page 53, you learned how the Presto planner converts a query in textual form into an executable and optimized query plan. You learned about various optimization rules in "Optimization Rules" on page 57, and their importance for query performance at execution time. You also saw implementation rules in "Implementation Rules" on page 60, without which a query plan would not be executable at all.

We walked the path from the beginning, where query text is received from the user, to the end, where the final execution plan is ready. Along the way, we saw selected plan transformations, which are critical because they make the plan execute orders of magnitude faster, or make the plan executable at all.

Now let's take a closer look at plan transformations that make their decisions based not only on the shape of the query but also, and more importantly, on the shape of the data being queried. This is what the Presto state-of-the-art *cost-based optimizer (CBO)* does.

The Cost Concept

Earlier, we used an example query as our work model. Let's use a similar approach, again for convenience and to ease understanding. As you can see in Example 4-8, certain query clauses, which are not relevant for this section, are removed. This allows you to focus on the cost-based decisions of the query planner.

Example 4-8. Example query for cost-based optimization

```
SELECT
    n.name AS nation_name,
    avg(extendedprice) as avg_price
FROM nation n, orders o, customer c, lineitem l
WHERE n.nationkey = c.nationkey
  AND c.custkey = o.custkey
  AND o.orderkey = l.orderkey
GROUP BY n.nationkey, n.name;
```

Without cost-based decisions, the query planner rules optimize the initial plan for this query to produce a plan, as shown in Example 4-9. This plan is determined solely by the lexical structure of the SQL query. The optimizer used only the syntactic information; hence it is sometimes called the *syntactic optimizer*. The name is meant to be humorous, highlighting the simplicity of the optimizations. Since the query plan is based only on the query, you can hand-tune or optimize the query by adjusting the syntactic order of the tables in the query.

Example 4-9. Query join order from the syntactic optimizer

```
- Aggregate[by nationkey...; orders_sum := sum(totalprice)]
  - InnerJoin[o.orderkey = l.orderkey]
  - InnerJoin[c.custkey = o.custkey]
    - InnerJoin[n.nationkey = c.nationkey]
      - TableScan[nation]
      - TableScan[customer]
    - TableScan[orders]
  - TableScan[lineitem]
```

Now let's say the query was written differently, changing only the order of the WHERE conditions:

```
SELECT
    n.name AS nation_name,
    avg(extendedprice) as avg_price
FROM nation n, orders o, customer c, lineitem l
WHERE c.custkey = o.custkey
  AND o.orderkey = l.orderkey
  AND n.nationkey = c.nationkey
GROUP BY n.nationkey, n.name;
```

The plan ends up with a different join order as a result:

```
- Aggregate[by nationkey...; orders_sum := sum(totalprice)]
  - InnerJoin[n.nationkey = c.nationkey]
  - InnerJoin[o.orderkey = l.orderkey]
    - InnerJoin[c.custkey = o.custkey]
      - TableScan[customer]
      - TableScan[orders]
    - TableScan[lineitem]
  - TableScan[nation]
```

The fact that a simple change of ordering conditions affects the query plan, and therefore the performance of the query, is cumbersome for the SQL analyst. Creating efficient queries then requires internal knowledge of the way Presto processes the queries. A query author should not be required to have this knowledge to get the best performance out of Presto. Beyond people writing queries, tools such as Apache Superset, Tableau, Qlik, or MicroStrategy do not write the queries to be optimal for Presto.

The cost-based optimizer ensures that the two variants of the query produce the same optimal query plan for processing by Presto's execution engine.

From a time complexity perspective, it does not matter whether you join, for example, the nation table with customer— or, vice versa, the customer table with nation. Both tables need to be processed, and in the case of hash-join implementation, total running time is proportional to the number of output rows. However, time complexity is not the only thing that matters. This is generally true for programs working with data, but it is especially true for large database systems. Presto needs to be concerned about memory usage and network traffic as well. To reason about memory and network usage of the join, Presto needs to better understand how the join is implemented.

CPU time, memory requirements, and network bandwidth usage are the three dimensions that contribute to query execution time, both in single-query and concurrent workloads. These dimensions constitute the cost in Presto.

Cost of the Join

When joining two tables over the equality condition (=), Presto implements an extended version of the algorithm known as a *hash join* (*https://en.wikipedia.org/wiki/Hash_join*). One of the joined tables is called the *build* side. This table is used to build a lookup hash table with the join condition columns as the key. Another joined table is called the *probe* side. Once the lookup hash table is ready, rows from the probe side are processed, and the hash table is used to find matching build-side rows in constant time. By default, Presto uses three-level hashing in order to parallelize processing as much as possible:

1. Both joined tables are distributed across the worker nodes, based on the hash values of the join condition columns. Rows that should be matched have the same values on join condition columns, so they are assigned to the same node. This reduces the size of the problem by the number of nodes being used at this stage. This *node-level data assignment* is the first level of hashing.

2. At a node level, the build side is further scattered across build-side worker threads, again using a hash function. Building a hash table is a CPU-intensive process, and using multiple threads to do the job greatly improves throughput.

3. Each worker thread ultimately produces one partition of the final lookup hash table. Each partition is a hash table itself. The partitions are combined into a two-level lookup hash table so that we avoid scattering the probe side across multiple threads as well. The probe side is still processed in multiple threads, but the threads get their work assigned in batches, which is faster than partitioning the data by using a hash function.

As you can see, the build side is kept in memory to facilitate fast, in-memory data processing. Of course, a memory footprint is also associated, proportional to the size of the build side. This means that the build side must fit into the memory available on the node. This also means that less memory is available to other operations and to other queries. This is the memory cost associated with the join. There is also the network cost. In the algorithm described previously, both joined tables are transferred over the network to facilitate node-level data assignment.

The cost-based optimizer can select which table should be the build table, controlling the memory cost of the join. Under certain conditions, the optimizer can also avoid sending one of the tables over the network, thus reducing network bandwidth usage (reducing the network cost). To do its job, the cost-based optimizer needs to know the size of the joined tables, which is provided as the table statistics.

Table Statistics

In "Connector-Based Architecture" on page 47, you learned about the role of connectors. Each table is provided by a connector. Besides table schema information and access to actual data, the connector can provide table and column statistics:

- Number of rows in a table
- Number of distinct values in a column
- Fraction of NULL values in a column
- Minimum and maximum values in a column
- Average data size for a column

Of course, if some information is missing—for example, the average text length in a varchar column is not known—a connector can still provide other information, and the cost-based optimizer uses what is available.

With an estimation of the number of rows in the joined tables and, optionally, average data size for columns, the cost-based optimizer already has sufficient knowledge to determine the optimal ordering of the tables in our example query. The CBO can start with the biggest table (lineitem) and subsequently join the other tables—orders, then customer, then nation:

```
- Aggregate[by nationkey...; orders_sum := sum(totalprice)]
  - InnerJoin[l.orderkey = o.orderkey]
    - InnerJoin[o.custkey = c.custkey]
      - InnerJoin[c.nationkey = n.nationkey]
        - TableScan[lineitem]
        - TableScan[orders]
      - TableScan[customer]
    - TableScan[nation]
```

Such a plan is good and should be considered because every join has the smaller relation as the build side, but it is not necessarily optimal. If you run the example query, using a connector that provides table statistics, you can enable the cost-based optimizer with the session property:

```
SET SESSION join_reordering_strategy = 'AUTOMATIC';
```

With the table statistics available from the connector, Presto may come up with a different plan:

```
- Aggregate[by nationkey...; orders_sum := sum(totalprice)]
  - InnerJoin[l.orderkey = o.orderkey]
    - TableScan[lineitem]
    - InnerJoin[o.custkey = c.custkey]
      - TableScan[orders]
      - InnerJoin[c.nationkey = n.nationkey]
        - TableScan[customer]
        - TableScan[nation]
```

This plan was chosen because it avoids sending the biggest table (lineitem) three times over the network. The table is scattered across the nodes only once.

The final plan depends on the actual sizes of joined tables and the number of nodes in a cluster, so if you're trying this out on your own, you may get a different plan than the one shown here.

Cautious readers notice that the join order is selected based only on the join conditions, the links between tables, and the data size of the tables, including number of rows and average data size for each column. Other statistics are critical for optimizing more involved query plans, which contain intermediate operations between table scans and the joins—for example, filters, aggregations, and non-inner joins.

Filter Statistics

As you just saw, knowing the sizes of the tables involved in a query is fundamental to properly reordering the joined tables in the query plan. However, knowing just the table sizes is not enough. Consider a modification of our example query, in which the user added another condition like l.partkey = 638, in order to drill down in their data set for information about orders for a particular item:

```
SELECT
    n.name AS nation_name,
    avg(extendedprice) as avg_price
FROM nation n, orders o, customer c, lineitem l
WHERE n.nationkey = c.nationkey
  AND c.custkey = o.custkey
  AND o.orderkey = l.orderkey
  AND l.partkey = 638
GROUP BY n.nationkey, n.name;
```

Before the condition was added, lineitem was the biggest table, and the query was planned to optimize handling of that table. But now, the filtered lineitem is one of the smallest joined relations.

Looking at the query plan shows that the filtered lineitem table is now small enough. The CBO puts the table on the build side of the join, so that it serves as a filter for other tables:

```
- Aggregate[by nationkey...; orders_sum := sum(totalprice)]
  - InnerJoin[l.orderkey = o.orderkey]
    - InnerJoin[o.custkey = c.custkey]
      - TableScan[customer]
      - InnerJoin[c.nationkey = n.nationkey]
        - TableScan[orders]
        - Filter[partkey = 638]
          - TableScan[lineitem]
    - TableScan[nation]
```

To estimate the number of rows in the filtered lineitem table, the CBO again uses statistics provided by a connector: the number of distinct values in a column and fraction of NULL values in a column. For the partkey = 638 condition, no NULL value satisfies the condition, so the optimizer knows that the number of rows gets reduced by the fraction of NULL values in the partkey column. Further, if you assume roughly uniform distribution of values in the column, you can derive the final number of rows:

```
filtered rows = unfiltered rows * (1 - null fraction)
    / number of distinct values
```

Obviously, the formula is correct only when the distribution of values is uniform. However, the optimizer does not need to know the number of rows; it just needs to know the estimation of it, so being somewhat off is not a problem in general. Of course, if an item is bought much more frequently than others—say, Starburst candies —the estimation may be too far off, and the optimizer may choose a bad plan. Currently, when this happens, you have to disable the CBO.

In the future, connectors can be able to provide information about the data distribution to handle cases like this. For example, if a histogram were available for the data, then the CBO could more accurately estimate the filtered rows.

Table Statistics for Partitioned Tables

One special case of filtered table deserves being mentioned separately: partitioned tables. Data may be organized into *partitioned tables* in a Hive/HDFS warehouse accessed by the Hive connector; see "Hive Connector for Distributed Storage Data Sources" on page 93. When the data is filtered by a condition on partitioning keys, only matching partitions are read during query executions. Furthermore, since the table statistics are stored in Hive on a per-partition basis, the CBO gets statistics information only for partitions that are read, so it's more accurate.

Of course, every connector can provide this kind of improved stats for filtered relations. We are referring only to the way the Hive connector provides statistics here.

Join Enumeration

So far, we've discussed how the CBO leverages data statistics, in order to come up with an optimal plan for executing a query. In particular, it chooses an optimal join order, which affects the query performance substantially for two primary reasons:

Hash join implementation
> The hash join implementation is asymmetric. It is important to carefully choose which input is the build side and which input is the probe side.

Distributed join type
> It is important to carefully choose whether to broadcast or redistribute the data to the join inputs.

Broadcast Versus Distributed Joins

In the previous section, you learned about the hash join implementation and the importance of the build and probe sides. Because Presto is a distributed system, joins can be done in parallel across a cluster of workers, where each worker processes a fraction of the join. For a distributed join to occur, the data may need to be distributed across the network, and different strategies are available that vary in efficiency, depending on the data shape.

Broadcast join strategy

In a *broadcast join strategy*, the build side of the join is broadcast to all the worker nodes that are performing the join in parallel. In other words, each join gets a complete copy of the data for the build side, as displayed in Figure 4-12. This is semantically correct only if the probe side remains distributed across the workers without duplication. Otherwise, duplicate results are created.

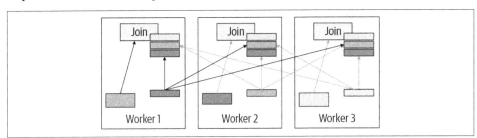

Figure 4-12. Broadcast join strategy visualization

The broadcast join strategy is advantageous when the build side is small, allowing for a cost-effective transmission of data. The advantage is also greater when the probe side is very large because it avoids having to redistribute the data as is necessary in the distributed join case.

Distributed join strategy

In a *distributed join strategy*, the input data to both the build side and the probe side are redistributed across the cluster such that the workers perform the join in parallel. The difference in data transmission over the network is that each worker receives a unique fraction of the data set, rather than a copy of the data as performed in the broadcast join case. The data redistribution must use a partitioning algorithm such that the matching join key values are sent to the same node. For example, say we have the following data sets of join keys on a particular node:

```
Probe: {4, 5, 6, 7, 9, 10, 11, 14}
Build: {4, 6, 9, 10, 17}
```

Consider a simple partitioning algorithm:

```
if joinkey mod 3 == 0 then send to Worker 1
if joinkey mod 3 == 1 then send to Worker 2
if joinkey mod 3 == 2 then send to Worker 3
```

The partitioning results in these probes and builds on Worker 1:

```
Probe:{6, 9}
Build:{6, 9}
```

Worker 2 deals with different probes and builds:

```
Probe: {4, 7, 10}
Build: {4, 10}
```

And, finally, Worker 3 deals with a different subset:

```
Probe:{5, 11, 14}
Build: {17}
```

By partitioning the data, the CBO guarantees that the joins can be computed in parallel without having to share information during the processing. The advantage of a distributed join is that it allows Presto to compute a join whereby both sides are very large and there is not enough memory on a single machine to hold the entirety of the probe side in memory. The disadvantage is the extra data being sent over the network.

The decision between a broadcast join and distributed join strategy must be costed. Each strategy has trade-offs, and we must take into account the data statistics in order to cost the optimal one. Furthermore, this also needs to be decided during the join reordering process. Depending on the join order and where filters are applied, the data shape changes. This could lead to cases in which a distributed join between two data sets may be best in one join order scenario, but a broadcast join maybe better in a different scenario. The join enumeration algorithm takes this into consideration.

The join enumeration algorithm used by Presto is rather complex and beyond the scope of this book. It is documented in detail on a Starburst blog post (*https://www.starburstdata.com/technical-blog/presto-join-enumeration*). It breaks the problem into subproblems with smaller partitions, finds the correct join usage with recursions, and aggregates the results up to a global result.

Working with Table Statistics

In order to leverage the CBO in Presto, your data must have statistics. Without data statistics, the CBO cannot do much; it requires data statistics to estimate rows and costs of the different plans.

Because Presto does not store data, producing statistics for Presto is connector-implementation dependent. As of the time of this writing, the Hive connector provides data statistics to Presto. Other data sources, such as the relational database connectors, could also provide statistics. For example, PostgreSQL can collect and store statistics of its data. The PostgreSQL connector implementation could be extended to provide these statistics to Presto's CBO. However, at the time of this writing, it is not available in open source. We expect that, over time, more connectors will support statistics, and you should continue to refer to the Presto documentation for up-to-date information.

For the Hive connectors, you can use the following ways to collect statistics:

- Use Presto's ANALYZE command to collect statistics.
- Enable Presto to gather statistics when writing data to a table.
- Use Hive's ANALYZE command to collect statistics.

It is important to note that Presto stores statistics in the Hive metastore, the same place that Hive uses to store statistics. So if you're sharing the same tables between Hive and Presto, they overwrite each others' statistics. This is something you should take into consideration when determining how to manage statistics collection.

Presto ANALYZE

Presto provides an ANALYZE command to collect statistics for a connector; for example, the Hive connector. When run, Presto computes column-level statistics by using its execution engine and stores the statistics in the Hive metastore. The syntax is as follows:

```
ANALYZE table_name [ WITH ( property_name = expression [, ...] ) ]
```

For example, if you want to collect and store statistics from the flights table, you can run the following:

```
ANALYZE hive.ontime.flights;
```

In the partitioned case, we can use the WITH clause if we want to analyze only a particular partition:

```
ANALYZE hive.ontime.flights WITH (partitions = ARRAY[ARRAY['01-01-2019']])
```

The nested array is needed when you have more than one partition key, and you'd like each key to be an element in the next array. The topmost array is used if you have multiple partitions you want to analyze. The ability to specify a partition is very useful in Presto. For example, you may have some type of ETL process that creates new partitions. As new data comes in, statistics could become stale, as they do not incorporate the new data. However, by updating statistics for the new partition, you don't have to reanalyze all the previous data.

Gathering Statistics When Writing to Disk

If you have tables for which the data is always written through Presto, statistics can be collected during write operations. For example, if you run a CREATE TABLE AS, or an INSERT SELECT query, Presto collects the statistics as it is writing the data to disk (HDFS or S3, for example) and then stores the statistics in the Hive metastore.

This is a useful feature, as it does not require you to run the manual step of ANALYZE. The statistics are never stale. However, for this to work properly and as expected, the data in the table must always be written by Presto.

The overhead of this process has been extensively benchmarked and tested, and it shows negligible impact to performance. To enable the feature, you can add the following property into your catalog properties file by using the Hive connector:

```
hive.collect-column-statistics-on-write=true
```

Hive ANALYZE

Outside of Presto, you can still use the Hive ANALYZE command to collect the statistics for Presto. The computation of the statistics is performed by the Hive execution engine and not the Presto execution engine, so the results may vary, and there is always the risk of Presto behaving differently when using statistics generated by Hive versus Presto. It's generally recommended to use Presto to collect statistics. But there may be reasons for using Hive, such as if the data lands as part of a more complex pipeline and is shared with other tools that may want to use the statistics. To collect statistics by using Hive, you can run the following commands:

```
hive> ANALYZE TABLE hive.ontime.flights COMPUTE STATISTICS;
hive> ANALYZE TABLE hive.ontime.flights COMPUTE STATISTICS FOR COLUMNS;
```

For complete information on the Hive `ANALYZE` command, you can refer to the official Hive documentation (*https://cwiki.apache.org/confluence/display/Hive/StatsDev*).

Displaying Table Statistics

Once you have collected the statistics, it is often useful to view them. You may want to do this to confirm that statistics have been collected, or perhaps you are debugging a performance issue and want to see the statistics being used.

Presto provides a `SHOW STATS` command:

```
SHOW STATS FOR hive.ontime.flights;
```

Alternatively, if you want to see the statistics on a subset of data, you can provide a filtering condition. For example:

```
SHOW STATS FOR (SELECT * FROM hive.ontime.flights WHERE year > 2010);
```

Conclusion

Now you understand the Presto architecture, with a coordinator receiving user requests and then using workers to assemble all the data from the data sources.

Each query is translated into a distributed query plan of tasks in numerous stages. The data is returned by the connectors in splits and processed in multiple stages until the final result is available and provided to the user by the coordinator.

If you are interested in the Presto architecture in even more detail, you can dive into the paper "Presto: SQL on Everything" by the Presto creators, published at the IEEE International Conference on Data Engineering (ICDE) and available on the website; see "Website" on page 12.

Next, you are going to learn more about deploying a Presto cluster in Chapter 5, hooking up more data sources with different connectors in Chapters 6 and 7, and writing powerful queries in Chapter 8.

Production-Ready Deployment

Following the installation of Presto from the *tar.gz* archive in Chapter 2, and your new understanding of the Presto architecture from Chapter 4, you are now ready to learn more about the details of installing a Presto cluster. You can then take that knowledge and work toward a production-ready deployment of a Presto cluster with a coordinator and multiple worker nodes.

Configuration Details

The Presto configuration is managed in multiple files discussed in the following sections. They are all located in the *etc* directory located within the installation directory by default.

The default location of this folder, as well of as each individual configuration file, can be overridden with parameters passed to the launcher script, discussed in "Launcher" on page 77.

Server Configuration

The file *etc/config.properties* provides the configuration for the Presto server. A Presto server can function as a coordinator, or a worker, or both at the same time. Dedicating a single server to perform only coordinator work, and adding a number of other servers as dedicated workers, provides the best performance and creates a Presto *cluster*.

The contents of the file are of critical importance, specifically since they determine the role of the server as a worker or coordinator, which in turn affects resource usage and configuration.

All worker configurations in a Presto cluster should be identical.

The following are the basic allowed Presto server configuration properties. In later chapters, as we discuss features such as authentication, authorization, and resource groups, we cover additional optional properties.

`coordinator=true|false`
> Allows this Presto instance to function as a coordinator and therefore accept queries from clients and manage query execution. Defaults to `true`. Setting the value to `false` dedicates the server as worker.

`node-scheduler.include-coordinator=true|false`
> Allows scheduling work on the coordinator. Defaults to `true`. For larger clusters, we suggest setting this property to `false`. Processing work on the coordinator can impact query performance because the server resources are not available for the critical task of scheduling, managing, and monitoring query execution.

`http-server.http.port=8080` *and* `http-server.https.port=8443`
> Specifies the ports used for the server for the HTTP/HTTPS connection. Presto uses HTTP for all internal and external communication.

`query.max-memory=5GB`
> The maximum amount of distributed memory that a query may use. This is described in greater detail in Chapter 12.

`query.max-memory-per-node=1GB`
> The maximum amount of user memory that a query may use on any one machine. This is described in greater detail in Chapter 12.

`query.max-total-memory-per-node=2GB`
> The maximum amount of user and system memory that a query may use on any one server. System memory is the memory used during execution by readers, writers, network buffers, etc. This is described in greater detail in Chapter 12.

`discovery-server.enabled=true`
> Presto uses the discovery service to find all the nodes in the cluster. Every Presto instance registers with the discovery service on startup. To simplify deployment and avoid running an additional service, the Presto coordinator can run an embedded version of the discovery service. It shares the HTTP server with Presto and thus uses the same port. Typically set to `true` on the coordinator. Required to be disabled on all workers by removing the property.

```
discovery.uri=http://localhost:8080
```
The URI to the discovery server. When running the embedded version of discovery in the Presto coordinator, this should be the URI of the Presto coordinator, including the correct port. This URI must not end in a slash.

Logging

The optional Presto logging configuration file, *etc/log.properties*, allows setting the minimum log level for named logger hierarchies. Every logger has a name, which is typically the fully qualified name of the Java class that uses the logger. Loggers use the Java class hierarchy. The packages used for all components of Presto can be seen in the source code, discussed in "Source Code, License, and Version" on page 14.

For example, consider the following log levels file:

```
io.prestosql=INFO
io.prestosql.plugin.postgresql=DEBUG
```

The first line sets the minimum level to `INFO` for all classes inside `io.prestosql`, including nested packages such as `io.prestosql.spi.connector` and `io.pres tosql.plugin.hive`. The default level is `INFO`, so the preceding example does not actually change logging for any packages in the first line. Having the default level in the file just makes the configuration more explicit. However, the second line overrides the logging configuration for the PostgreSQL connector to debug-level logging.

There are four levels, `DEBUG`, `INFO`, `WARN`, and `ERROR`, sorted by decreasing verbosity. Throughout the book, we may refer to setting logging when discussing topics such as troubleshooting in Presto.

 When setting the logging levels, keep in mind that `DEBUG` levels can be verbose. Only set `DEBUG` on specific lower-level packages that you are actually troubleshooting to avoid creating large numbers of log messages, negatively impacting the performance of the system.

After starting Presto, you find the various log files in the *var/log* directory within the installation directory, unless you specified another location in the *etc/node.properties* file:

launcher.log
This log, created by the launcher (see "Launcher" on page 77), is connected to standard out (`stdout`) and standard error (`stderr`) streams of the server. It contains a few log messages from the server initialization and any errors or diagnostics produced by the JVM.

server.log

This is the main log file used by Presto. It typically contains the relevant information if the server fails during initialization, as well as most information concerning the actual running of the application, connections to data sources, and more.

http-request.log

This is the HTTP request log, which contains every HTTP request received by the server. These include all usage of the Web UI, Presto CLI, as well as JDBC or ODBC connection discussed in Chapter 3, since all of them operate using HTTP connections. It also includes authentication and authorizations logging.

All log files are automatically rotated and can also be configured in more detail in terms of size and compression.

Node Configuration

The node properties file, *etc/node.properties*, contains configuration specific to a single installed instance of Presto on a server—a node in the overall Presto cluster.

The following is a small example file:

```
node.environment=production
node.id=ffffffff-ffff-ffff-ffff-ffffffffffff
node.data-dir=/var/presto/data
```

The following parameters are the allowed Presto configuration properties:

`node.environment=demo`

The *required* name of the environment. All Presto nodes in a cluster must have the same environment name. The name shows up in the Presto Web UI header.

`node.id=some-random-unique-string`

An optional unique identifier for this installation of Presto. This must be unique for every node. This identifier should remain consistent across reboots or upgrades of Presto, and therefore be specified. If omitted, a random identifier is created with each restart.

`node.data-dir=/var/presto/data`

The optional filesystem path of the directory, where Presto stores log files and other data. Defaults to the *var* folder inside the installation directory.

JVM Configuration

The JVM configuration file, *etc/jvm.config*, contains a list of command-line options used for starting the JVM running Presto.

The format of the file is a list of options, one per line. These options are not interpreted by the shell, so options containing spaces or other special characters should not be quoted.

The following provides a good starting point for creating *etc/jvm.config*:

```
-server
-mx16G
-XX:+UseG1GC
-XX:G1HeapRegionSize=32M
-XX:+UseGCOverheadLimit
-XX:+ExplicitGCInvokesConcurrent
-XX:+HeapDumpOnOutOfMemoryError
-XX:+ExitOnOutOfMemoryError
-Djdk.attach.allowAttachSelf=true
```

Because an `OutOfMemoryError` typically leaves the JVM in an inconsistent state, we write a heap dump for debugging and forcibly terminate the process when this occurs.

The `-mx` option is an important property in this file. It sets the maximum heap space for the JVM. This determines how much memory is available for the Presto process.

The configuration to allow the JDK/JVM to attach to itself is required for Presto usage since the update to Java 11.

More information about memory and other JVM settings is discussed in Chapter 12.

Launcher

As mentioned in Chapter 2, Presto includes scripts to start and manage Presto in the *bin* directory. These scripts require Python.

The `run` command can be used to start Presto as a foreground process.

In a production environment, you typically start Presto as a background daemon process:

```
$ bin/launcher start
Started as 48322
```

The number 48322 you see in this example is the assigned process ID (PID). It differs at each start.

You can stop a running Presto server, which causes it to shut down gracefully:

```
$ bin/launcher stop
Stopped 48322
```

When a Presto server process is locked or experiences other problems, it can be useful to forcefully stop it with the kill command:

```
$ bin/launcher kill
Killed 48322
```

You can obtain the status and PID of Presto with the status command:

```
$ bin/launcher status
Running as 48322
```

If Presto is not running, the status command returns that information:

```
$ bin/launcher status
Not running
```

Besides the mentioned commands, the launcher script supports numerous options that can be used to customize the configuration file locations and other parameters. The --help option can be used to display the full details:

```
$ bin/launcher --help
Usage: launcher [options] command

Commands: run, start, stop, restart, kill, status

Options:
  -h, --help                 show this help message and exit
  -v, --verbose              Run verbosely
  --etc-dir=DIR              Defaults to INSTALL_PATH/etc
  --launcher-config=FILE     Defaults to INSTALL_PATH/bin/launcher.properties
  --node-config=FILE         Defaults to ETC_DIR/node.properties
  --jvm-config=FILE          Defaults to ETC_DIR/jvm.config
  --config=FILE              Defaults to ETC_DIR/config.properties
  --log-levels-file=FILE     Defaults to ETC_DIR/log.properties
  --data-dir=DIR             Defaults to INSTALL_PATH
  --pid-file=FILE            Defaults to DATA_DIR/var/run/launcher.pid
  --launcher-log-file=FILE   Defaults to DATA_DIR/var/log/launcher.log (only in
                             daemon mode)
  --server-log-file=FILE     Defaults to DATA_DIR/var/log/server.log (only in
                             daemon mode)
  -D NAME=VALUE              Set a Java system property
```

Other installation methods use these options to modify paths. For example, the RPM package, discussed in "RPM Installation" on page 80, adjusts the path to better comply with Linux filesystem hierarchy standards and conventions. You can use them for similar needs, such as complying with enterprise-specific standards, using specific mount points for storage, or simply using paths outside the Presto installation directory to ease upgrades.

Cluster Installation

In Chapter 2, we discussed installing Presto on a single machine, and in Chapter 4, you learned more about how Presto is designed and intended to be used in a distributed environment.

For any real use, other than for demo purposes, you need to install Presto on a cluster of machines. Fortunately, the installation and configuration is similar to installing on a single machine. It requires a Presto installation on each machine, either by installing manually or by using a deployment automation system like Ansible.

So far, you've deployed a single Presto server process to act as both a coordinator and a worker. For the cluster installation, you need to install and configure one coordinator and multiple workers.

Simply copy the downloaded *tar.gz* archive to all machines in the cluster and extract it.

As before, you have to add the *etc* folder with the relevant configuration files. A set of example configuration files for the coordinator and the workers is available in the *cluster-installation* directory of the support repository of the book; see "Book Repository" on page 15. The configuration files need to exist on every machine you want to be part of the cluster.

The configurations are the same as the simple installation for the coordinator and workers, with some important differences:

- The `coordinator` property in *config.properties* is set to `true` on the coordinator and set to `false` on the workers.
- The `node-scheduler` is set to exclude the coordinator.
- The `discovery-uri` property has to point to the IP address or hostname of the coordinator on all workers and the coordinator itself.
- The discovery server has to be disabled on the workers, by removing the property.

The main configuration file, *etc/config.properties*, suitable for the coordinator:

```
coordinator=true
node-scheduler.include-coordinator=false
http-server.http.port=8080
query.max-memory=5GB
query.max-memory-per-node=1GB
query.max-total-memory-per-node=2GB
discovery-server.enabled=true
discovery.uri=http://<coordinator-ip-or-host-name>:8080
```

Note the difference of the configuration file, *etc/config.properties*, suitable for the workers:

```
coordinator=false
http-server.http.port=8080
query.max-memory=5GB
query.max-memory-per-node=1GB
query.max-total-memory-per-node=2GB
discovery.uri=http://<coordinator-ip-or-host-name>:8080
```

With Presto installed and configured on a set of nodes, you can use the launcher to start Presto on every node. Generally, it is best to start the Presto coordinator first, followed by the Presto workers:

```
$ bin/launcher start
```

As before, you can use the Presto CLI to connect to the Presto server. In the case of a distributed setup, you need to specify the address of the Presto coordinator using the `--server` option. If you are running the Presto CLI on the Presto coordinator node directly, you do not need to specify this option, as it defaults to `localhost:8080`:

```
$ presto --server <coordinator-ip-or-host-name>:8080
```

You can now verify that the Presto cluster is running correctly. The `nodes` system table contains the list of all the active nodes that are currently part of the cluster. You can query it with a SQL query:

```
presto> SELECT * FROM system.runtime.nodes;
 node_id  |        http_uri        | node_version | coordinator | state
---------+------------------------+--------------+-------------+--------------------
 c00367d  | http://<http_uri>:8080 | 330          | true        | active
 9408e07  | http://<http_uri>:8080 | 330          | false       | active
 90dfc04  | http://<http_uri>:8080 | 330          | false       | active
(3 rows)
```

The list includes the coordinator and all connected workers in the cluster. The coordinator and each worker expose status and version information by using the REST API at the endpoint */v1/info*; for example, *http://worker-or-coordinator-host-name/v1/info*.

You can also confirm the number of active workers using the Presto Web UI.

RPM Installation

Presto can be installed using the RPM Package Manager (RPM) on various Linux distributions such as CentOS, Red Hat Enterprise Linux, and others.

The RPM package is available on the Maven Central Repository at *https://repo.maven.apache.org/maven2/io/prestosql/presto-server-rpm*. Locate the RPM in the folder with the desired version and download it.

You can download the archive with `wget`; for example, for version 330:

```
$ wget https://repo.maven.apache.org/maven2/ \
io/prestosql/presto-server-rpm/330/presto-server-rpm-330.rpm
```

With administrative access, you can install Presto with the archive in single-node mode:

```
$ sudo rpm -i presto-server-rpm-*.rpm
```

The `rpm` installation creates the basic Presto configuration files and a service control script to control the server. The script is configured with `chkconfig`, so that the service is started automatically on the operating system boot. After installing Presto from the RPM, you can manage the Presto server with the `service` command:

```
service presto [start|stop|restart|status]
```

Installation Directory Structure

When using the RPM-based installation method, Presto is installed in a directory structure more consistent with the Linux filesystem hierarchy standards. This means that not everything is contained within the single Presto installation directory structure as we have seen so far. The service is configured to pass the correct paths to Presto with the launcher script:

/usr/lib/presto/
> The directory contains the various libraries needed to run the product. Plug-ins are located in a nested *plugin* directory.

/etc/presto
> This directory contains the general configuration files such as *node.properties*, *jvm.config*, and *config.properties*. Catalog configurations are located in a nested *catalog* directory.

/etc/presto/env.sh
> This file sets the Java installation path used.

/var/log/presto
> This directory contains the log files.

/var/lib/presto/data
> This is the data directory.

/etc/rc.d/init.d/presto
> This directory contains the service scripts for controlling the server process.

The *node.properties* file requires the following two additional properties, since our directory structure is different from the defaults used by Presto:

```
catalog.config-dir=/etc/presto/catalog
plugin.dir=/usr/lib/presto/plugin
```

Configuration

The RPM package installs Presto acting as coordinator and worker out of the box, identical to the *tar.gz* archive. To create a working cluster, you can update the configuration files on the nodes in the cluster manually, use the presto-admin (*https://github.com/prestosql/presto-admin*) tool, or use a generic configuration management and provisioning tool such as Ansible.

Uninstall Presto

If Presto is installed using RPM, you can uninstall it the same way you remove any other RPM package:

```
$ rpm -e presto
```

When removing Presto, all files and configurations, apart from the logs directory */var/log/presto*, are deleted. Create a backup copy if you wish to keep anything.

Installation in the Cloud

A typical installation of Presto involves running at least one cluster with a coordinator and multiple workers. Over time, the number of workers in the cluster, as well as the number of clusters, can change based on the demand from users.

The number and type of connected data sources, as well as their location, also has a major impact on choosing where to install and run your Presto cluster. Typically, it is desirable that the Presto cluster has a high-bandwidth, low-latency network connectivity to the data sources.

The simple requirements of Presto, discussed in Chapter 2, allow you to run Presto in many situations. You can run it on different machines such as physical servers or virtual machines, as well as Docker containers.

Presto is known to work on private cloud deployments as well as on many public cloud providers including Amazon Web Services (AWS), Google Cloud Platform (GCP), Microsoft Azure, and others.

Using containers allows you to run Presto on Kubernetes (k8s) clusters such as Amazon Elastic Kubernetes Service (Amazon EKS), Microsoft Azure Kubernetes Service (AKS), Google Kubernetes Engine (GKE), Red Hat Open Shift, and any other Kubernetes deployments.

An advantage of these cloud deployments is the potential for a highly dynamic cluster, where workers are created and destroyed on demand. Tooling for such use cases has been created by different users, including cloud vendors embedding Presto in their offerings and other vendors offering Presto tooling and support.

 The Presto project does not provide a complete set of suitable resources and tooling for running a Presto cluster in a turn-key, hands-off fashion. Organizations typically create their own packages, configuration management setups, container images, k8s operators, or whatever is necessary, and they use tools such as Concord (*https://concord.walmartlabs.com*) or Terraform (*https://www.terraform.io*) to create and manage the clusters. Alternatively, you can consider relying on the support and offerings from a company like Starburst.

Cluster Sizing Considerations

An important aspect of getting Presto deployed is sizing the cluster. In the longer run, you might even work toward multiple clusters for different use cases. Sizing the Presto cluster is a complex task and follows the same patterns and steps as other applications:

1. Decide on an initial size, based on rough estimates and available infrastructure.
2. Ensure that the tooling and infrastructure for the cluster is able to scale the cluster.
3. Start the cluster and ramp up usage.
4. Monitor utilization and performance.
5. React to the findings by changing cluster scale and configuration.

The feedback loop around monitoring, adapting, and continued use allows you to get a good understanding of the behavior of your Presto deployment.

Many factors influence your cluster performance, and the combination of these is specific to each Presto deployment:

- Resources like CPU and memory for each node
- Network performance within the cluster and to data sources and storage
- Number and characteristics of connected data sources
- Queries run against the data sources and their scope, complexity, number, and resulting data volume
- Storage read/write performance of the data sources
- Active users and their usage patterns

Once you have your initial cluster deployed, make sure you take advantage of using the Presto Web UI for monitoring. Chapter 12 provides more tips.

Conclusion

As you've now learned, Presto installation and running a cluster requires just a handful of configuration files and properties. Depending on your actual infrastructure and management system, you can achieve a powerful setup of one or even multiple Presto clusters. Check out real-world examples in Chapter 13.

Of course, you are still missing a major ingredient of configuring Presto. And that is the connections to the external data sources that your users can then query with Presto and SQL. In Chapter 6 and Chapter 7, you get to learn all about the various data sources, the connectors to access them, and the configuration of the catalogs that point at specific data sources using the connectors.

Connectors

In Chapter 3, you configured a catalog to use a connector to access a data source in Presto—specifically, the TPC-H benchmark data—and then learned a bit about how to query that data with SQL.

Catalogs are an important aspect of using Presto. They define the connection to the underlying data source and storage system, and use concepts such as connector, schema, and table. These fundamental concepts are described in Chapter 4, and their use with SQL is discussed in more detail in Chapter 8.

A *connector* translates the query and storage concepts of an underlying data source, such as a relational database management system (RDBMS), object storage, or a key-value store, to the SQL and Presto concepts of tables, columns, rows, and data types. These can be simple SQL-to-SQL translations and mappings but also much more complicated translations from SQL to object storage or NoSQL systems. These can also be user defined.

You can think of a connector the same way you think of a driver for a database. It translates the user input into operations that the underlying database can execute. Every connector implements the Presto service provider interface (SPI). This enables Presto to allow you to use the same SQL tooling to work with whatever underlying data source the connector exposes and makes Presto a SQL-on-Anything system.

Query performance is also influenced by the connector implementation. The most basic connector makes a single connection to the data source and provides the data to Presto. However, a more advanced connector can break a statement into multiple connections, performing operations in parallel to allow for better performance. Another advanced feature of a connector is to provide table statistics, that can then be used by the cost-based optimizer to create highly performant query plans.. Such a connector is, however, more complex to implement.

Presto provides numerous connectors:

- Connectors for RDBMS systems such as PostgreSQL or MySQL—see "RDBMS Connector Example PostgreSQL" on page 87

- A Hive connector suitable for querying systems by using the Hadoop Distributed File System (HDFS) and similar object storage systems—see "Hive Connector for Distributed Storage Data Sources" on page 93

- Numerous connectors to nonrelational data sources—see "Non-Relational Data Sources" on page 104

- `tpch` and `tpcds` connectors designed to serve TPC benchmark data—see "Presto TPC-H and TPC-DS Connectors" on page 92

- A connector for Java Management Extensions, or JMX—see "Presto JMX Connector" on page 104

In this chapter, you learn more about some of these connectors, available from the Presto project. More than two dozen connectors are shipped in Presto today, and more are created by the Presto team and the user community. Commercial, proprietary connectors are also available to further extend the reach and performance of Presto. Finally, if you have a custom data source, or one that there is not a connector for, you can implement your own connector by implementing the necessary SPI calls and drop it into the plug-ins directory in Presto.

One important aspect of the catalog and connector usage is that all of them become available to SQL statements and queries in Presto at the same time. This means that you can create queries that span data sources. For example, you can combine data from a relational database with the data in files stored in your object storage backend. These *federated queries* are discussed in more detail in "Query Federation in Presto" on page 122.

Configuration

As discussed in "Adding a Data Source" on page 23, every data source you want to access needs to be configured as a catalog by creating a catalog file. The name of the file determines the name of the catalog when writing queries.

The mandatory property `connector.name` indicates which connector is used for the catalog. The same connector can be used multiple times in different catalogs; for example, to access different RDBMS server instances with different databases all using the same technology such as PostgreSQL. Or if you have two Hive clusters, you can configure two catalogs in a single Presto cluster that both use the Hive connector, allowing you to query data from both Hive clusters.

RDBMS Connector Example PostgreSQL

Presto contains connectors to both open source and proprietary RDBMSs, including MySQL, PostgreSQL, AWS Redshift, and Microsoft SQL Server. Presto queries these data sources with the connectors by using each system's respective JDBC drivers.

Let's look at a simple example using PostgreSQL. A PostgreSQL instance may consist of several databases. Each database contains schemas, which contain objects such as tables and views. When configuring Presto with PostgreSQL, you choose the database that is exposed as a catalog in Presto.

After creating a simple catalog file pointing at a specific database in the server, *etc/catalog/postgresql.properties* shown next, and restarting Presto, you can find out more information. You can also see that the postgresql connector is configured as the required connector.name:

```
connector.name=postgresql
connection-url=jdbc:postgresql://db.example.com:5432/database
connection-user=root
connection-password=secret
```

 The user and password in the catalog properties file determines the access rights to the underlying data source. This can be used to, for example, restrict access to read-only operations or to restrict available tables.

You can list all catalogs to confirm that the new catalog is available, and inspect details with the Presto CLI, or a database management tool using the JDBC driver (as explained in "Presto Command-Line Interface" on page 25 and "Presto JDBC Driver" on page 30):

```
SHOW CATALOGS;
  Catalog
-----------
 system
 postgresql
(2 rows)

SHOW SCHEMAS IN postgresql;
  Catalog
-----------
 public
 airline
(2 rows)

USE postgresql.airline
SHOW TABLES;
  Table
```

```
---------
 airport
 carrier
(2 rows)
```

In this example, you see we connected to a PostgreSQL database that contains two schemas: public and airline. And then within the airline schema are two tables, airport and carrier. Let's try running a query. In this example, we issue a SQL query to Presto, where the table exists in a PostgreSQL database. Using the PostgreSQL connector, Presto is able to retrieve the data for processing, returning the results to the user:

```
SELECT code, name FROM airport WHERE code = 'ORD';
 code |             name
------+------------------------------
 ORD  | Chicago O'Hare International
(1 row)
```

As displayed in Figure 6-1, the client submits the query to the Presto coordinator. It offloads the work to a worker, which sends the entire SQL query statement to PostgrSQL using JDBC. The PostgreSQL JDBC driver is contained within the PostgresSQL connector. PostgreSQL processes the query and returns the results over JDBC. The connector reads the results and writes them to the Presto internal data format. Presto continues the processing on the worker, provides it to the coordinator, and then returns the results to the user.

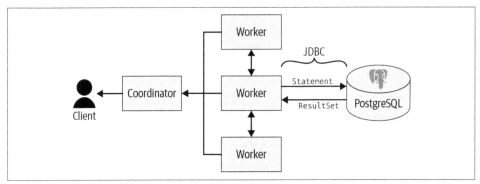

Figure 6-1. Presto cluster interaction with PostgreSQL using JDBC in the connector

Query Pushdown

As we saw in the previous example, Presto is able to offload processing by pushing the SQL statement down into the underlying data source. This is known as *query pushdown*, or *SQL pushdown*. This is advantageous, as the underlying system can reduce the amount of data returned to Presto, avoiding unnecessary memory, CPU, and network costs. Furthermore, systems like PostgreSQL typically have indexes on certain filter columns, allowing for faster processing. However, it is not always possible to push the entire SQL statement down into the data source. Currently, the Presto Connector SPI limits the types of operations that can be pushed down to filter and column projections:

```
SELECT state, count(*)
FROM airport
WHERE country = 'US'
GROUP BY state;
```

Given the preceding Presto query, the PostgreSQL connector constructs the SQL query to push down to PostgreSQL:

```
SELECT state
FROM airport
WHERE country = 'US';
```

There are two important places to look when queries are pushed by a RDBMS connector. The columns in the SELECT list are set to specifically what is needed by Presto. In this case, we need only the state column for processing the GROUP BY in Presto. We also push the filter country = 'US', which means we do not need to perform further processing of the country column in Presto. You notice that the aggregations are not pushed down to PostgreSQL. This is because Presto is not able to push any other form of queries down, and the aggregations must be performed in Presto. This can be advantageous because Presto is a distributed query processing engine, whereas PostgreSQL is not.

If you do want to push additional processing down to the underlying RDBMS source, you can accomplish this by using views. If you encapsulate the processing in a view in PostgreSQL, it is exposed as a table to Presto, and the processing occurs within PostgreSQL. For example, let's say you create the view in PostgreSQL:

```
CREATE view airline.airports_per_us_state AS
SELECT state, count(*) AS count_star
FROM airline.airport
WHERE country = 'US'
GROUP BY state;
```

When you run SHOW TABLES in Presto, you see this view:

```
SHOW TABLES IN postgresql.airline;
  Table
---------
 airport
 carrier
 airports_per_us_state
(3 rows)
```

Now you can just query the view, and all processing is pushed down to PostgreSQL, since the view appears as an ordinary table to Presto:

```
SELECT * FROM airports_per_us_state;
```

Parallelism and Concurrency

Currently, all RDBMS connectors use JDBC to make a single connection to the underlying data source. The data is not read in parallel, even if the underlying data source is a parallel system. For parallel systems, like Teradata or Vertica, you have to write parallel connectors that can take advantage of how those systems store the data in a distributed fashion.

When accessing multiple tables from the same RDBMS, a JDBC connection is created and used for each table in the query. For example, if the query is performing a join between two tables in PostgreSQL, Presto creates two different connections over JDBC to retrieve the data, as displayed in Figure 6-2. They run in parallel, send their results back, and then the join is performed in Presto.

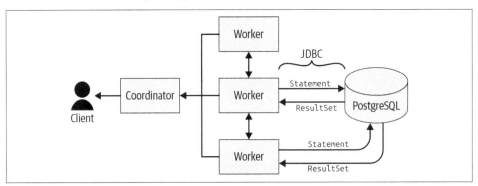

Figure 6-2. Multiple JDBC connections used to access different tables in PostgreSQL

As with aggregations, joins cannot be pushed down. However, if you want to take advantage of the performance enhancements possible in the underlying PostgreSQL system, you can create a view in PostgreSQL, or even add native indices for further improvements.

Other RDBMS Connectors

Currently, the Presto open source project has four RDBMS connectors. The MySQL, PostgreSQL, AWS Redshift, and Microsoft SQL Server connectors are already included in the plug-ins directory of Presto and ready to be configured. If you have multiple servers, or want to separate access, you can configure multiple catalogs in Presto for each instance. You just need to name the *.properties* file differently. As usual, the name of the properties file determines the name of the catalog:

```
SHOW CATALOGS;
  Catalog
------------
 system
 mysql-dev
 mysql-prod
 mysql-site
(2 rows)
```

Nuances exist among different RDBMSs. Let's take a look at how each is configured in their catalog configuration files.

In MySQL, there is no difference between a database and a schema, and the catalog file and the JDBC connection string basically point at the specific MySQL server instance:

```
connector.name=mysql
connection-url=jdbc:mysql://example.net:3306
connection-user=root
connection-password=secret
```

PostgreSQL makes a clear distinction, and an instance can contain multiple databases that contain schemas. The JDBC connection points at a specific database:

```
connector.name=postgresql
connection-url=jdbc:postgresql://example.net:5432/database
connection-user=root
connection-password=secret
```

The AWS Redshift catalog looks similar to PostgreSQL's. In fact, Redshift uses the PostgreSQL JDBC driver, since it is based on the open source PostgreSQL code and the JDBC driver is compatible and can be used:

```
connector.name=redshift
connection-url=jdbc:postgresql://example.net:5439/database
connection-user=root
connection-password=secret
```

Microsoft SQL Server connection strings look similar to the MySQL string. However, SQL Server does have the notion of databases and schemas, and the example simply connects to the default database:

```
connector.name=sqlserver
connection-url=jdbc:sqlserver://example.net:1433
connection-user=root
connection-password=secret
```

Using a different database like sales has to be configured with a property:

```
connection-url=jdbc:sqlserver://example.net:1433;databaseName=sales
```

Security

Currently, the only way to authenticate for RDBMS connectors is by storing the username and password in the catalog configuration file. Since the machines in the Presto cluster are designed to be a trusted system, this should be sufficient for most uses. In order to keep Presto and the connected data sources secure, it's important to secure access to the machines and configuration files. It should be treated the same way as a private key. All users of Presto use the same connection to the RDBMS.

If you do not want to store a password in cleartext, there are ways to pass through the username and password from the Presto client. We discuss this further in Chapter 10.

In conclusion, using Presto with RDBMSs is easy and allows you to expose all the systems in one place and query them all at the same time. This usage alone is already providing a significant benefit of Presto usage. Of course, it gets much more interesting when you add more data sources with other connectors. So let's continue to learn more.

Presto TPC-H and TPC-DS Connectors

You have already discovered the TPC-H connector usage in Chapter 2. Let's have a closer look.

The TPC-H and the TPC-DS connector are built into Presto and provide a set of schemas to support the TPC Benchmark H (TPC-H) and the TPC Benchmark DS (TPC-DS). These database benchmark suites from the Transaction Processing Performance Council (*http://tpc.org*) are industry standard benchmarks for database systems, used to measure the performance of highly complex decision support databases.

The connectors can be used to test the capabilities and query syntax of Presto without configuring access to an external data source. When you query a TPC-H or TPC-DS schema, the connector generates some data on the fly by using a deterministic algorithm.

Create a catalog properties file, *etc/catalog/tpch.properties*, to configure the TPC-H connector:

```
connector.name=tpch
```

Configuration is similar for the TPC-DS connector; for example, with *etc/catalog /tpcds.properties*:

```
connector.name=tpcds
```

Both connectors expose schemas that include the same data sets in terms of structure:

```
SHOW SCHEMAS FROM tpch;
        Schema
--------------------
 information_schema
 sf1
 sf100
 sf1000
 sf10000
 sf100000
 sf300
 sf3000
 sf30000
 tiny
(10 rows)
```

Table 6-1 shows how the different schemas contain increasingly larger numbers of records in transactional tables such as orders.

Table 6-1. Example record counts for order table in different tpch schemas

Schema	Count
tiny	15000
sf1	1500000
sf3	4500000
sf100	150000000

You can use these data sets for learning more about SQL supported by Presto, as discussed in Chapter 8 and Chapter 9, without the need to connect another database.

Another important use case of these connectors is the simple availability of the data. You can use the connectors for development and testing, or even on a production Presto deployment. With the huge data amounts easily available, you can build queries that put a significant load on your Presto cluster. This allows you to better understand the performance of your cluster, tune and optimize it, and ensure that it performs over time and across version updates and other changes.

Hive Connector for Distributed Storage Data Sources

As you learned in "A Brief History of Presto" on page 16, Presto is designed to run fast queries at Facebook scale. Given that Facebook had a massive storage in its Hive data warehouse, it is only natural that the Hive connector is one of the first connectors that was developed with Presto.

Apache Hadoop and Hive

Before you read about the Hive connector, and its suitability for numerous object storage formats, you need to brush up on your knowledge about Apache Hadoop (*https://hadoop.apache.org*) and Apache Hive (*https://hive.apache.org*) a bit.

If you're not that familiar with Hadoop and Hive and want to learn more, we recommend the official websites of the projects, videos and other resources on the web, and some of the great books available. For example, *Programming Hive (https://oreil.ly/ liekE)* by Edward Capriolo et al. (O'Reilly) has proven to be a great guide to us.

For now, we need to discuss certain Hadoop and Hive concepts to provide enough context for the Presto usage.

At its very core, Hadoop consists of the Hadoop Distributed File System (HDFS) and application software, such a Hadoop MapReduce, to interact with the data stored in HDFS. Apache YARN is used to manage the resources needed by Hadoop applications. *Hadoop* is the leading system for distributed processing of large data sets across clusters of computers. It is capable of scaling the system while maintaining a highly available service on top of a cluster of computers.

Originally, data processing was performed by writing MapReduce programs. They followed a specific programming model that enables the data processing to be naturally distributed across the cluster. This model works well and is robust. However, writing MapReduce programs for analytical questions is cumbersome. It also does not transfer well for existing infrastructure, tooling, and users that rely on SQL and data warehousing.

Hive provides an alternative to the usage of MapReduce. It was created as a method to provide a SQL layer of abstraction on top of Hadoop to interact with data in HDFS using a SQL-like syntax. Now the large set of users who know and understand SQL can interact with data stored in HDFS.

Hive data is stored as files, often referred to as *objects*, in HDFS. These files use various formats, such as ORC, Parquet, and others. The files are stored using a particular directory and file layout that Hive understands; for example, partitioned and bucketed tables. We refer to the layout as a Hive-style table format.

Hive metadata describes how data stored in HDFS maps to schemas, tables, and columns to be queried via SQL. This metadata information is persisted in a database such as MySQL or PostgreSQL and is accessible via the *Hive Metastore Service (HMS)*.

The Hive runtime provides the SQL-like query language and distributed execution layer to execute the queries. The Hive runtime translates the query into a set of MapReduce programs that can run on a Hadoop cluster. Over time, Hive has evolved to provide other execution engines such as Apache Tez and Spark that the query is translated to.

Hadoop and Hive are widely used across the industry. With their use, the HDFS format has become a supported format for many other distributed storage systems such as Amazon S3 and S3-compatible stores, Azure Data Lake Storage, Azure Blob Storage, Google Cloud Storage, and many others.

Hive Connector

The *Hive connector* for Presto allows you to connect to an HDFS object storage cluster. It leverages the metadata in HMS and queries and processes the data stored in HDFS.

Probably the most common use case of Presto is to leverage the Hive connector to read data from distributed storage such as HDFS or cloud storage.

 Presto and the Presto Hive connector do not use the Hive runtime at all. Presto is a replacement for it and is suitable for running interactive queries.

The Hive connector allows Presto to read and write from distributed storage such as HDFS. However, it is not constrained to HDFS but designed to work with distributed storage in general. Currently, you can configure the Hive connector to work with HDFS, AWS S3, Azure Blob Storage, Azure Data Lake Storage, Google Cloud Storage, and S3-compatible storage. S3-compatible storage may include MinIO, Ceph, IBM Cloud Object Storage, SwiftStack, Cloudian, Riak CS, LeoFS, OpenIO, and others. A variety of these compatible stores exist. As long as they implement the S3 API and behave the same way, Presto does not need to know the difference for the most part.

Because of the widespread use of Hadoop and other compatible systems using HDFS and the expanded feature set of the Hive connector to support them, it can be considered the main connector for querying object storage with Presto and is therefore of critical importance for many, if not most, Presto users.

Architecturally, the Hive connector is a bit different from RBDMS and other connectors since it does not use the Hive engine itself at all. It therefore cannot push SQL processing to Hive. Instead, it simply uses the metadata in HMS and accesses the data directly on HDFS, using the HDFS client provided with the Hadoop project. It also assumes the Hive table format in the way the data is organized in the distributed storage.

In all cases, the schema information is accessed from HMS, and the data layout is the same as with a Hive data warehouse. The concepts are the same, but the data is simply stored in a location other than HDFS. However, unlike Hadoop, these non-Hadoop distributed filesystems do not always have an HMS equivalent to store the metadata for use by Presto. To leverage the Hive-style table format, you must configure Presto to use HMS from an existing Hadoop cluster or to your own standalone HMS. This can mean that you use a replacement for HMS such as AWS Glue or run a minimal Hadoop deployment with HMS only.

Using HMS to describe data in blob storage other than HDFS allows the Hive connector to be used to query these storage systems. This unlocks the data stored in these systems to all the power of SQL usage via Presto and any tool capable of using SQL.

Configuring a catalog to use the Hive connector requires you to create a catalog properties file with the desired name, for example, *etc/catalog/s3.properties*, *etc/catalog/gcs.properties*, *etc/catalog/minio.properties*, or even just *etc/catalog/hdfs.properties* or *etc/catalog/objectstorage.properties*. In the following, we assume the use of *etc/catalog/hive.properties*. At a minimum, you need to configure the connector name and the URL for HMS:

```
connector.name=hive-hadoop2
hive.metastore.uri=thrift://example.net:9083
```

Numerous other configuration properties apply for different use cases, some of which you learn more about soon. When in doubt, always make sure to check out the documentation; see "Documentation" on page 13. Let's get into some of those details next.

Hive-Style Table Format

Once the connector is configured, you can create a schema from Presto,f for example, in HDFS:

```
CREATE SCHEMA hive.web
WITH (location = 'hdfs://starburst-oreilly/web')
```

The schema, sometimes still called a *database*, can contain multiple tables. You can read more about them in the next section. The schema creation typically creates only the metadata about the schema in the HMS:

```
...
hdfs://starburst-oreilly/web/customers
hdfs://starburst-oreilly/web/clicks
hdfs://starburst-oreilly/web/sessions
...
```

Using Amazon S3 is not much different. You just use a different protocol string:

```
CREATE SCHEMA hive.web
WITH (location = 's3://example-org/web')

...
s3://example-org/web/customers
s3://example-org/web/clicks
s3://example-org/web/sessions
...
```

Managed and External Tables

After the schema, we need to learn more about the content in the schema, organized as tables. Hive distinguishes between managed tables and external tables. A *managed table* is managed by Hive, and therefore also by Presto potentially, and is created along with its data under the location of the database's directory. An *external table* is not managed by Hive and explicitly points to another location outside the directory that Hive manages.

The main difference between a managed table and an external table is that Hive, and therefore Presto, owns the data in the managed table. If you drop a managed table, the metadata in the HMS and the data are deleted. If you drop an external table, the data remains, and only the metadata about the table is deleted.

The types of tables you use really comes down to the way you plan to use Presto. You may be using Presto for data federation, your data warehouse or data lake, both, or some other mix. You need to decide who owns the data. It could be Presto working with the HMS, or it could be Hadoop and HMS, or Spark, or other tools in an ETL pipeline. In all cases, the metadata is managed in HMS.

The decision about which system owns and manages HMS and the data is typically based on your data architecture. In the early use cases of Presto, Hadoop often controls the data life cycle. But as more use cases leverage Presto as the central tool, many users shift their pattern, and Presto takes over control.

Some new Presto users start by querying an existing Hadoop deployment. In this case, it starts off as more of a data federation use, and Hadoop owns the data. You then configure the Hive connector to expose the existing tables in Hadoop to Presto for querying. You use external tables. Typically, you do not allow Presto to write to these tables in this case.

Other Presto users may start to migrate away from Hadoop and completely toward Presto, or they may start new with another object storage system, specifically, often a cloud-based system. In this case, it is best to start creating the data definition language (DDL) via Presto to let Presto own the data.

Let's consider the following DDL for a Presto table:

```
CREATE TABLE hive.web.page_views (
  view_time timestamp,
  user_id bigint,
  page_url varchar,
  view_date date,
  country varchar
)
```

In this example, the table `page_views` stores data under a directory also named *page_views*. This *page_views* directory is either a subdirectory under the directory defined by `hive.metastore.warehouse.dir` or is a different directory if you defined the schema location when creating the schema.

Here is an HDFS example:

```
hdfs:/user/hive/warehouse/web/page_views/...
```

And here's an Amazon S3 example:

```
s3://example-org/web/page_views/...
```

Next, let's consider DDL for a Presto table that points to existing data. This data is created and managed by another means, such as by Spark or an ETL process where the data lands in storage. In this case, you may create an external table via Presto pointing to the external location of this data:

```
CREATE TABLE hive.web.page_views (
  view_time timestamp,
  user_id bigint,
  page_url varchar,
  view_date date,
  country varchar
)
WITH (
  external_location = 's3://starburst-external/page_views'
)
```

This inserts the metadata about the table into the HMS, including the external path and a flag that signals to Presto and HMS that the table is external and therefore managed by another system.

As a result, the data, located in *s3://example-org/page_views*, may already exist. Once the table is created in Presto, you can start querying it. When you configure the Hive connector to an existing Hive warehouse, you see the existing tables and are able to query from them immediately.

Alternatively, you could create the table in an empty directory and expect the data to be loaded later, either by Presto or by an external source. In either case, Presto expects that the directory structure is already created; otherwise, the DDL errors. The most common case for creating an external table is when data is shared with other tools.

Partitioned Data

So far, you have learned how the data for a table, whether managed or external, is stored as one or more files in a directory. *Data partitioning* is an extension of this and is a technique used to horizontally divide a logical table into smaller pieces of data known as *partitions*.

The concept itself derives from partitioning schemes in RDBMSs. Hive introduced this technique for data in HDFS as a way to achieve better query performance and manageability of the data.

Partitioning is now a standard data organization strategy in distributed filesystems, such as HDFS, and in object storage, such as S3.

Let's use this table example to demonstrate partitioning:

```
CREATE TABLE hive.web.page_views (
  view_time timestamp,
  user_id bigint,
  page_url varchar,
  view_date date
)
WITH (
  partitioned_by = ARRAY['view_date']
)
```

 The columns listed in the partitioned_by clause must be the last columns as defined in the DDL. Otherwise, you get an error from Presto.

As with nonpartitioned tables, the data for the page_views table is located within .../ *page_views*. Using partitioning changes the way the table layout is structured. With partitioned tables, additional subdirectories are added within the table subdirectory. In the following example, you see the directory structure as defined by the partition keys:

```
...
.../page_views/view_date=2019-01-14/...
.../page_views/view_date=2019-01-15/...
.../page_views/view_date=2019-01-16/...
...
```

Presto uses this same Hive-style table format. Additionally, you can chose to partition on multiple columns:

```
CREATE TABLE hive.web.page_views (
  view_time timestamp,
  user_id bigint,
  page_url varchar,
  view_date date,
  country varchar
)
WITH (
  partitioned_by = ARRAY['view_date', 'country']
)
```

When choosing multiple partitioned columns, Presto creates a hierarchical directory structure:

```
...
.../page_views/view_date=2019-01-15/country=US…
.../page_views/view_date=2019-01-15/country=PL…
.../page_views/view_date=2019-01-15/country=UA...
.../page_views/view_date=2019-01-16/country=US…
.../page_views/view_date=2019-01-17/country=AR...
...
```

Partitioning gives you improved query performance, especially as your data grows in size. For example, let's take the following query:

```
SELECT DISTINCT user_id
FROM page_views
WHERE view_date = DATE '2019-01-15' AND country = 'US';
```

When this query is submitted, Presto recognizes the partition columns in the WHERE clause and uses the associated value to read only the *view_date=2019-01-15/country=US* subdirectory. By reading only the partition you need, potentially large performance savings can result. If your data is small today, the performance gain might not be noticeable. But as your data grows, the improved performance is significant.

Loading Data

So far, you've learned about the Hive-style table format, including partitioned data. How do you get the data into the tables? It really depends on who owns the data. Let's start under the assumption that you are creating the tables in Presto and loading the data with Presto:

```
CREATE TABLE hive.web.page_views (
  view_time timestamp,
  user_id bigint,
  page_url varchar,
  view_date date,
  country varchar
)
WITH (
  partitioned_by = ARRAY['view_date', 'country']
)
```

To load data via Presto, Presto supports INSERT INTO ... VALUES, INSERT INTO ... SELECT, and CREATE TABLE AS SELECT. Although INSERT INTO exists, it has limited use, since it creates a single file and single row for each statement. It is often good to use as you learn Presto.

INSERT SELECT and CREATE TABLE AS perform the same function. Which one you use is a matter of whether you want to load into an existing table or create the table as you're loading. Let's take, for example, INSERT SELECT where you may be querying data from a nonpartitioned external table and loading into a partitioned table in Presto:

```
presto:web> INSERT INTO page_views_ext SELECT * FROM page_views;
INSERT: 16 rows
```

 The preceding example shows inserting new data into an external table. By default, Presto disallows writing to an external table. To enable it, you need to set `hive.non-managed-table-writes-enabled` to `true` in your catalog configuration file.

If you're familiar with Hive, Presto does what is known as *dynamic partitioning*: the partitioned directory structure is created the first time Presto detects a partition column value that doesn't have a directory.

You can also create an external partitioned table in Presto. Say a directory structure with data in S3 is as follows:

```
...
s3://example-org/page_views/view_date=2019-01-14/...
s3://example-org/page_views/view_date=2019-01-15/...
s3://example-org/page_views/view_date=2019-01-16/...
...
```

We create the external table definition:

```
CREATE TABLE hive.web.page_views (
  view_time timestamp,
  user_id bigint,
  page_url varchar,
  view_date date
)
WITH (
  partitioned_by = ARRAY['view_date']
)
```

Now let's query from it:

```
presto:web> SELECT * FROM page_views;
 view_time | user_id | page_url | view_date
-----------+---------+----------+-----------
(0 rows)
```

What happened? Even though we know there is data in it, the HMS does not recognize the partitions. If you're familiar with Hive, you know about the `MSCK REPAIR TABLE` command to autodiscover all the partitions. Fortunately, Presto has its own command as well to autodiscover and add the partitions:

```
CALL system.sync_partition_metadata(
  'web',
  'page_views',
  'FULL'
)
...
```

Now that you have added the partitions, let's try again:

```
presto:web> SELECT * FROM page_views;
        view_time        | user_id | page_url | view_date
-------------------------+---------+----------+-----------
 2019-01-25 02:39:09.987 |    123  | ...      | 2019-01-14
 ...
 2019-01-25 02:39:11.807 |    123  | ...      | 2019-01-15
 ...
```

Alternatively, Presto provides the ability to create partitions manually. This is often cumbersome because you have to use the command to define each partition separately:

```
CALL system.create_empty_partition[w][x](
  'web',
  'page_views',
  ARRAY['view_date'],
  ARRAY['2019-01-14']
)
...
```

Adding empty partitions is useful when you want to create the partitions outside Presto via an ETL process and then want to expose the new data to Presto.

Presto also supports dropping partitions simply by specifying the partition column value in the WHERE clause of a DELETE statement. And in this example, the data stays intact because it is an external table:

```
DELETE FROM hive.web.page_views
WHERE view_date = DATE '2019-01-14'
```

It is important to emphasize that you do not have to manage your tables and data with Presto, but you can if desired. Many users leverage Hive, or other tools, to create and manipulate data, and use Presto only to query the data.

File Formats and Compression

Presto supports many of the common file formats used in Hadoop/HDFS, including the following:

- ORC

- PARQUET

- AVRO

- JSON

- TEXTFILE

- RCTEXT

- RCBINARY

- CSV

- SEQUENCEFILE

The three most common file formats used by Presto are ORC, Parquet, and Avro data files. The readers for ORC, Parquet, RC Text, and RC Binary formats are heavily optimized in Presto for performance.

The metadata in HMS contains the file format information so that Presto knows what reader to use when reading the data files. When creating a table in Presto, the default data type is set to ORC. However, the default can be overridden in the CREATE TABLE statement as part of the WITH properties:

```
CREATE TABLE hive.web.page_views (
   view_time timestamp,
   user_id bigint,
   page_url varchar,
   ds_date,
   country varchar
)
WITH (
   format = 'ORC'
)
```

The default storage format for all tables in the catalog can be set with the hive.storage-format configuration in the catalog properties file.

By default, the GZIP compression codec is used by Presto for writing files. You can change the code to use SNAPPY or NONE by setting the hive.compression-codec configuration in the catalog properties file.

MinIO Example

MinIO (*https://min.io*) is an S3-compatible, lightweight distributed storage system you can use with Presto and the Hive connector. If you want to explore its use in more detail, you can check out our example project (*https://github.com/starburstdata/presto-minio*).

If your HDFS is secured with Kerberos, you can learn more about configuring the Hive connector in "Kerberos Authentication with the Hive Connector" on page 225.

Non-Relational Data Sources

Presto includes connectors to query variants of nonrelational data sources. These data sources are often referred to as *NoSQL systems* and can be key-value stores, column stores, stream processing systems, document stores, and other systems.

Some of these data sources provide SQL-like query languages such as CQL for Apache Cassandra (*https://cassandra.apache.org*). Others provide only specific tools or APIs to access the data or include entirely different query languages such as the Query Domain Specific Language used in Elasticsearch. The completeness of these languages is often limited and not standardized.

Presto connectors for these NoSQL data sources allow you to run SQL queries for these systems as if they were relational. This allows you to use applications such as business intelligence tools or allow those who know SQL to query these data sources. This includes use of joins, aggregations, subqueries, and other advanced SQL capabilities against these data sources.

In the next chapter, you learn more about some of these connectors:

- NoSQL system such as Elasticsearch or MongoDB—"Document Store Connector Example: Elasticsearch" on page 120
- Streaming systems such as Apache Kafka—"Streaming System Connector Example: Kafka" on page 118
- Key-value store systems such as Apache Accumulo—"Key-Value Store Connector Example: Accumulo" on page 110 and Apache Cassandra—"Apache Cassandra Connector" on page 117
- Apache HBase with Apache Phoenix connector—"Connecting to HBase with Phoenix" on page 109

Let's skip over these for now and talk about some simpler connectors and related aspects first.

Presto JMX Connector

The JMX connector can easily be configured for use in the catalog properties file *etc/catalog/jmx.properties*:

```
connector.name=jmx
```

The JMX connector exposes runtime information about the JVMs running the Presto coordinator and workers. It uses Java Management Extensions (JMX) and allows you to use SQL in Presto to access the available information. It is especially useful for monitoring and troubleshooting purposes.

The connector exposes a `history` schema for historic, aggregate data, a `current` schema with up-to-date information and the `information_schema` schema for metadata.

The easiest way to learn more is to use Presto statements to investigate the available tables:

```
SHOW TABLES FROM jmx.current;
                Table
------------------------------------------------------------------
 com.sun.management:type=diagnosticcommand
 com.sun.management:type=hotspotdiagnostic
 io.airlift.discovery.client:name=announcer
 io.airlift.discovery.client:name=serviceinventory
 io.airlift.discovery.store:name=dynamic,type=distributedstore
 io.airlift.discovery.store:name=dynamic,type=httpremotestore
 ....
```

As you can see, the table names use the Java classpath for the metrics emitting classes and parameters. This means that you need to use quotes when referring to the table names in SQL statements. Typically, it is useful to find out about the available columns in a table:

```
DESCRIBE jmx.current."java.lang:type=runtime";
 Column               |  Type   | Extra | Comment
----------------------+---------+-------+---------
 bootclasspath        | varchar |       |
 bootclasspathsupported | boolean |     |
 classpath            | varchar |       |
 inputarguments       | varchar |       |
 librarypath          | varchar |       |
 managementspecversion | varchar |      |
 name                 | varchar |       |
 objectname           | varchar |       |
 specname             | varchar |       |
 specvendor           | varchar |       |
 specversion          | varchar |       |
 starttime            | bigint  |       |
 systemproperties     | varchar |       |
 uptime               | bigint  |       |
 vmname               | varchar |       |
 vmvendor             | varchar |       |
 vmversion            | varchar |       |
 node                 | varchar |       |
 object_name          | varchar |       |
(19 rows)
```

This allows you to get information nicely formatted:

```
SELECT vmname, uptime, node FROM  jmx.current."java.lang:type=runtime";
            vmname           |  uptime  |      node
---------------------------+---------+--------------
 OpenJDK 64-Bit Server VM | 1579140 | ffffffff-ffff
(1 row)
```

Notice that only one node is returned in this query since this is a simple installation of a single coordinator/worker node, as described in Chapter 2.

The JMX connector exposes a lot of information about the JVM in general, including as Presto specific aspects. You can start exploring the available information by looking at the tables starting with `presto`; for example, with `DESCRIBE jmx.current."presto.execution:name=queryexecution";`.

Here are a few other describe statements worth checking out:

```
DESCRIBE jmx.current."presto.execution:name=querymanager";
DESCRIBE jmx.current."presto.memory:name=clustermemorymanager";
DESCRIBE jmx.current."presto.failuredetector:name=heartbeatfailuredetector";
```

To learn more about monitoring Presto by using the Web UI and other related aspects, you can head over to Chapter 12.

Black Hole Connector

The *black hole connector* can easily be configured for use in a catalog properties file such as *etc/catalog/blackhole.properties*:

```
connector.name=blackhole
```

It acts as a sink for any data, similar to the null device in Unix operating systems, */dev/null*. This allows you to use it as a target for any insert queries reading from other catalogs. Since it does not actually write anything, you can use this to measure read performance from those catalogs.

For example, you can create a test schema in `blackhole` and create a table from the `tpch.tiny` data set. Then you read a data set from the `tpch.sf3` data and insert it into the `blackhole` catalog:

```
CREATE SCHEMA blackhole.test;
CREATE TABLE blackhole.test.orders AS SELECT * from tpch.tiny.orders;
INSERT INTO blackhole.test.orders SELECT * FROM tpch.sf3.orders;
```

This operation essentially measures read performance from the `tpch` catalog, since it reads 1.5 million order records and then sends them to `blackhole`. Using other schemas like `tcph.sf100` increases the data-set size. This allows you to assess the performance of your Presto deployment.

A similar query with a RDBMS, object storage, or a key-value store catalog can be helpful for query development and performance testing and improvements.

Memory Connector

The *memory connector* can be configured for use in a catalog properties file; for example, *etc/catalog/memory.properties*:

```
connector.name=memory
```

You can use the memory connector like a temporary database. All data is stored in memory in the cluster. Stopping the cluster destroys the data. Of course, you can also actively use SQL statements to remove data in a table or even drop the table altogether.

Using the memory connector is useful for testing queries or temporary storage. For example, we use it as a simple replacement for the need to have an external data source configured when using the Iris data set; see "Iris Data Set" on page 15.

While useful for testing and small tasks, the memory connector is *not* suitable for large data sets and production usage, especially when distributed across a cluster. For example, the data might be distributed across different worker nodes, and a crash of a worker results in loss of that data. Use the memory connector only for temporary data.

Other Connectors

As you now know, the Presto project includes many connectors, yet sometimes you end up in a situation where you need just one more connector for that one specific data source.

The good news is that you are not stuck. The Presto team, and the larger Presto community, are constantly expanding the list of available connectors, so by the time you read this book, the list is probably longer than it is now.

Connectors are also available from parties outside the Presto project itself. This includes other community members and users of Presto, who wrote their own connectors and have not yet contributed them back, or cannot contribute for one reason or another.

Connectors are also available from commercial vendors of database systems, so asking the owner or creator of the system you want to query is a good idea. And the Presto community includes commercial vendors, such as Starburst, which bundle Presto with support and extensions, including additional or improved connectors.

Last, but not least, you have to keep in mind that Presto is a welcoming community around the open source project. So you can, and are encouraged to, look at the code of the existing connectors, and create new connectors as desired. Ideally, you can even work with the project and contribute a connector back to the project to enable simple maintenance and usage going forward.

Conclusion

Now you know a lot more about the power of Presto to access a large variety of data sources. No matter what data source you access, Presto makes the data available to you for querying with SQL and SQL-powered tools. In particular, you learned about the crucial Hive connector, used to query distributed storage such as HDFS or cloud storage systems. In the next chapter, Chapter 7, you can learn more details about a few other connectors that are widely in use.

Detailed documentation for all the connectors is available on the Presto website; see "Website" on page 12. And if you do not find what you are looking for, you can even work with the community to create your own connector or enhance existing connectors.

Advanced Connector Examples

Now you know what functionality connectors provide to Presto and how to configure them from Chapter 6. Let's expand that knowledge to some of the more complex usage scenarios and connectors. These are typically connectors that need to be smart enough to translate storage patterns and ideas from the underlying data source, which do not easily map to the table-oriented model from SQL and Presto.

Learn more by jumping right to the section about the system you want to connect to with Presto and query with SQL:

After these connectors, you can round out your understanding by learning about query federation and the related ETL usage in "Query Federation in Presto" on page 122.

Connecting to HBase with Phoenix

The distributed, scalable, big data store Apache HBase (*http://hbase.apache.org*) builds on top of HDFS. Users are, however, not restricted to use low-level HDFS and access it with the Hive connector. The Apache Phoenix project (*https://phoenix.apache.org*) provides a SQL layer to access HBase, and thanks to the Presto Phoenix connector, you can therefore access HBase databases from Presto just like any other data source.

As usual, you simply need a catalog file like *etc/catalog/bigtables.properties*:

```
connector.name=phoenix
phoenix.connection-url=jdbc:phoenix:zookeeper1,zookeeper2:2181:/hbase
```

The connection URL is a JDBC connection string to the database. It includes a list of the Apache ZooKeeper nodes, used for the discovery of the HBase nodes.

Phoenix schemas and tables are mapped to Presto schemas and tables, and you can inspect them with the usual Presto statements:

```
SHOW SCHEMAS FROM bigtable;
SHOW TABLES FROM bigtable.example;
SHOW COLUMNS FROM bigtable.examples.user;
```

Now you are ready to query any HBase tables and use them in the downstream tooling, just like the data from any other data source connected to Presto.

Using Presto allows you to query HBase with the performance benefits of a horizontally scaled Presto. Any queries you create have access to HBase and any other catalog, allowing you to combine HBase data with other sources into federated queries.

Key-Value Store Connector Example: Accumulo

Presto includes connectors for several key-value data stores. A *key-value store* is a system for managing a dictionary of records stored and retrieved by using a unique key. Imagine a hash table for which a record is retrieved by a key. This record may be a single value, multiple values, or even a collection.

Several key-value store systems exist that have a range of functionality. One widely used system is the open source, wide column store database Apache Cassandra (*https://cassandra.apache.org*), for which a Presto connector is available. You can find more information in "Apache Cassandra Connector" on page 117.

Another example we now discuss in more detail is Apache Accumulo (*https://accu mulo.apache.org*). It is a highly performant, widely used, open source key-value store that can be queried with a Presto connector. The general concepts translate to other key-value stores.

Inspired by Google's BigTable, Apache Accumulo is a sorted, distributed key-value store for scalable stores and retrieval. Accumulo stores key-value data on HDFS sorted by the key.

Figure 7-1 shows how a key in Accumulo consists of a triplet of row ID, column, and timestamp. The key is sorted first by the key and the column in ascending lexicographic order, and then timestamps in descending order.

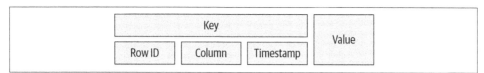

Figure 7-1. A key-value pair in Accumulo

Accumulo can be further optimized by utilizing column families and locality groups. Most of this is transparent to Presto, but knowing the access patterns of your SQL queries may help you optimize your creation of Accumulo tables. This is identical to optimizing the tables for any other application using Accumulo.

Let's take a look at the logical representation of a relational table in Table 7-1.

Table 7-1. Relational or logic view of the data in Accumulo

rowid	flightdate	flightnum	origin	dest
1234	2019-11-02	2237	BOS	DTW
5678	2019-11-02	133	BOS	SFO
...	...	...	...	...

Because Accumulo is a key-value store, it stores this representation of data on disk differently from the logic view, as shown in Table 7-2. This nonrelational storage makes it less straightforward to determine how Presto can read from it.

Table 7-2. View of how Accumulo stores data

rowid	column	value
1234	flightdate:flightdate	2019-11-02
1234	flightnum:flightnum	2237
1234	origin:origin	BOS
1234	dest:dest	DTW
5678	flightdate:flightdate	2019-11-02
5678	flightnum:flightnum	133
5678	origin:origin	BOS
5678	dest:dest	SFO
...	...	...

The Presto Accumulo connector handles mapping the Accumulo data model into a relational one that Presto can understand.

Figure 7-2 shows that Accumulo uses HDFS for storage and ZooKeeper to manage metadata about the tables.

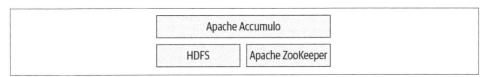

Figure 7-2. Basic Accumulo architecture consisting of distributed Accumulo, HDFS, and Apache ZooKeeper

At its core, Accumulo is a distributed system that consists of a master node and multiple tablet servers, as displayed in Figure 7-3. Tablet servers contain and expose tablets, which are horizontally partitioned pieces of a table. Clients connect directly to the tablet server to scan the data that is needed.

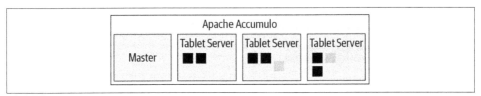

Figure 7-3. Accumulo architecture with master node and multiple tablet servers

Just like Accumulo itself, the Presto Accumulo connector uses ZooKeeper. It reads all information such as tables, views, table properties, and column definitions from the ZooKeeper instance used by Accumulo.

Let's take a look at how to scan data in Accumulo from Presto. In Accumulo, key pairs can be read from a table by using the Scanner object. The scanner starts reading from the table at a particular key and ends at another key, or at the end of the table. The scanners can be configured to read only the exact columns needed. Recall from the RDBMS connectors that only the columns needed are added to the SQL query generated to push into the database.

Accumulo also has the notion of a BatchScanner object. This is used when reading from Accumulo over multiple ranges. This is more efficient because it is able to use multiple workers to communicate with Accumulo, displayed in Figure 7-4.

The user first submits the query to the coordinator, and the coordinator communicates with Accumulo to determine the splits from the metadata. It determines the splits by looking for the ranges from the available index in Accumulo. Accumulo returns the row IDs from the index, and Presto stores these ranges in the split. If an index cannot be used, one split is used for all the ranges in a single tablet. Last, the worker uses the information to connect to the specific tablet servers and pulls the data in parallel from Accumulo. This pulls the database by using the BatchScanner utility from Accumulo.

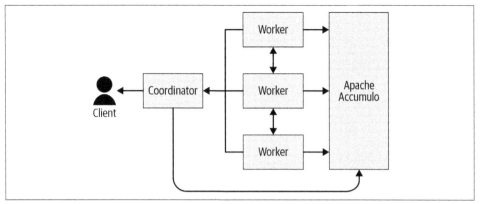

Figure 7-4. Multiple workers accessing Accumulo in parallel

Once the data is pulled back from the workers, the data is put into a relational format that Presto understands, and the remainder of the processing is completed by Presto. In this case, Accumulo is being used for the data storage. Presto provides the higher-level SQL interface for access to the data in Accumulo.

If you were writing an application program yourself to retrieve the data from Accumulo, you'd write something similar to the following Java snippet. You set the ranges to be scanned and define which columns to fetch:

```
ArrayList<Range> ranges = new ArrayList<Range>();
ranges.add(new Range("1234"));
ranges.add(new Range("5678"));

BatchScanner scanner = client.createBatchScanner("flights", auths, 10);
scanner.setRangers(ranges);
scanner.fetchColumn("flightdate");
scanner.fetchColumn("flightnum");
scanner.fetchColumn("origin");

  for (Entry<Key,Value> entry : scanner) {
    // populate into Presto format
  }
}
```

The concept of pruning columns that do not need to be read is similar to the RDBMS connectors. Instead of pushing down SQL, the Accumulo connector uses the Accumulo API to set what columns to fetch.

Using the Presto Accumulo Connector

To use Accumulo, create a catalog properties file (for example, *etc/catalog/accumulo.properties*) that references the Accumulo connector and configures the Accumulo access including the connection to ZooKeeper:

```
connector.name=accumulo
accumulo.instance=accumulo
accumulo.zookeepers=zookeeper.example.com:2181
accumulo.username=user
accumulo.password=password
```

Using our flights example from earlier, let's create a table in Accumulo with Presto, using the Presto CLI, or a RDBMS management tool connected to Presto via JDBC:

```
CREATE TABLE accumulo.ontime.flights (
    rowid VARCHAR,
    flightdate VARCHAR,
    flightnum, INTEGER,
    origin VARCHAR
    dest VARCHAR
);
```

When you create this table in Presto, the connector actually creates a table in Accumulo and the metadata about the table in ZooKeeper.

It is also possible to create a column family. A *column family* in Accumulo is an optimizer for applications that accesses columns together. By defining column families, Accumulo arranges how columns are stored on disk such that the frequently accessed columns, as part of a column family, are stored together. If you want to create a table using column families, you can specify this as a table property, specified in the WITH statement:

```
CREATE TABLE accumulo.ontime.flights (
    rowid VARCHAR,
    flightdate VARCHAR,
    flightnum, INTEGER,
    origin VARCHAR
    dest VARCHAR
)
WITH
    column_mapping = 'origin:location:origin,dest:location:dest'
);
```

By using column_mapping, you are able to define a column family location with column qualifiers origin and dest, which are the same as the Presto column names.

When the column_mapping table property is not used, Presto auto-generates a column family and column qualifier to be the same name as the Presto column name. You can observe the Accumulo column family and column qualifier by running the DESCRIBE command on the table.

The Presto Accumulo connector supports INSERT statements:

```
INSERT INTO accumulo.ontime.flights VALUES
    (2232, '2019-10-19', 118, 'JFK', 'SFO');
```

This is a convenient way to insert data. However, it is currently low throughput when data is written to Accumulo from Presto. For better performance, you need to use the native Accumulo APIs. The Accumulo connector has utilities outside Presto for assisting with higher performance of inserting data. You can find more information about loading data by using the separate tool in the Presto documentation.

The table we created in the preceding example is an *internal table*. The Presto Accumulo connector supports both internal and external tables. The only difference between the types is that dropping of an external table deletes only the metadata and not the data itself. External tables allow you to create Presto tables that already exist in Accumulo. Furthermore, if you need to change the schema, such as to add a column, you can simply drop the table and re-create it in Presto without losing the data. It's worth noting that Accumulo can support this schema evolution when each row does not need to have the same set of columns.

Using external tables requires a bit more work because the data is already stored in a particular way. For example, you must use the `column_mapping` table property when using external tables. You must set the `external` property to `true` when creating the table:

```
CREATE TABLE accumulo.ontime.flights (
    rowid VARCHAR,
    flightdate VARCHAR,
    flightnum, INTEGER,
    origin VARCHAR
    dest VARCHAR
)
WITH
    external = true,
    column_mapping = 'origin:location:origin,dest:location:dest'
);
```

Predicate Pushdown in Accumulo

In the Accumulo connector, Presto can take advantage of the secondary indexes built in Accumulo. To achieve this, the Accumulo connector requires a custom server-side iterator on each Accumulo tablet server. The iterator is distributed as a JAR file that you have to copy into the *$ACCUMULO_HOME/lib/ext* on each tablet server. You can find the exact details of how to do this in the Presto documentation.

Indexes in Accumulo are used to look up the row IDs. These can be used to read the values from the actual table. Let's look at an example:

```
SELECT flightnum, origin
FROM flights
WHERE flightdate BETWEEN DATE '2019-10-01' AND 2019-11-05'
AND origin = 'BOS';
```

Without an index, Presto reads the entire data set from Accumulo and then filters it within Presto. The workers get splits that contain the Accumulo range to read. This range is the entire range of the tablet. Where there is an index, such as the example index in Table 7-3, the number of ranges to process can be significantly reduced.

Table 7-3. Example index on the flights table

2019-08-10	flightdate_flightdate:2232	[]
2019-10-19	flightdate_flightdate:2232	[]
2019-11-02	flightdate_flightdate:1234	[]
2019-11-02	flightdate_flightdate:5478	[]
2019-12-01	flightdate_flightdate:1111	[]
SFO	origin_origin:2232	[]
BOS	origin_origin:3498	[]
BOS	origin_origin:1234	[]
BOS	origin_origin:5678	[]
ATL	origin_origin:1111	[]
...	...	...

The coordinator uses the WHERE clause filters flightdate BETWEEN DATE '2019-10-01' AND 2019-11-05' AND origin = 'BOS' to scan the index to obtain the row IDs for the table. The row IDs are then packed into the split that the worker later uses to access the data in Accumulo. In our example, we have secondary indexes on flightdate and origin and we collected the row IDs {2232, 1234, 5478} and {3498, 1234, 5678}. We take the intersection from each index and know that we have to only scan row IDs {1234, 5678}. This range is then placed into the split for processing by the worker, which can access the individual values directly, as seen in the detailed view of the data in Table 7-4.

Table 7-4. Detail view with the individual values for origin, dest, and others

Rowid	Column	Value
2232	flightdate:flightdate	2019-10-19
2232	flightnum:flightnum	118
2232	origin:origin	JFK
2232	dest:dest	SFO
1234	flightdate:flightdate	2019-11-02
1234	flightnum:flightnum	2237

Rowid	Column	Value
1234	origin:origin	BOS
1234	dest:dest	DTW
5678	flightdate:flightdate	2019-11-02
5678	flightnum:flightnum	133
5678	origin:origin	BOS
5678	dest:dest	SFO
3498	flightdate:flightdate	2019-11-10
3498	flightnum:flightnum	133
3498	origin:origin	BOS
3498	dest:dest	SFO
...	...	...

To take advantage of predicate pushdown, we need to have indexes on the columns we want to push down predicates for. Through the Presto connector, indexing on columns can be easily enabled with the `index_columns` table property:

```
CREATE TABLE accumulo.ontime.flights (
    rowid VARCHAR,
    flightdate VARCHAR,
    flightnum, INTEGER,
    origin VARCHAR
    dest VARCHAR
)
WITH
    index_columns = 'flightdate,origin'
);
```

In this section on Apache Accumulo, you learned about key-value storage and how Presto can be used to query it with standard SQL. Let's see another, much more widespread system that can benefit from Presto: Apache Cassandra.

Apache Cassandra Connector

Apache Cassandra (*https://cassandra.apache.org*) is a distributed, wide column store that supports massive amounts of data. Its fault tolerant architecture and the linear scalability have led to wide adoption of Cassandra.

The typical approach to work with the data in Cassandra is to use the custom query language created for Cassandra: Cassandra Query Language (CQL). While CQL on the surface looks quite a bit like SQL, it practically misses many of the useful features of SQL, such as joins. Overall, it is different enough to make using standard tools that rely on SQL impossible.

By using the Cassandra connector, however, you can allow SQL querying of your data in Cassandra. Minimal configuration is a simple catalog file like *etc/catalog/sitedata* for a Cassandra cluster tracking all user interaction on a website, for example:

```
connector.name=cassandra
cassandra.contact-points=sitedata.example.com
```

With this simple configuration in place, users can query the data in Cassandra. Any keyspace in Cassandra (for example, `cart`) is exposed as a schema in Presto, and tables such as `users` can be queried with normal SQL now:

```
SELECT * FROM sitedata.cart.users;
```

The connector supports numerous configuration properties that allow you to adapt the catalog to your Cassandra cluster, enable authentication and TLS for the connection, and more.

Streaming System Connector Example: Kafka

Streaming systems and publish-subscribe (pub/sub) systems are designed for handling real-time data feeds. For example, Apache Kafka was created to be a high-throughput and low-latency platform at LinkedIn. Publishers write messages to Kafka for the subscribers to consume. Such a system is generally useful for data pipelines between systems. The Presto Kafka connector is used to read data from Kafka. Currently, you cannot use the connector to publish data.

Using the connector, you can use SQL to query data on a Kafka topic and even join it with other data. The typical use case with Presto is ad hoc querying of the live Kafka topic streams to inspect and better understand the current status and data flowing through the system. Using Presto makes this much easier and accessible for data analysts and other users who typically don't have any specific Kafka knowledge but do know how to write SQL queries.

Another, less common use case for Presto with Kafka is the migration of data from Kafka. Using a `CREATE TABLE AS` or an `INSERT SELECT` statement, you can read data from the Kafka topic, transform the data using SQL, and then write it to HDFS, S3, or other storage.

Since Kafka is a streaming system, the exposed topics constantly change their content as new data comes in. This has to be taken into account when querying Kafka topics with Presto. Performing a migration of the data with Presto to HDFS or another database system with permanent storage allows you to preserve the information passing through your Kafka topics.

Once the data is permanently available in the target database or storage, Presto can be used to expose it to analytical tools such as Apache Superset; see "Queries, Visualizations, and More with Apache Superset" on page 229.

Using the Kafka connector works like any other connector. Create a catalog (for example, *etc/catalog/trafficstream.properties*) that uses the Kafka connector, configures any other required details, and points at your Kafka cluster:

```
connector.name=kafka
kafka.table-names=web.pages,web.users
kafka.nodes=trafficstream.example.com:9092
```

Now every topic from Kafka web.pages and web.users is available as a table in Presto. At any time, that table exposes the entire Kafka topic with all messages currently in the topic. Each message in the topic shows up as a row in the table in Presto. The data is now easily available with SQL queries on Presto, using catalog, schema, and table names:

```
SELECT * FROM trafficstream.web.pages;
SELECT * FROM trafficstream.web.users;
```

Essentially, you can inspect your Kafka topics as they are streamed live with simple SQL queries.

If you want to migrate the data to another system, such as an HDFS catalog, you can start with a simple CREATE TABLE AS (CTAS) query:

```
CREATE TABLE hdfs.web.pages
WITH (
    format = 'ORC',
    partitioned_by = ARRAY['view_date']
)
AS
SELECT *
FROM trafficstream.web.pages;
```

Once the table exists, you can insert more data into it by running insert queries regularly:

```
INSERT INTO hdfs.web.pages
SELECT *
FROM trafficstream.web.pages;
```

To avoid duplicate copying, you can keep track of some of the internal columns from Kafka that are exposed by the connector. Specifically, you can use _partition_id, _partition_offset, _segment_start, _segment_end, and _segment_count. The specific setup you use to run the query regularly depends on your Kafka configuration for removing messages as well as the tools used to run the queries, such as Apache Airflow, described in "Workflows with Apache Airflow" on page 231.

The mapping of Kafka topics, which are exposed as tables, and their contained message, can be defined with a JSON file for each topic located in *etc/kafka/schema.tablename.json*. For the preceding example, you can define the mapping in *etc/kafka/web.pages.json*.

Kafka messages within a topic use different formats, and the Kafka connector includes decoders for the most common formats, including Raw, JSON, CSV, and Avro (*https://avro.apache.org*).

Detailed information for the configuration properties, mapping, and other internal columns is available in the Presto documentation; see "Documentation" on page 13.

Using Presto with Kafka opens up new analysis and insights into the data streamed through Kafka and defines another valuable usage of Presto. Another stream processing system supported by Presto for similar usage is Amazon Kinesis.

Document Store Connector Example: Elasticsearch

Presto includes connectors for well-known document storage systems such as Elasticsearch or MongoDB. These systems support storage and retrieval of information in JSON-like documents. Elasticsearch is better suited for indexing and searching documents. MongoDB is a general-purpose document store.

Overview

The Presto connectors allow users to use SQL to access these systems and query data in them, even though no native SQL access exists.

Elasticsearch clusters are often used to store log data or other event streams for longer-term or even permanent storage. These data sets are often very large, and they can be a useful resource for better understanding the system emitting the log data in operation and in a wide variety of scenarios.

Elasticsearch and Presto are a powerful and performant combination, since both systems can scale horizontally. Presto scales by breaking up a query and running parts of it across many workers in the cluster.

Elasticsearch typically operates on its own cluster and scales horizontally as well. It can shard the index across many nodes and run any search operations in a distributed manner. Tuning the Elasticsearch cluster for performance is a separate topic that requires an understanding of the number of documents in the search index, the number of nodes in the cluster, the replica sets, the sharding configuration, and other details.

However, from a client perspective, and therefore also from the perspective of Presto, this is all transparent, and Elasticsearch simply exposes the cluster with a URL of the Elasticsearch server.

Configuration and Usage

Configuring Presto to access Elasticsearch is performed with the creation of a catalog file such as *etc/catalog/search.properties*:

```
connector.name=elasticsearch
elasticsearch.host=searchcluster.example.com
```

This configuration relies on default values for the port, the schema, and other details, but is sufficient for querying the cluster. The connector supports numerous data types from Elasticsearch out of the box. It automatically analyzes each index, configures each as a table, exposes the table in the `default` schema, creates the necessary nested structures and row types, and exposes it all in Presto. Any document in the index is automatically unpacked into the table structure in Presto. For example, an index called `server` is automatically available as a table in the catalog's `default` schema, and you can query Presto for more information about the structure:

```
DESCRIBE search.default.server;
```

Users can start querying the index straightaway. The information schema, or the `DESCRIBE` command, can be used to understand the created tables and fields for each index/schema.

Fields in Elasticsearch schemas commonly contain multiple values as arrays. If the automatic detection does not perform as desired, you can add a field property definition of the index mapping. Furthermore, the `_source` hidden field contains the source document from Elasticsearch, and if desired, you can use the functions for JSON document parsing (see "JSON Functions" on page 183) as well as collection data types (see "Collection Data Types" on page 149). These can generally be helpful when working with the documents in an Elasticsearch cluster, which are predominately JSON documents.

In Elasticsearch, you can expose the data from one or more indexes as `alias`. This can also be filtered data. The Presto connector supports alias usage and exposes them just like any other index as a table.

Query Processing

Once you issue a query from Presto to Elasticsearch, Presto actually takes advantage of its cluster infrastructure in addition to the already clustered Elasticsearch to increase performance even more.

Presto queries Elasticsearch to understand all the Elasticsearch shards. It then uses this information when creating the query plan. It breaks the query into separate splits that are targeted at the specific shards, and then issues the separate queries to the shards all in parallel. Once the results come back, they are combined in Presto and returned to the user. This means that Presto combined with Elasticsearch can use SQL for querying and be more performant than Elasticsearch on its own.

Also note that this individual connection to specific shards also happens in typical Elasticsearch clusters where the cluster runs behind a load balancer and is just exposed via a DNS hostname.

Full-Text Search

Another powerful feature of the connector for Elasticsearch is support for full-text search. It allows you to use Elasticsearch query strings within a SQL query issued from Presto.

For example, imagine an index full of blog posts on a website. The documents are stored in the blogs index. And maybe those posts consist of numerous fields such as title, intro, post, summary, and authors. With the full-text search, you can write a simple query that searches the whole content in all the fields for specific terms such as presto:

```
SELECT * FROM "blogs: +presto";
```

The query string syntax from Elasticsearch supports weighting different search terms and other features suitable for a full-text search.

Summary

Another powerful feature, specific to users of Amazon Elasticsearch Service, is the support for AWS Identity and Access Management. Find out more details about this configuration as well as securing the connection to the Elasticsearch cluster with TLS and other tips from the Presto documentation; see "Documentation" on page 13.

Using Presto with Elasticsearch allows you to analyze the rich data in your index with the powerful tools around SQL support. You can write queries manually or hook up rich analytical tools. This allows you to understand the data in the cluster better than previously possible.

Similar advantages are available when you connect MongoDB to Presto, taking advantage of the Presto MongoDB connector.

Query Federation in Presto

After reading about all the use cases for Presto in "Presto Use Cases" on page 7, and learning about all the data sources and available connectors in Presto, you are now ready to learn more about query federation in Presto. A *federated query* is a query that accesses data in more than one data source.

This query can be used to tie together the content and information from multiple RDBMS databases, such as an enterprise backend application database running on PostgreSQL with a web application database on MySQL. It could also be a data warehouse on PostgreSQL queried with data from the source also running in PostgreSQL or elsewhere.

The much more powerful examples, however, arise when you combine queries from a RDBMS with queries running against other nonrelational systems. Combine the data from your data warehouse with information from your object storage, filled with data from your web application at massive scale. Or relate the data to content in your key-value store or your NoSQL database. Your object storage data lake can suddenly be exposed with SQL, and the information can become the basis for better understanding your overall data.

Query federation can help you truly understand the data in those systems.

In the following example, you learn about the use case of joining data in distributed storage with data in a relational database management system. You can find information about the necessary setup in "Flight Data Set" on page 16.

With this data, you can ask questions such as, "What is the average delay of airplanes by year?" by using a SQL query:

```
SELECT avg(depdelayminutes) AS delay, year
FROM flights_orc
GROUP BY year
ORDER BY year DESC;
```

Another question is, "What are the best days of the week to fly out of Boston in the month of February?":

```
SELECT dayofweek, avg(depdelayminutes) AS delay
FROM flights_orc
WHERE month=2 AND origincityname LIKE '%Boston%'
GROUP BY dayofmonth
ORDER BY dayofweek;
```

Because the notion of multiple data sources and query federation is an integral part of Presto, we encourage you to set up an environment and explore the data. These queries serve as inspiration for you to create additional queries on your own.

We use the two example analytical queries on the airline data to demonstrate query federation in Presto. The setup we provide uses data stored in S3 and accessed by configuring Presto with the Hive connector. However, if you prefer, you can store the data in HDFS, Azure Storage, or Google Cloud Storage and use the Hive connector to query the data.

In this first example query, we want Presto to return the top 10 airline carriers with the most flights from the data in HDFS:

```
SELECT uniquecarrier, count(*) AS ct
FROM flights_orc
GROUP BY uniquecarrier
ORDER BY count(*) DESC
LIMIT 10;
 uniquecarrier |    ct
---------------+----------
   WN          | 24096231
   DL          | 21598986
   AA          | 18942178
   US          | 16735486
   UA          | 16377453
   NW          | 10585760
   CO          |  8888536
   OO          |  7270911
   MQ          |  6877396
   EV          |  5391487
(10 rows)
```

While the preceding query provides us the results for the top 10 airline carriers with the most flights, it requires you to understand the values of uniquecarrier. It would be better if a more descriptive column provided the full airline carrier name instead of the abbreviations. However, the airline data source we are querying from does not contain such information. Perhaps if another data source with the information does exist, we can combine the data source to return more comprehensible results.

Let's look at another example. Here, we want Presto to return the top 10 airports that had the most departures:

```
SELECT origin, count(*) AS ct
FROM flights_orc
GROUP BY origin
ORDER BY count(*) DESC
LIMIT 10;
 origin |   ct
--------+---------
   ATL  | 8867847
   ORD  | 8756942
   DFW  | 7601863
   LAX  | 5575119
   DEN  | 4936651
   PHX  | 4725124
   IAH  | 4118279
   DTW  | 3862377
   SFO  | 3825008
   LAS  | 3640747
(10 rows)
```

As with the previous query, the results require some domain expertise. For example, you need to understand that the origin column contains airport codes. The code is meaningless to people with less expertise analyzing the results.

Let's enhance our results by combining them with additional data in a relational database. We use PostgreSQL in our examples, but similar steps are applicable for any relational database.

As with the airline data, our GitHub repository includes the setup for creating and loading tables in a relational database as well as configuring the Presto connector to access it. We've chosen to configure Presto to query from a PostgreSQL database that contains additional airline data. The table `carrier` in PostgreSQL provides a mapping of the airline code to the more descriptive airline name. You can use this additional data with our first example query.

Let's take a look at table `carrier` in PostgreSQL:

```
SELECT * FROM carrier LIMIT 10;
 code |                  description
------+-----------------------------------------------
 02Q  | Titan Airways
 04Q  | Tradewind Aviation
 05Q  | Comlux Aviation, AG
 06Q  | Master Top Linhas Aereas Ltd.
 07Q  | Flair Airlines Ltd.
 09Q  | Swift Air, LLC
 0BQ  | DCA
 0CQ  | ACM AIR CHARTER GmbH
 0GQ  | Inter Island Airways, d/b/a Inter Island Air
 0HQ  | Polar Airlines de Mexico d/b/a Nova Air
(10 rows)
```

This table contains `code` column code along with a `description` column. Using this information, we can use our first example query for the `flights_orc` table and modify it to join with the data in the PostgreSQL `carrier` table:

```
SELECT f.uniquecarrier, c.description, count(*) AS ct
FROM hive.ontime.flights_orc f,
    postgresql.airline.carrier c
WHERE c.code = f.uniquecarrier
GROUP BY f.uniquecarrier, c.description
ORDER BY count(*) DESC
LIMIT 10;
 uniquecarrier |         description         |    ct
---------------+-----------------------------+----------
 WN            | Southwest Airlines Co.      | 24096231
 DL            | Delta Air Lines Inc.        | 21598986
 AA            | American Airlines Inc.      | 18942178
 US            | US Airways Inc.             | 16735486
 UA            | United Air Lines Inc.       | 16377453
 NW            | Northwest Airlines Inc.     | 10585760
 CO            | Continental Air Lines Inc.  |  8888536
 OO            | SkyWest Airlines Inc.       |  7270911
 MQ            | Envoy Air                   |  6877396
```

```
      EV              | ExpressJet Airlines Inc.   |  5391487
   (10 rows)
```

Voilà! Now that we have written a single SQL query to federate data from S3 and PostgreSQL, we're able to provide more valuable results of the data to extract meaning. Instead of having to know or separately look up the airline codes, the descriptive airline name is in the results.

In the query, you have to use fully qualified names when referencing the tables. When utilizing the USE command to set the default catalog and schema, a nonqualified table name is linked to that catalog and schema. However, anytime you need to query outside for the catalog and schema, the table name must be qualified. Otherwise, Presto tries to find it within the default catalog and schema, and returns an error. If you are referring to a table within the default catalog and schema, it is not required to fully qualify the table name. However, it's recommended as best practice whenever referring to data sources outside the default scope.

Next, let's look at the table airport in PostgreSQL. This table is used as part of federating our second example query:

```
SELECT code, name, city FROM airport LIMIT 10;
 code |           name            |         city
------+---------------------------+----------------------
 01A  | Afognak Lake Airport      | Afognak Lake, AK
 03A  | Bear Creek Mining Strip   | Granite Mountain, AK
 04A  | Lik Mining Camp           | Lik, AK
 05A  | Little Squaw Airport      | Little Squaw, AK
 06A  | Kizhuyak Bay              | Kizhuyak, AK
 07A  | Klawock Seaplane Base     | Klawock, AK
 08A  | Elizabeth Island Airport  | Elizabeth Island, AK
 09A  | Augustin Island           | Homer, AK
 1B1  | Columbia County           | Hudson, NY
 1G4  | Grand Canyon West         | Peach Springs, AZ
 (10 rows)
```

Looking at this data from PostgreSQL, you see that the code column can be used to join with our second query on the flight_orc table. This allows you to use the additional information in the airport table with the query to provide more details:

```
SELECT f.origin, c.name, c.city, count(*) AS ct
FROM hive.ontime.flights_orc f,
    postgresql.airline.airport c
WHERE c.code = f.origin
GROUP BY origin, c.name, c.city
ORDER BY count(*) DESC
LIMIT 10;
 origin |                     name                      |         city          |   ct
--------+-----------------------------------------------+-----------------------+---------
  ATL   | Hartsfield-Jackson Atlanta International       | Atlanta, GA           | 8867847
  ORD   | Chicago OHare International                    | Chicago, IL           | 8756942
  DFW   | Dallas/Fort Worth International                | Dallas/Fort Worth, TX | 7601863
```

```
LAX    | Los Angeles International                | Los Angeles, CA     | 5575119
DEN    | Denver International                     | Denver, CO          | 4936651
PHX    | Phoenix Sky Harbor International         | Phoenix, AZ         | 4725124
IAH    | George Bush Intercontinental/Houston    | Houston, TX         | 4118279
DTW    | Detroit Metro Wayne County              | Detroit, MI         | 3862377
SFO    | San Francisco International              | San Francisco, CA   | 3825008
LAS    | McCarran International                   | Las Vegas, NV       | 3640747
(10 rows)
```

Presto! As with our first example, we can provide more meaningful information by federating across two disparate data sources. Here, we are able to add in the name of the airport instead of the user relying on airport codes that are hard to interpret.

With this quick example of query federation, you see that the combination of different data sources and the central querying in one location, in Presto, can provide tremendous improvements to your query results. Our example only enhanced the appearance and readability of the results. However, in many cases, using richer, larger data sets, the federation of queries, and combination of data from different sources can result in complete new understanding of the data.

Now that we've gone through some examples of query federation from an end-user perspective, let's discuss the architecture of how this works. We build on top of some of the concepts you learned about in Chapter 4 on the Presto architecture.

Presto is able to coordinate the hybrid execution of the query across the data sources involved in the query. In the example earlier, we were querying between distributed storage and PostgreSQL. For distributed storage via the Hive connector, Presto reads the data files directly, whether it's from HDFS, S3, Azure Blob Storage, etc. For a relational database connector such as the PostgreSQL connector, Presto relies on PostgreSQL to perform as part of the execution. Let's use our query from earlier, but to make it more interesting, we add a new predicate that refers to a column in the PostgreSQL airport table:

```
SELECT f.origin, c.name, c.city, count(*) AS ct
FROM hive.ontime.flights_orc f,
  postgresql.airline.airport c
WHERE c.code = f.origin AND c.state = 'AK'
GROUP BY origin, c.name, c.city
ORDER BY count(*) DESC
LIMIT 10;
```

The logical query plan resembles something similar to Figure 7-5. You see the plan consists of scanning both the flights_orc and airport tables. Both inputs are fed into the join operator. But before the airport data is fed into the join, a filter is applied because we want to look at the results only for airports in Alaska. After the join, the aggregation and grouping operation is applied. And then finally the TopN operator performs the ORDER BY and LIMIT combined.

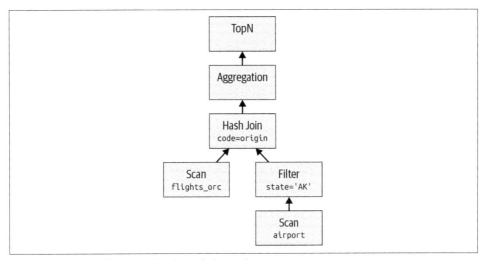

Figure 7-5. Logical query plan for a federated query

In order for Presto to retrieve the data from PostgreSQL, it sends a query via JDBC. For example, in the naive approach, the following query is sent to PostgreSQL:

```
SELECT * FROM airline.airport;
```

However, Presto is smarter than this, and the Presto optimizer tries to reduce the amount of data transferred between systems. In this example, Presto queries only the columns it needs from the PostgreSQL table, as well as pushes down the predicate into the SQL that is sent to PostgreSQL.

So now the query sent from Presto to PostgreSQL pushes more processing to PostgreSQL:

```
SELECT code, city, name FROM airline.airport WHERE state = 'AK';
```

As the JDBC connector to PostgreSQL returns data to Presto, Presto continues processing the data for the part that is executed in the Presto query engine.

Some simpler queries such as SELECT * FROM public.airport are entirely pushed down into the underlying data source, shown in Figure 7-6, such that the query execution happens outside Presto, and Presto acts as a pass-through.

Currently, more complex SQL pushdown is not supported. For example, aggregations or joins that involve only the RDBMS data could be pushed into the RDBMS to eliminate data transfer to Presto.

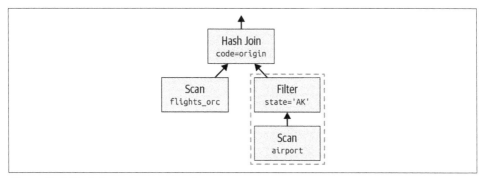

Figure 7-6. Pushdown in a query plan

Extract, Transform, Load and Federated Queries

Extract, transform, load (ETL) is a term used to describe the technique of copying data from data sources and landing it into another data source. Often there is a middle step of transforming the data from the source in preparation for the destination. This may include dropping columns, making calculations, filtering and cleaning up data, joining in data, performing pre-aggregations, and other ways to prepare and make it suitable for querying the destination.

Presto is not intended to be a full-fledged ETL tool comparable to a commercial solution. However, it can assist by avoiding the need for ETL. Because Presto can query from the data source, there may no longer be a need to move the data. Presto queries the data where it lives to alleviate the complexity of managing the ETL process.

You may still desire to do some type of ETL transformations. Perhaps you want to query on pre-aggregated data, or you don't want to put more load on the underlying system. By using the `CREATE TABLE AS` or `INSERT SELECT` constructs, you can move data from one data source into another.

A large advantage of using Presto for ETL workloads and use cases is the support for other data sources beyond relational databases.

Conclusion

You really have a good understanding about connectors in Presto now. It is time to put them to good use. Configure your catalogs and get ready to learn more about querying the data sources.

This brings us to our next topic, everything about SQL use in Presto. SQL knowledge is crucial to your successful use of Presto, and we cover all you need to know in Chapter 8 and Chapter 9.

Using SQL in Presto

After installing and running Presto, you first learned about the central feature of first-class SQL support in Presto in "SQL with Presto" on page 36. Go back and check out that content again if you need an overview or a reminder.

From Chapter 6 about connectors, you know that you can query a lot of data sources with SQL in Presto.

In this chapter, you get to dive deep into the details of SQL support of Presto, including a set of data definition language (DDL) statements for creating and manipulating database objects such as schemas, tables, columns, and views. You learn more about the supported data types and SQL statements. In Chapter 9, you learn about operators and functions for more advanced usage.

Overall, the goal of this chapter is not to serve as a reference guide for SQL but rather demonstrate the SQL capabilities in Presto. For the latest and most complete information about SQL on Presto, you can refer to the official Presto documentation (see "Documentation" on page 13).

> You can take advantage of all SQL support by using the Presto CLI, or any application using the JDBC driver or ODBC drivers, all discussed in Chapter 3.

Impact from Connector

All operations performed in Presto depend on the connector to the data source and its support for specific commands. For example, if the connector to the data source does not support the DELETE statement, any usage results in a failure.

In addition, the connection typically uses a specific user or another authorization, and specific restrictions continue to apply. For example, if the user does not have access rights beyond reading the data, or even data only from a specific schema, other operations such as deleting data or writing new data fails.

Presto Statements

Before you dive into querying data in Presto, it's important to know what data is even available, where, and in what data types. *Presto statements* allow you gather that type of information and more. Presto statements query its system tables and information for metadata about configured catalogs, schemas, and more. These statements work in the same context as all SQL statements.

The FROM and FOR clauses in the statements need the input of a fully qualified table, catalog, or schema, unless a default is set with USE.

The LIKE clause, which can be used to restrict the result, uses pattern matching syntax like that of the SQL LIKE command.

Command sections in [ ] are optional. The following Presto statements are available:

SHOW CATALOGS [LIKE *pattern*]
> List the available catalogs.

SHOW SCHEMAS [FROM *catalog*] [LIKE *pattern*]
> List the schemas in a catalog.

SHOW TABLES [FROM *schema*] [LIKE *pattern*]
> List the tables in a schema.

SHOW FUNCTIONS
> Display a list of all available SQL functions.

SHOW COLUMNS FROM *table* or DESCRIBE *table*
> List the columns in a table along with their data type and other attributes.

USE *catalog.schema* or USE *schema*
> Update the session to use the specified catalog and schema as the default. If a catalog is not specified, the schema is resolved using the current catalog.

SHOW STATS FOR *table_name*

Show statistics like data size and counts for the data in a specific table.

EXPLAIN

Generate the query plan and detail the individual steps.

Let's have a look at some examples that can come in handy in your own use:

```
SHOW SCHEMAS IN tpch LIKE '%3%';
 Schema
---------
 sf300
 sf3000
 sf30000
(3 rows)

DESCRIBE tpch.tiny.nation;
  Column   |    Type     | Extra | Comment
-----------+-------------+-------+--------
 nationkey | bigint      |       |
 name      | varchar(25) |       |
 regionkey | bigint      |       |
 comment   | varchar(152)|       |
(4 rows)
```

The EXPLAIN statement is actually a bit more powerful than indicated in the previous list. Here is the full syntax:

```
EXPLAIN [ ( option [, ...] ) ] <query>
    options: FORMAT { TEXT | GRAPHVIZ | JSON}
             TYPE { LOGICAL | DISTRIBUTED | IO | VALIDATE }
```

You can use the EXPLAIN statement to display the query plan:

```
EXPLAIN
SELECT name FROM tpch.tiny.region;
                              Query Plan
-----------------------------------------------------------------------
Output[name]
│   Layout: [name:varchar(25)]
│   Estimates: {rows: 5 (59B), cpu: 59, memory: 0B, network: 59B}
└─ RemoteExchange[GATHER]
   │   Layout: [name:varchar(25)]
   │   Estimates: {rows: 5 (59B), cpu: 59, memory: 0B, network: 59B}
   └─ TableScan[tpch:region:sf0.01]
          Layout: [name:varchar(25)]
          Estimates: {rows: 5 (59B), cpu: 59, memory: 0B, network: 0B}
          name := tpch:name
```

Working with these plans is helpful for performance tuning and for better understanding what Presto is going to do with your query. You can learn more about this in Chapter 4 and Chapter 12.

A very simple use case of EXPLAIN is to check whether the syntax of your query is even valid:

```
EXPLAIN (TYPE VALIDATE)
SELECT name FROM tpch.tiny.region;
```

Presto System Tables

The *Presto system tables* do not need to be configured with a catalog file. All schemas and tables are automatically available with the system catalog.

You can query the schemas and tables to find out more about the running instance of Presto by using the statements discussed in "Presto Statements" on page 132. The available information includes data about the runtime, nodes, catalog, and more. Inspecting the available information allows you to better understand and work with Presto at runtime.

 The Presto Web UI exposes information from the system tables in a web-based user interface. Find out more details in "Monitoring with the Presto Web UI" on page 239.

The system tables contain schemas:

```
SHOW SCHEMAS IN system;
       Schema
--------------------
 information_schema
 jdbc
 metadata
 runtime
(4 rows)
```

For the purposes of query tuning, the tables `system.runtime.queries` and `system.runtime.tasks` are the most useful:

```
DESCRIBE system.runtime.queries;
          Column              |      Type      | Extra | Comment
------------------------------+----------------+-------+---------
 query_id                     | varchar        |       |
 state                        | varchar        |       |
 user                         | varchar        |       |
 source                       | varchar        |       |
 query                        | varchar        |       |
 resource_group_id            | array(varchar) |       |
 queued_time_ms               | bigint         |       |
 analysis_time_ms             | bigint         |       |
 distributed_planning_time_ms | bigint         |       |
 created                      | timestamp      |       |
```

```
started                     | timestamp  |       |
last_heartbeat              | timestamp  |       |
end                         | timestamp  |       |
(13 rows)

DESCRIBE system.runtime.tasks;
        Column              |    Type    | Extra | Comment
----------------------------+------------+-------+---------
node_id                     | varchar    |       |
task_id                     | varchar    |       |
stage_id                    | varchar    |       |
query_id                    | varchar    |       |
state                       | varchar    |       |
splits                      | bigint     |       |
queued_splits               | bigint     |       |
running_splits              | bigint     |       |
completed_splits            | bigint     |       |
split_scheduled_time_ms     | bigint     |       |
split_cpu_time_ms           | bigint     |       |
split_blocked_time_ms       | bigint     |       |
raw_input_bytes             | bigint     |       |
raw_input_rows              | bigint     |       |
processed_input_bytes       | bigint     |       |
processed_input_rows        | bigint     |       |
output_bytes                | bigint     |       |
output_rows                 | bigint     |       |
physical_written_bytes      | bigint     |       |
created                     | timestamp  |       |
start                       | timestamp  |       |
last_heartbeat              | timestamp  |       |
end                         | timestamp  |       |
(23 rows)
```

The preceding table descriptions show the underlying data explained in more detail in "Monitoring with the Presto Web UI" on page 239. The system.runtime.queries table provides information about current and past queries executed in Presto. The system.runtime.tasks table provides the lower-level details for the tasks in Presto. This is similar to the information output on the Query Details page of the Presto Web UI.

Following are a few useful examples for queries from the system tables.

List nodes in Presto cluster:

```
SELECT * FROM system.runtime.nodes;
```

Show all failed queries:

```
SELECT * FROM system.runtime.queries WHERE state='FAILED';
```

Show all running queries, including their query_id:

```
SELECT * FROM system.runtime.queries WHERE state='RUNNING';
```

The system tables also provide a mechanism to kill a running query:

```
CALL system.runtime.kill_query(query_id => 'queryId', message => 'Killed');
```

In addition to all the information about Presto at runtime, the cluster, the worker nodes, and more, Presto connectors also have the ability to expose system data about the connected data source. For example, the Hive connector discussed in "Hive Connector for Distributed Storage Data Sources" on page 93 can be configured as a connector in a `datalake` catalog. It automatically exposes data about Hive in the system tables:

```
SHOW TABLES FROM datalake.system;
```

This information contains aspects such as used partitions.

Catalogs

A *Presto catalog* represents a data source configured with a catalog properties file using a connector, as discussed in Chapter 6. Catalogs contain one or more schemas, which provide a collection of tables.

For example, you can configure a PostgreSQL catalog to access a relational database on PostgreSQL. Or you can configure a JMX catalog to provide access to JMX information via the JMX connector. Other examples of catalogs include a catalog using the Hive connector to connect to an HDFS object storage data source. When you run a SQL statement in Presto, you are running it against one or more catalogs.

It is possible to have multiple catalogs using the same connector. For example, you can create two separate catalogs to expose two PostgreSQL databases running on the same server.

When addressing a table in Presto, the fully qualified table name is always rooted in a catalog. For example, a fully qualified table name of `hive.test_data.test` refers to the `test` table in the `test_data` schema in the `hive` catalog.

You can see a list of available catalogs in your Presto server by accessing the system data:

```
SHOW CATALOGS;
 Catalog
 ---------
 blackhole
 hive
 jmx
 postgresql
 kafka
 system
(6 rows)
```

Catalogs, schemas, and table information are not stored by Presto; Presto does not have its own catalog. It is the responsibility of the connector to provide this information to Presto. Typically, this is done by querying the catalog from the underlying database or by another configuration in the connector. The connector handles this and simply provides the information to Presto when requested.

Schemas

Within a catalog, Presto contains schemas. *Schemas* hold tables, views, and various other objects and are a way to organize tables. Together, the catalog and schema define a set of tables that can be queried.

When accessing a relational database such as MySQL with Presto, a schema translates to the same concept in the target database. Other types of connectors may choose to organize tables into schemas in a way that makes sense for the underlying data source. The connector implementation determines how the schema is mapped in the catalog. For example, a database in Hive is exposed as a schema in Presto for the Hive connector.

Typically, schemas already exist when you configure a catalog. However, Presto also allows creation and other manipulation of schemas.

Let's look at the SQL statement to create a schema:

```
CREATE SCHEMA [ IF NOT EXISTS ] schema_name
[ WITH ( property_name = expression [, ...] ) ]
```

The WITH clause can be used to associate properties with the schema. For example, for the Hive connector, creating a schema actually creates a database in Hive. It is sometimes desirable to override the default location for the database as specified by hive.metastore.warehouse.dir:

```
CREATE SCHEMA hive.web
WITH (location = 's3://example-org/web/')
```

Refer to the latest Presto documentation for the list of schema properties, or query the list in Presto:

```
SELECT * FROM system.metadata.schema_properties;
-[ RECORD 1 ]-+-----------------------------
catalog_name  | hive
property_name | location
default_value |
type          | varchar
description   | Base file system location URI
```

You can change the name of an existing schema:

```
ALTER SCHEMA name RENAME TO new_name
```

Deleting a schema is also supported:

```
DROP SCHEMA [ IF EXISTS ] schema_name
```

Specify IF EXISTS when you do not want the statement to error if the schema does not exist. Before you can successfully drop a schema, you need to drop the tables in it. Some database systems support a CASCADE keyword that indicates the DROP statement to drop everything within the object such as a schema. Presto does *not* support CASCADE at this stage.

Information Schema

The *information schema* is part of the SQL standard and supported in Presto as a set of views providing metadata about schemas, tables, columns, views, and other objects in a catalog. The views are contained within a schema named information_schema. Each Presto catalog has its own information_schema. Commands such as SHOW TABLES, SHOW SCHEMA, and others are shorthand for the same information you can retrieve from the information schema.

The information schema is essential for using third-party tools such as business intelligence tools. Many of these tools query the information schema so they know what objects exist.

The information schema has eight total views. These are the same in each connector. For some connectors that don't support certain features (for example, roles), queries to the information_schema in that connector may result in an unsupported error:

```
SHOW TABLES IN system.information_schema;
      Table
-----------------
applicable_roles
columns
enabled_roles
roles
schemata
table_privileges
tables
views
(8 rows)
```

You can query the list of tables in the schema. Notice that the information schema tables are returned as well:

```
SELECT * FROM hive.information_schema.tables;
 table_catalog |    table_schema     |     table_name     | table_type
---------------+---------------------+--------------------+------------
 hive          | web                 | nation             | BASE TABLE
 hive          | information_schema  | enabled_roles      | BASE TABLE
 hive          | information_schema  | roles              | BASE TABLE
 hive          | information_schema  | columns            | BASE TABLE
 hive          | information_schema  | tables             | BASE TABLE
 hive          | information_schema  | views              | BASE TABLE
 hive          | information_schema  | applicable_roles   | BASE TABLE
 hive          | information_schema  | table_privileges   | BASE TABLE
 hive          | information_schema  | schemata           | BASE TABLE
(9 rows)
```

Additionally, you can view the columns for a particular table by leveraging the WHERE clause in these queries:

```
SELECT table_catalog, table_schema, table_name, column_name
FROM hive.information_schema.columns
WHERE table_name = 'nation';
 table_catalog |    table_schema     |     table_name     | column_name
---------------+---------------------+--------------------+------------
 hive          | web                 | nation             | regionkey
 hive          | web                 | nation             | comment
 hive          | web                 | nation             | nationkey
 hive          | web                 | nation             | name
...
```

Tables

Now that you understand catalogs and schemas, let's learn about table definitions in Presto. A *table* is a set of unordered rows, which are organized into named columns with specific data types. This is the same as in any relational database, in which the table consists of rows, columns, and data types for those columns. The mapping from source data to tables is defined by the catalog.

The connector implementation determines how a table is mapped into a schema. For example, exposing PostgreSQL tables in Presto is straightforward because PostgreSQL natively supports SQL and the concepts of tables. However, it requires more creativity to implement a connector to other systems, especially if they lack a strict table concept by design. For example, the Apache Kafka connector exposes Kafka topics as tables in Presto.

Tables are accessed in SQL queries by using a fully qualified name, such as *catalog-name.schema-name.table-name*.

Let's take a look at `CREATE TABLE` for creating a table in Presto:

```
CREATE TABLE [ IF NOT EXISTS ]
table_name (
  { column_name data_type [ COMMENT comment ]
  [ WITH ( property_name = expression [, ...] ) ]
  | LIKE existing_table_name [ { INCLUDING | EXCLUDING } PROPERTIES ] }
  [, ...]
)
[ COMMENT table_comment ]
[ WITH ( property_name = expression [, ...] ) ]
```

This general syntax should look familiar to you if you know SQL. In Presto, the optional `WITH` clause has an important use. Other systems such as Hive have extended the SQL language so that users can specify logic or data that cannot be otherwise expressed in standard SQL. Following this approach violates the underlying philosophy of Presto to stay as close to the SQL standard as possible. It also makes supporting many connectors unmanageable, and has therefore been replaced with having table and column properties use the `WITH` clause.

Once you have created the table, you can use the `INSERT INTO` statement from standard SQL.

For example, in the iris data set creation script, first a table is created; see "Iris Data Set" on page 15. Then values are inserted directly from the query:

```
INSERT INTO iris (
  sepal_length_cm,
  sepal_width_cm,
  petal_length_cm,
  petal_width_cm,
  species )
VALUES
  ( ...
```

If the data is available via a separate query, you can use `SELECT` with `INSERT`. Say, for example, you want to copy the data from a memory catalog to an existing table in PostgreSQL:

```
INSERT INTO postgresql.flowers.iris
SELECT * FROM memory.default.iris;
```

The `SELECT` statement can include conditions and any other supported features for the statement.

Table and Column Properties

Let's learn how the WITH clause is used by creating a table by using the Hive connector from "Hive Connector for Distributed Storage Data Sources" on page 93 (see Table 8-1).

Table 8-1. Table properties supported by the Hive connector

Property name	Property description
external_location	The filesystem location for an external Hive table; e.g., on S3 or Azure Blob Storage
format	The file storage format for the underlying data such as ORC, AVRO, PARQUET, etc.

Using the properties from Table 8-1, let's create a table in Hive with Presto that is identical to the way the table is created in Hive.

Let's start with this Hive syntax:

```
CREATE EXTERNAL TABLE page_views(
  view_time INT,
  user_id BIGINT,
  page_url STRING,
  view_date DATE,
  country STRING)
 STORED AS ORC
 LOCATION 's3://example-org/web/page_views/';
```

Compare this to using SQL in Presto:

```
CREATE TABLE hive.web.page_views(
  view_time timestamp,
  user_id BIGINT,
  page_url VARCHAR,
  view_date DATE,
  country VARCHAR
)
WITH (
  format = 'ORC',
  external_location = 's3://example-org/web/page_views'
);
```

As you can see, the Hive DDL has extended the SQL standard. Presto, however, uses properties for the same purpose and therefore adheres to the SQL standard.

You can query the system metadata of Presto to list the available table properties:

```
SELECT * FROM system.metadata.table_properties;
```

To list the available column properties, you can run the following query:

```
SELECT * FROM system.metadata.column_properties;
```

Copying an Existing Table

You can create a new table by using an existing table as a template. The LIKE clause creates a table with the same column definition as an existing table. Table and column properties are not copied by default. Since the properties are important in Presto, we suggest copying them as well by using INCLUDING PROPERTIES in the syntax. This feature is useful when performing some type of transformation of the data by using Presto:

```
CREATE TABLE hive.web.page_view_bucketed(
  comment VARCHAR,
  LIKE hive.web.page_views INCLUDING PROPERTIES
)
WITH (
  bucketed_by = ARRAY['user_id'],
  bucket_count = 50
)
```

Use the SHOW statement to inspect the newly created table definition:

```
SHOW CREATE TABLE hive.web.page_view_bucketed;
                    Create Table
---------------------------------------------
CREATE TABLE hive.web.page_view_bucketed (
    comment varchar,
    view_time timestamp,
    user_id bigint,
    page_url varchar,
    view_date date,
    country varchar
)
WITH (
    bucket_count = 50,
    bucketed_by = ARRAY['user_id'],
    format = 'ORC',
    partitioned_by = ARRAY['view_date','country'],
    sorted_by = ARRAY[]
)
(1 row)
```

You can compare this to the original table you copied:

```
SHOW CREATE TABLE hive.web2.page_views;
                    Create Table
---------------------------------------------
CREATE TABLE hive.web.page_views (
    view_time timestamp,
    user_id bigint,
    page_url varchar,
    view_date date,
    country varchar
)
```

```
WITH (
   format = 'ORC',
   partitioned_by = ARRAY['view_date','country']
)
(1 row)
```

Creating a New Table from Query Results

The CREATE TABLE AS (CTAS) statement can be used to create a new table that contains the results of a SELECT query. The column definitions for the table are created
dynamically by looking at the result column data from the query. The statement can
be used for creating temporary tables, or as part of a process to create transformed
tables:

```
CREATE TABLE [ IF NOT EXISTS ] table_name [ ( column_alias, ... ) ]
[ COMMENT table_comment ]
[ WITH ( property_name = expression [, ...] ) ]
AS query
[ WITH [ NO ] DATA ]
```

By default, the new table is populated with the result data from the query.

CTAS can be used for transforming tables and data. For example, you can load un-
partitioned data in TEXTFILE format into a new partitioned table with data in ORC
format:

```
CREATE TABLE hive.web.page_views_orc_part
WITH (
   format = 'ORC',
   partitioned_by = ARRAY['view_date','country']
)
AS
SELECT *
FROM hive.web.page_view_text
```

The next example shows creating a table from the resulting sessionization query over
the page_views table:

```
CREATE TABLE hive.web.user_sessions
AS
SELECT user_id,
       view_time,
       sum(session_boundary)
         OVER (
           PARTITION BY user_id
           ORDER BY view_time) AS session_id
FROM (SELECT user_id,
             view_time,
             CASE
               WHEN to_unixtime(view_time) -
                   lag(to_unixtime(view_time), 1)
                     OVER(
```

```
                     PARTITION BY user_id
                     ORDER BY view_time) >= 30
         THEN 1
         ELSE 0
         END AS session_boundary
    FROM page_views) T
ORDER BY user_id,
        session_id
```

 Occasionally, you need to create a copy of a table definition only. You can do this by using CTAS and adding a WITH NO DATA clause at the end of the statement.

Modifying a Table

The ALTER TABLE statement can perform actions such as renaming a table, adding a column, dropping a column, or renaming a column in a table:

```
ALTER TABLE name RENAME TO new_name

ALTER TABLE name ADD COLUMN column_name data_type
  [ COMMENT comment ] [ WITH ( property_name = expression [, ...] ) ]

ALTER TABLE name DROP COLUMN column_name

ALTER TABLE name RENAME COLUMN column_name TO new_column_name
```

It is important to note that depending on the connector and authorization model for the connector, these operations may not be allowed when using the default behavior. For example, the Hive connector restricts these operations by default.

Deleting a Table

Using the DROP TABLE statement, you can delete a table:

```
DROP TABLE  [ IF EXISTS ] table_name
```

Depending on the connector implementation, this may or may not drop the underlying data. You should refer to the connector documentation for further explanation.

Table Limitations from Connectors

So far in this chapter, we've gone over the various SQL statements Presto supports. However, it does not mean that every data source in Presto supports all statements and syntax possibilities or provides the same semantics.

The connector implementation and the capabilities and semantics of the underlying data source have a large impact on the possibilities.

If you try a statement or operation that is not supported by a particular connector, Presto returns an error. For example, the system schema and tables are used to expose information about the Presto system. It does not support table creation, since that simply does not make sense for internal system data tables. If you attempt to create a table anyway, you receive an error:

```
CREATE TABLE system.runtime.foo(a int);
Query failed: This connector does not support creating tables
```

Views

Views are virtual tables based on the result set of a SQL query. They are well supported in many RDBMSs. However, Presto does not have any support for creating, editing, or removing views.

Presto treats views from an underlying data source like tables. This allows you to use views for some very useful purposes:

- Exposing data from multiple tables in an easier consumable view
- Restricting data available with views that have limited columns and/or rows
- Providing processed, transformed data conveniently

Using views automatically requires the underlying data source to take full ownership of the data in the view, and therefore the processing to create the view and keep it up-to-date. As a result, using views can enable you to push the processing of a query to the RDBMS in a few steps:

1. Discover a performance problem on a SQL query on table data running in Presto.
2. Troubleshoot the system by looking at the EXPLAIN plan of the execution.
3. Realize that a specific subquery causes a bottleneck.
4. Create a view that preprocesses the subquery.
5. Use that view in your SQL query, replacing a table.
6. Enjoy the performance benefits.

Session Information and Configuration

When using Presto, all configuration is maintained in a user-specific context called a *session*. This session contains key-value pairs that signify the configuration of numerous aspects used for the current interaction of the user with Presto.

You can use SQL commands to interact with that information. For starters, you can just view what the current configuration is, and even use LIKE patterns to narrow down the options you are interested in:

```
SHOW SESSION LIKE 'query%';
```

This query returns information about the properties `query_max_cpu_time`, `query_max_execution_time`, `query_max_run_time`, and `query_priority`, including the current value, the default value, the data type (`integer`, `boolean`, or `varchar`), and a brief description of the property.

The list of properties is long and includes many configuration options for Presto behavior, such as memory and CPU limits for queries, query planning algorithms, and cost-based optimizer usage.

As a user, you can change these properties, which affects the performance for the current user session. You can set specific options for specific queries or workloads, or test them for global rollout into the main file-based Presto configuration in `config.prop erties` used by the cluster.

For example, you can activate the experimental algorithm to use collocated joins for query planning:

```
SET SESSION  collocated_join = true;
SET SESSION
```

You can confirm that the setting worked:

```
SHOW SESSION LIKE 'colocated_join';
      Name       | Value | Default ...
-----------------+-------+---------
 colocated_join  | true  | false   ...
```

To undo the setting and get back to the default value, you can reset the session property:

```
SET SESSION  colocated_join;
RESET SESSION
```

Data Types

Presto supports most of the data types described by the SQL standard, which are also supported by many relational databases. In this section, we discuss data type support in Presto.

Not all Presto connectors support all Presto data types. And Presto may not support all the types from the underlying data source either. The way the data types are translated to and from the underlying data source and into Presto depends on the connector implementation. The underlying data sources may not support the same type, or the same type may be named differently. For example, the MySQL connector maps the Presto REAL type to a MySQL FLOAT.

In some cases, data types need to be converted. Some connectors convert an unsupported type into a Presto VARCHAR—basically, a string representation of the source data—or ignore reading the column entirely. Specific details are available in the connector documentation and source code.

Back to the long list of well-supported data types. Tables 8-2 through 8-6 describe the data types in Presto and provide example data where applicable.

Table 8-2. Boolean data type

Type	Description	Example
BOOLEAN	Boolean value of true or false	True

Table 8-3. Integer data type

Type	Description	Example
TINYINT	8-bit signed integer, minimum value of -2^7, maximum value of 2^{7-1}	42
SMALLINT	16-bit signed integer, minimum value of -2^{15}, maximum value of 2^{15-1}	42
INTEGER, INT	32-bit signed integer, minimum value of -2^{31}, maximum value of 2^{31-1}	42
BIGINT	64-bit signed integer, minimum value of -2^{63}, maximum value of 2^{63-1}	42

Table 8-4. Floating-point data types

Type	Description	Example
REAL	32-bit floating-point, follows the IEEE Standard 754 for Binary Floating-Point Arithmetic	2.71828
DOUBLE	64-bit floating-point, follows the IEEE Standard 754 for Binary Floating-Point Arithmetic	2.71828

Table 8-5. Fixed-precision data types

Type	Description	Example
DECIMAL	Fixed-precision decimal number	123456.7890

Table 8-6. String data types

Type	Description	Example
VARCHAR or VARCHAR(*n*)	Variable-length string of characters. There is an optional maximum length when defined as VARCHAR(*n*), where *n* is a positive integer representing the maximum number of characters.	"Hello World"
CHAR CHAR(*n*)	A fixed-length string of characters. There is an optional length when defined as CHAR(*n*), where *n* is a positive integer defining the length of the character. CHAR is equivalent to CHAR(1).	"Hello World "

Unlike VARCHAR, CHAR always allocates *n* characters. Here are some characteristics and errors you should be aware of:

- If you are casting a character string with less than *n* characters, trailing spaces are added.

- If you are casting a character string with more than *n* characters, it is truncated without error.

- If you insert a VARCHAR or CHAR longer than defined in the column into a table, an error occurs.

- If you insert a CHAR that is shorter than as defined in the column into a table, the value is space padded to match the defined length.

- If you insert a VARCHAR that is shorter than as defined in the column into a table, the exact length of the string is stored. Leading and trailing spaces are included when comparing CHAR values.

The following examples highlight these behaviors:

```
SELECT length(cast('hello world' AS char(100)));
 _col0
 -----
   100
(1 row)

SELECT cast('hello world' AS char(15)) || '~';
      _col0
 ---------------
 hello world    ~
(1 row)

SELECT cast('hello world' AS char(5));
 _col0
 -------
 hello
(1 row)

SELECT length(cast('hello world' AS varchar(15)));
 _col0
```

```
  -------
      11
(1 row)

SELECT cast('hello world' AS varchar(15)) || '~';
    _col0
 --------------
 hello world~
(1 row)

SELECT cast('hello world' as char(15)) = cast('hello world' as char(14));
 _col0
 -------
 false
(1 row)

SELECT cast('hello world' as varchar(15)) = cast('hello world' as varchar(14));
 _col0
 -------
 true
(1 row)

CREATE TABLE varchars(col varchar(5));
CREATE TABLE

INSERT INTO into varchars values('1234');
INSERT: 1 row

INSERT INTO varchars values('123456');
Query failed: Insert query has mismatched column types:
Table: [varchar(5)], Query: [varchar(6)]
```

Collection Data Types

As data becomes increasingly vast and complex, it is sometimes stored in more complex data types such as arrays and maps. Many RDBMS systems, and specifically also some NoSQL systems, support complex data types natively. Presto supports some of these collection data types, listed in Table 8-7. It also provides support for the UNNEST operation detailed in "Unnesting Complex Data Types" on page 182.

Table 8-7. Collection data types

Collection data type	Example
ARRAY	ARRAY[*apples, oranges, pears*]
MAP	MAP(ARRAY[*a, b, c*], ARRAY[1, 2, 3])
JSON	{"a":1,"b":2,"c":3}
ROW	ROW(1, 2, 3)

Temporal Data Types

Table 8-8 describes temporal data types, or data types related to dates and time.

Table 8-8. Temporal data types

Type	Description	Example
DATE	A calendar date representing the year, month, and day	DATE '1983-10-19'
TIME	A time of day representing hour, minute, second, and millisecond.	TIME '02:56:15.123'
TIME WITH TIMEZONE	A time of day representing hour, minute, second, and millisecond, including a time zone.	
TIMESTAMP	A date and time.	
TIMESTAMP WITH TIMEZONE	A date and time with a time zone.	
INTERVAL YEAR TO MONTH	An interval span of years and months.	INTERVAL '1-2' YEAR TO MONTH
INTERVAL DAY TO SECOND	An interval span of days, hours, minutes, seconds, and milliseconds.	INTERVAL '5' DAY to SECOND

In Presto, TIMESTAMP is represented as a Java Instant type representing the amount of time before or after the Java epoch. This should be transparent to the end user as values are parsed and displayed in a different format.

For types that do not include time-zone information, the values are parsed and displayed according to the Presto session time zone. For types that include the time-zone information, the values are parsed and displayed using the time zone.

String literals can be parsed by Presto into a TIMESTAMP, TIMESTAMP WITH TIMEZONE, TIME, TIME WITH TIMEZONE, or DATE. Tables 8-9 through 8-11 describe the formats accepted for parsing. If you want to use ISO 8601, you can use the from _iso8601_timestamp or from_iso8601_date functions.

Table 8-9. Supported string literals for parsing to timestamp data types

TIMESTAMP	TIMESTAMP WITH TIMEZONE
yyyy-M-d	yyyy-M-d ZZZ
yyyy-M-d H:m	yyyy-M-d H:m ZZZ
yyyy-M-d H:m:s	yyyy-M-d H:m:s ZZZ
yyyy-M-d H:m:s.SSS	yyyy-M-d H:m:s.SSS ZZZ

Table 8-10. Supported string literals for parsing to time data types

TIME	TIMESTAMP WITH TIMEZONE
H:m	H:m ZZZ
H:m:s	H:m:s ZZZ
H:m:s.SSS	H:m:s.SSS ZZZ

Table 8-11. Supported string literals for parsing to date data type

DATE
YYYY-MM-DD

When printing the output for TIMESTAMP, TIMESTAMP WITH TIMEZONE, TIME, TIME WITH TIMEZONE, or DATE, Presto uses the output formats in Table 8-12. If you want to output in strict ISO 8601 format, you can use the to_iso8601 function.

Table 8-12. Temporal output formats

Data type	Format
TIMESTAMP	yyyy-MM-dd HH:mm:ss.SSS ZZZ
TIMESTAMP WITH TIMEZONE	yyyy-MM-dd HH:mm:ss.SSS ZZZ
TIME	yyyy-MM-dd HH:mm:ss.SSS ZZZ
TIME WITH TIMEZONE	yyyy-MM-dd HH:mm:ss.SSS ZZZ
DATE	YYYY-MM-DD

Time Zones

The time zone adds important additional temporal information. Presto supports TIME WITH TIMEZONE, but it is often best to use time zones with a DATE or TIMESTAMP. This enables accounting of daylight saving time with the DATE format.

Following are some sample time-zone strings:

- America/New_York
- America/Los_Angeles
- Europe/Warsaw
- +08:00
- -10:00

Let's look at some examples:

```
SELECT TIME '02:56:15 UTC';
     _col0
-----------------
 02:56:15.000 UTC
(1 row)

SELECT TIME '02:56:15 UTC' AT TIME ZONE 'America/Los_Angeles';
             _col0
---------------------------------
 18:56:15.000 America/Los_Angeles

SELECT TIME '02:56:15 UTC' AT TIME ZONE '-08:00';
       _col0
--------------------
 18:56:15.000 -08:00
(1 row)

SELECT TIMESTAMP '1983-10-19 07:30:05.123';
         _col0
-----------------------
 1983-10-19 07:30:05.123
(1 row)

SELECT TIMESTAMP '1983-10-19 07:30:05.123 America/New_York' AT TIME ZONE 'UTC';
           _col0
---------------------------
 1983-10-19 11:30:05.123 UTC
(1 row)
```

Intervals

The data type INTERVAL can be either YEAR TO MONTH or DAY TO SECOND, as shown in Tables 8-13 and 8-14.

Table 8-13. Years-to-months intervals

YEAR TO MONTH
INTERVAL '<years>-<months>' YEAR TO MONTH
INTERVAL '<years>' YEAR TO MONTH
INTERVAL '<years>' YEAR
INTERVAL '<months>' MONTH

Table 8-14. Days-to-seconds intervals

DAY TO SECOND
INTERVAL '<days> <time>' DAY TO SECOND
INTERVAL '<days>' DAY TO SECOND
INTERVAL '<days>' DAY
INTERVAL '<hours>' HOUR
INTERVAL '<minutes>' MINUTE
INTERVAL '<seconds>' SECOND

The following examples highlight some behaviors we've described:

```
SELECT INTERVAL '1-2' YEAR TO MONTH;
 _col0
 ------
 1-2
(1 row)

SELECT INTERVAL '4' MONTH;
 _col0
 -------
 0-4
(1 row)

SELECT INTERVAL '4-1' DAY TO SECOND;
Query xyz failed: Invalid INTERVAL DAY TO SECOND value: 4-1

SELECT INTERVAL '4' DAY TO SECOND;
      _col0
 ---------------
 4 00:00:00.000
(1 row)

SELECT INTERVAL '4 01:03:05.44' DAY TO SECOND;
      _col0
 ---------------
 4 01:03:05.440
(1 row)

SELECT INTERVAL '05.44' SECOND;
      _col0
 ---------------
 0 00:00:05.440
(1 row)
```

Type Casting

Sometimes it is necessary to explicitly change a value or literal to a different data type. This is called *type casting* and is performed by the CAST function:

```
CAST(value AS type)
```

Now let's say you need to compare a DATE to a literal string:

```
SELECT *
FROM hive.web.page_views
WHERE view_date > '2019-01-01';
Query failed: line 1:42: '>' cannot be applied to date, varchar(10)
```

This query fails because Presto does not have a greater than (>) comparison operator that knows how to compare a date and a string literal. However, it has a comparison function that knows how to compare two dates. Therefore, we need to use the CAST function to coerce one of the types. In this example, it makes the most sense to convert the string to a date:

```
SELECT *
FROM hive.web.page_views
WHERE view_date > CAST('2019-01-01' as DATE);
      view_time          | user_id | page_url | view_data  | country
-------------------------+---------+----------+------------+---------
 2019-01-26 20:40:15.477 |       2 | http://  | 2019-01-26 | US
 2019-01-26 20:41:01.243 |       3 | http://  | 2019-01-26 | US
...
```

Presto provides another conversion function, try_cast. It attempts to perform the type coercion, but unlike CAST, which returns an error if the cast fails, try_cast returns a null value. This can be useful when an error is not necessary:

```
try_cast(value AS type)
```

Let's take, for example, coercing a character literal to a number type:

```
SELECT cast('1' AS integer);
 _col0
-------
     1
(1 row)

SELECT cast('a' as integer);
Query failed: Cannot cast 'a' to INT

SELECT try_cast('a' as integer);
 _col0
------
 NULL
(1 row)
```

SELECT Statement Basics

The SELECT statement is of critical importance, as it allows you to return data from one or multiple tables in a table format, at minimum collapsing down to one row or potentially just one value.

SELECT queries with Presto have the additional complexity to include tables from different catalogs and schemas—completely different data sources. You learned about this in "Query Federation in Presto" on page 122.

Now you are going to dive into the details and learn about all the power available. Let's start with a syntax overview:

```
[ WITH with_query [, ...] ]
SELECT [ ALL | DISTINCT ] select_expr [, ...]
[ FROM from_item [, ...] ]
[ WHERE condition ]
[ GROUP BY [ ALL | DISTINCT ] grouping_element [, ...] ]
[ HAVING condition]
[ { UNION | INTERSECT | EXCEPT } [ ALL | DISTINCT ] select ]
[ ORDER BY expression [ ASC | DESC ] [, ...] ]
[ LIMIT [ count | ALL ] ]
```

select_expr represents the data returned by the query in the form of a table column, a derived table column, a constant, or a general expression in zero, one, or more rows. A general expression can include functions, operators, columns, and constants. You can run a query with just a SELECT select_expr, for testing, but its usefulness beyond that is limited:

```
SELECT 1, 1+1, upper('lower');
 _col0 | _col1 | _col2
-------+-------+------
     1 |     2 | LOWER
(1 row)
```

SELECT select_expr [, ...] FROM from_item is the most basic form of the query. It allows you to retrieve all data from an underlying table, or only a selection of columns. It also allows you to calculate expressions on the underlying data.

Say we have two tables, also known as relations, nation and customer. The examples are taken from the TPC-H, discussed in "Presto TPC-H and TPC-DS Connectors" on page 92. For brevity, the example tables were truncated to have just a few rows and columns each. We use this data throughout the chapter over multiple examples of select queries.

You can return select columns and data from the nation table in the sf1 schema:

```
SELECT nationkey, name, regionkey
FROM tpch.sf1.nation;
 nationkey |      name      | regionkey
-----------+----------------+-----------
         0 | ALGERIA        |         0
         1 | ARGENTINA      |         1
         2 | BRAZIL         |         1
         3 | CANADA         |         1
         4 | EGYPT          |         4
         5 | ETHIOPIA       |         0
...
```

And now some sample data from the customer table.

```
SELECT custkey, nationkey, phone, acctbal, mktsegment
FROM tpch.tiny.customer;
 custkey | nationkey |       phone       | acctbal | mktsegment
---------+-----------+-------------------+---------+------------
     751 |         0 | 10-658-550-2257   | 2130.98 | FURNITURE
     752 |         8 | 18-924-993-6038   | 8363.66 | MACHINERY
     753 |        17 | 27-817-126-3646   | 8114.44 | HOUSEHOLD
     754 |         0 | 10-646-595-5871   | -566.86 | BUILDING
     755 |        16 | 26-395-247-2207   | 7631.94 | HOUSEHOLD
     756 |        14 | 24-267-298-7503   | 8116.99 | AUTOMOBILE
     757 |         3 | 13-704-408-2991   | 9334.82 | AUTOMOBILE
     758 |        17 | 27-175-799-9168   | 6352.14 | HOUSEHOLD
...
```

Beyond just returning select data, we can transform data with functions and return the result:

```
SELECT acctbal, round(acctbal) FROM tpch.sf1.customer;
 acctbal | _col1
---------+--------
 7470.96 | 7471.0
 8462.17 | 8462.0
 2757.45 | 2757.0
 -588.38 | -588.0
 9091.82 | 9092.0
 3288.42 | 3288.0
 2514.15 | 2514.0
 2259.38 | 2259.0
  -716.1 | -716.0
 7462.99 | 7463.0
(10 rows)
```

WHERE Clause

The WHERE clause is used as a filter in SELECT queries. It consists of a condition that evaluates to TRUE, FALSE, or UNKNOWN. During query execution, the condition is evaluated for each row. If the evaluation does not equal TRUE, the row is skipped and omitted from the result set. Otherwise, the row is emitted and sent back as part of the results to the user or for further processing.

The WHERE clause condition consists of one or more Boolean expressions connected by conjunctive ANDs and disjunctive ORs:

```
SELECT custkey, acctbal
FROM tpch.sf1.customer WHERE acctbal < 0;
 custkey | acctbal
---------+---------
   75016 | -735.89
   75027 | -399.78
   75028 | -222.92
   75034 | -679.38
   75037 | -660.07
...

SELECT custkey, acctbal FROM tpch.sf1.customer
WHERE acctbal > 0 AND acctbal < 500;
 custkey | acctbal
---------+---------
   75011 |  165.71
   75012 |   41.65
   75021 |   176.2
   75022 |  348.24
   75026 |   78.64
   75084 |   18.68
   75107 |  314.88
...
```

The WHERE clause condition is important because it is used for several query optimizations. In "Query Planning" on page 53, you can learn more about the query planning and optimizations. When querying multiple tables, you can connect them via conditions in the WHERE clause. Presto uses this information to determine efficient query execution plans.

GROUP BY and HAVING Clauses

The GROUP BY and HAVING clauses are common to use in analytical queries. GROUP BY is used to combine rows of the same value into a single row:

```
SELECT mktsegment
FROM tpch.sf1.customer
GROUP BY mktsegment;
 mktsegment
 -----------
 MACHINERY
 AUTOMOBILE
 HOUSEHOLD
 BUILDING
 FURNITURE
(5 rows)
```

For analytical queries in Presto, GROUP BY is often combined with aggregation functions. These functions are computed from the data in the rows that make up a single group. The following query calculates the total account balance of all customers, breaking it down by market segment.

```
SELECT mktsegment, round(sum(acctbal) / 1000000, 3) AS acctbal_millions
FROM tpch.sf1.customer
GROUP BY mktsegment;
 mktsegment | acctbal_millions
------------+------------------
 MACHINERY  |          134.439
 AUTOMOBILE |          133.867
 BUILDING   |          135.889
 FURNITURE  |          134.259
 HOUSEHOLD  |          135.873
```

Aggregation functions can also be used, even if the GROUP BY clause is not used. In this case, the entire relation serves as input to the aggregation function, so we can calculate the overall account balance:

```
SELECT round(sum(acctbal) / 1000000, 3) AS acctbal_millions
FROM tpch.sf1.customer;
 acctbal_millions
------------------
          674.327
```

The HAVING clause is similar to the WHERE clause. It is evaluated for each row, and rows are emitted only if the condition evaluates to TRUE. The HAVING clause is evaluated after the GROUP BY and operated on the grouped rows. The WHERE clause is evaluated before the GROUP BY and evaluated on the individual rows.

Here is the full query:

```
SELECT mktsegment,
       round(sum(acctbal), 1) AS acctbal_per_mktsegment
FROM tpch.tiny.customer
GROUP BY mktsegment
HAVING round(sum(acctbal), 1) > 5283.0;
 mktsegment | acctbal_per_mktsegment
------------+------------------------
 BUILDING   |              1444587.8
 HOUSEHOLD  |              1279340.7
 AUTOMOBILE |              1395695.7
 FURNITURE  |              1265282.8
 MACHINERY  |              1296958.6
(5 rows)
```

And here are the filtered results using the condition on grouped data:

```
SELECT mktsegment,
       round(sum(acctbal), 1) AS acctbal_per_mktsegment
FROM tpch.tiny.customer
GROUP BY mktsegment
HAVING round(sum(acctbal), 1) > 1300000;
 mktsegment | acctbal_per_mktsegment
------------+------------------------
 AUTOMOBILE |              1395695.7
 BUILDING   |              1444587.8
(2 rows)
```

ORDER BY and LIMIT Clauses

The ORDER BY clause contains expressions that are used to order the results. The clause, which can contain multiple expressions, is evaluated from left to right. Multiple expressions are typically used to break ties when the left expression evaluates to the same value for more than one row. The expressions can indicate the sort order to be ascending (e.g., A–Z, 1–100) or descending (e.g., Z–A, 100–1).

The LIMIT clause is used to return only the specified number of rows. Together with the ORDER BY clause, LIMIT can be used to find the first *N* results of an ordered set:

```
SELECT mktsegment,
       round(sum(acctbal), 2) AS acctbal_per_mktsegment
FROM tpch.sf1.customer
GROUP BY mktsegment
HAVING sum(acctbal) > 0
ORDER BY acctbal_per_mktsegment DESC
LIMIT 1;
 mktsegment | acctbal_per_mktsegment
------------+------------------------
 MACHINERY  |                19851.2
(1 row)
```

Often Presto is able to optimize executing `ORDER BY` and `LIMIT` as a combined step rather than separately.

`LIMIT` can be used without the `ORDER BY` clause, but most often they are used together. The reason is that the SQL standard, and therefore also Presto, does not guarantee any order of the results. This means that using `LIMIT` without an `ORDER BY` clause can return different nondeterministic results with each run of the same query. This becomes more apparent in a distributed system such as Presto.

JOIN Statements

SQL allows you to combine data from different tables by using `JOIN` statements. Presto supports the SQL standard joins such as `INNER JOIN`, `LEFT OUTER JOIN`, `RIGHT OUTER JOIN`, `FULL OUTER JOIN`, and `CROSS JOIN`. A full exploration of `JOIN` statements is beyond the scope of this book but is covered in many others.

Let's focus on a few examples and explore specific details relevant to Presto:

```
SELECT custkey, mktsegment, nation.name AS nation
FROM tpch.tiny.nation JOIN tpch.tiny.customer
ON nation.nationkey = customer.nationkey;
 custkey | mktsegment |   nation
---------+------------+-----------
     108 | BUILDING   | ETHIOPIA
     101 | MACHINERY  | BRAZIL
     106 | MACHINERY  | ARGENTINA
(3 rows)
```

Presto also has an implicit cross join: a list of tables is separated by commas, and the join is defined with conditions in the `WHERE` clause:

```
SELECT custkey, mktsegment, nation.name AS nation
FROM tpch.tiny.nation, tpch.tiny.customer
WHERE nation.nationkey = customer.nationkey;
 custkey | mktsegment |   name
---------+------------+-----------
     108 | BUILDING   | ETHIOPIA
     106 | MACHINERY  | ARGENTINA
     101 | MACHINERY  | BRAZIL
```

Joins can be one of the most expensive operations of query processing. When multiple joins are in a query, the joins can be processed by different permutations. The Q09 query from the TPCH benchmark is a good example of such a complex query:

```
SELECT
  nation,
  o_year,
  sum(amount) AS sum_profit
FROM (
      SELECT
```

```
        N.name AS nation,
        extract(YEAR FROM o.orderdate)AS o_year,
        l.extendedprice * (1 - l.discount) - ps.supplycost * l.quantity AS amount
      FROM
        part AS p,
        supplier AS s,
        lineitem AS l,
        partsupp AS ps,
        orders AS o,
        nation AS n
      WHERE
        s.suppkey = l.suppkey
        AND ps.suppkey = l.suppkey
        AND ps.partkey = l.partkey
        AND p.partkey = l.partkey
        AND o.orderkey = l.orderkey
        AND s.nationkey = n.nationkey
        AND p.name LIKE '%green%'
    ) AS profit
GROUP BY
  nation,
  o_year
ORDER BY
  nation,
  o_year DESC;
```

UNION, INTERSECT, and EXCEPT Clauses

UNION, INTERSECT, and EXCEPT are known as *set operations* in SQL. They are used to combine the data from multiple SQL statements into a single result.

While you can use joins and conditions to get the same semantics, it is often easier to use set operations. Presto executes them more efficiently than equivalent SQL.

As you learn the semantics of the set operations, it's usually easier to start with basic integers. You can start with UNION, which combines all values and removes duplicates:

```
SELECT * FROM (VALUES 1, 2)
UNION
SELECT * FROM (VALUES 2, 3);
 _col0
 ------
     2
     1
     3
(3 rows)
```

UNION ALL leaves any duplicates in place:

```
SELECT * FROM (VALUES 1, 2)
UNION ALL
SELECT * FROM (VALUES 2, 3);
```

```
     _col0
     -----
         1
         2
         2
         3
     (4 rows)
```

INTERSECT returns all elements found in both queries as a result:

```
SELECT * FROM (VALUES 1, 2)
INTERSECT
SELECT * FROM (VALUES 2, 3);
 _col0
 ------
     2
(1 row)
```

EXCEPT returns elements from the first query after removing all elements found in the second query:

```
SELECT * FROM (VALUES 1, 2)
EXCEPT
SELECT * FROM (VALUES 2, 3);
 _col0
 ------
     1
(1 row)
```

Each set operator supports use of an optional qualifier, ALL or DISTINCT. The DIS
TINCT keyword is the default and need not be specified. The ALL keyword is used as a
way to preserve duplicates. Currently, ALL is not supported for the INTERSECT and
EXCEPT operators.

Grouping Operations

You learned about the basic GROUP BY and aggregations. Presto also supports the
advanced grouping operations from the SQL standard. Using GROUPING SETS, CUBE,
and ROLLUP, users can perform aggregations on multiple sets in a single query.

Grouping sets allow you to group multiple lists of columns in the same query. For
example, let's say we want to group on (state, city, street), (state, city), and
(state). Without grouping sets, you have to run each group in its own separate
query and then combine the results. With grouping sets, Presto computes the grouping for each set. The result schema is the union of the columns across the sets. For
columns that are not part of a group, a null value is added.

ROLLUP and CUBE can be expressed using GROUPING SETS and are shorthand. ROLLUP is
used to generate group sets based on a hierarchy. For example ROLLUP(a, b, c)

generates grouping sets (a, b, c), (a, b), (a), (). The CUBE operation generates all possible combinations of the grouping. For example. CUBE (a, b, c) generates group sets (a, b, c), (a, b), (a, c), (b, c), (a), (b), (c), ().

For example, say you want to compute the total of account balances per market segment and compute the total account balances for all market segments:

```
SELECT mktsegment,
  round(sum(acctbal), 2) AS total_acctbal,
  GROUPING(mktsegment) AS id
FROM tpch.tiny.customer
GROUP BY ROLLUP (mktsegment)
ORDER BY id, total_acctbal;
 mktsegment | total_acctbal | id
------------+---------------+----
 FURNITURE  |     1265282.8 |  0
 HOUSEHOLD  |    1279340.66 |  0
 MACHINERY  |    1296958.61 |  0
 AUTOMOBILE |    1395695.72 |  0
 BUILDING   |     1444587.8 |  0
 NULL       |    6681865.59 |  1
(6 rows)
```

With ROLLUP, you can compute aggregations on different groups. In this example, the first five rows represent the total of account balances per market segment. The last row represents the total of all account balances. Because there is no group for mktsegment, that is left as NULL. The GROUPING function is used to identify which rows belong to which groups.

Without ROLLUP, you have to run this as two separate queries and combine them together. In this example, we can use UNION, which helps you to understand conceptually what ROLLUP is doing:

```
SELECT mktsegment,
       round(sum(acctbal), 2) AS total_acctbal,
       0 AS id
FROM tpch.tiny.customer
GROUP BY mktsegment
UNION
SELECT NULL, round(sum(acctbal), 2), 1
FROM tpch.tiny.customer
ORDER BY id, total_acctbal;
 mktsegment | total_acctbal | id
------------+---------------+----
 FURNITURE  |     1265282.8 |  0
 HOUSEHOLD  |    1279340.66 |  0
 MACHINERY  |    1296958.61 |  0
 AUTOMOBILE |    1395695.72 |  0
 BUILDING   |     1444587.8 |  0
 NULL       |    6681865.59 |  1
(6 rows)
```

WITH Clause

The WITH clause is used to define an inline view within a single query. This is often used to make a query more readable because the query may need to include the same nested query multiple times.

In this query, let's find the market segments whose total account balances are greater than the average of the market segments:

```
SELECT mktsegment,
       total_per_mktsegment,
       average
FROM
  (
    SELECT mktsegment,
       round(sum(acctbal)) AS total_per_mktsegment
    FROM tpch.tiny.customer
    GROUP BY 1
  ),
  (
    SELECT round(avg(total_per_mktsegment)) AS average
    FROM
      (
        SELECT mktsegment,
           sum(acctbal) AS total_per_mktsegment
        FROM tpch.tiny.customer
        GROUP BY 1
      )
  )
WHERE total_per_mktsegment > average;
 mktsegment | total_per_mktsegment |  average
------------+----------------------+----------
 BUILDING   |            1444588.0 | 1336373.0
 AUTOMOBILE |            1395696.0 | 1336373.0
(2 rows)
```

As you can see, this query is a bit complex. Using the WITH clause, we can simplify it as follows:

```
WITH
total AS (
  SELECT mktsegment,
     round(sum(acctbal)) AS total_per_mktsegment
  FROM tpch.tiny.customer
  GROUP BY 1
),
average AS (
  SELECT round(avg(total_per_mktsegment)) AS average
  FROM total
)
SELECT mktsegment,
  total_per_mktsegment,
```

```
  average
FROM total,
  average
WHERE total_per_mktsegment > average;
mktsegment | total_per_mktsegment |  average
-----------+----------------------+----------
 AUTOMOBILE |            1395696.0 | 1336373.0
 BUILDING   |            1444588.0 | 1336373.0
(2 rows)
```

In this example, the second inline view is referring to the first. You can see that the WITH inline view is executed twice. Currently, Presto does not materialize the results to share across multiple executions. In fact, it would have to be a cost-based decision on the complexity of the query, as it could be more efficient to execute a query multiple times than to store and retrieve the results.

Subqueries

Presto supports many common uses of subqueries. A *subquery* is an expression that serves as input into a higher-level expression. In SQL, subqueries can be placed into three categories:

- Scalar subqueries
- ANY/SOME
- ALL

Each category has two types, uncorrelated and correlated. A *correlated subquery* is one that references other columns from outside the subquery.

Scalar Subquery

A *scalar subquery* is one that returns a single value—one row and one column:

```
SELECT regionkey, name
FROM tpch.tiny.nation
WHERE regionkey =
  (SELECT regionkey FROM tpch.tiny.region WHERE name = 'AMERICA');
 regionkey |     name
-----------+---------------
         1 | ARGENTINA
         1 | BRAZIL
         1 | CANADA
         1 | PERU
         1 | UNITED STATES
(5 rows)
```

In this scalar example, the result from the subquery is 1. The WHERE condition essentially becomes regionkey = 1 and is evaluated for each row. Logically, the subquery is evaluated for every row in the `nation` table, for example, one hundred times for one hundred rows. However Presto is smart enough to evaluate the subquery only once and to use the static value all other times.

EXISTS Subquery

An `EXISTS` subquery evaluates to `true` if there are any rows. These queries are commonly used as correlated subqueries. While an uncorrelated subquery is possible for `EXISTS`, it is not as practical because anything that returns a single row evaluates to `true`:

```
SELECT name
FROM tpch.tiny.nation
WHERE regionkey IN (SELECT regionkey FROM tpch.tiny.region)
```

Another common form of `EXISTS` subqueries is `NOT EXISTS`. However, this is simply applying the negation to the result of the `EXISTS` subquery.

Quantified Subquery

ANY subqueries take the form expression operator quantifier (subquery). Valid operator values are <, >, <=, >=, =, or <>. The token `SOME` may be used in place of `ANY`. The most familiar form of this type of query is the *expression* IN *subquery*, which is equivalent to *expression* = ANY *subquery*.

```
SELECT name
FROM nation
WHERE regionkey = ANY (SELECT regionkey FROM region)
```

This query is equivalent to the following, where IN is the shorthand form:

```
SELECT name
FROM nation
WHERE regionkey IN (SELECT regionkey FROM region)
```

The subquery must return exactly one column. Today, Presto does not support the row expression subqueries, where more than one column is compared. Semantically, for a given row of the outer query, the subquery is evaluated and the expression is compared to each result row of the subquery. If at least one of these comparisons evaluates to TRUE, the result of the ANY subquery condition is TRUE. The result is FALSE if none of the comparisons evaluate to TRUE. This is repeated for each row of the outer query.

You should be aware of some nuances. If the expression is NULL, the result of the IN expression is NULL. Additionally, if no comparisons evaluate to TRUE, but there is a NULL value in the subquery, the IN expression evaluates to NULL. In most cases, this remains unnoticed because a result of FALSE or NULL filters out the row. However, if this IN expression is to serve as input to a surrounding expression that is sensitive to NULL values (e.g., surrounded with NOT), then it would matter.

ALL subqueries work similarly to ANY. For a given row of the outer query, the subquery is evaluated and the expression is compared to each result row of the subquery. If all of the comparisons evaluate to TRUE, the result of ALL is TRUE. If there is at least one FALSE evaluation, the result of ALL is FALSE.

As with ANY, some nuances are not obvious at first. When the subquery is empty and returns no rows, ALL evaluates to TRUE. If none of the comparisons return FALSE and at least one comparison returns NULL, the result of ALL is NULL. The most familiar form of ALL is <> ALL, which is equivalent to NOT IN.

Deleting Data from a Table

The DELETE statement can delete rows of data from a table. The statement provides an optional WHERE clause to restrict which rows are deleted. Without a WHERE clause, all the data is deleted from the table:

```
DELETE FROM table_name [ WHERE condition ]
```

Various connectors have limited or no support for deletion. For example, deletion is not supported by the Kafka connector. The Hive connector supports deletion only if a WHERE clause specifies a partition key that can be used to delete entire partitions:

```
DELETE FROM hive.web.page_views
WHERE view_date = DATE '2019-01-14' AND country = 'US'
```

Conclusion

Exciting what you can do with SQL in Presto, isn't it? With the knowledge from this chapter, you can already craft very complex queries and achieve some pretty complex analysis of any data exposed to Presto.

Of course, there is more. So read on in Chapter 9 to learn about functions, operators, and other features for querying your data with Presto.

CHAPTER 9
Advanced SQL

While you can certainly achieve a lot with the power of SQL statements, as covered in Chapter 8, you are really only scratching the surface of what you can do with more complex processing with queries in Presto. In this chapter, you are going to cover more advanced features such as functions, operators, and other features.

Functions and Operators Introduction

So far, you've learned about the basics, including catalogs, schemas, tables, data types, and various SQL statements. This knowledge is useful when querying data from one or more tables in one or more catalogs in Presto. In the examples, we focused mostly on writing the queries by using the data from the different attributes, or columns, in the table.

SQL functions and operators exist to enable more complex and comprehensive SQL queries. In this chapter, we focus on the functions and operators supported by Presto and provide examples of their use.

Functions and operators in SQL are internally equivalent. Functions generally use the syntax form *function_name*(*function_arg1*, ...) and operators use a different syntax, similar to operators in programming languages and mathematics. Operators are a syntactic abbreviation and improvement for commonly used functions. An example of an equivalent operator and function are the || operator and the concat() function. Both are used to concatenate strings.

Operators in SQL and in Presto come in two general types:

Binary operators

A binary operator takes the input of two operands to produce a single value result. The operator itself defines what the operand data types must be and what the result data type is. A binary operator is written in the format *operand operator operand*.

Unary operators

A unary operator takes the input of a single operator and produces a single value result. As with binary operators, the operator requires what the operand data type must be and what the result data type must be. A unary operator is written in the format *operator operand*.

With both binary and unary operators, the operand input may be the result of an operator itself creating a tree of operators. For example, in 2 × 2 × 2, the result of the first operator 2 × 2 is input to the second multiplier operator.

In the following sections of this chapter, you learn details about numerous functions and operators supported by Presto.

Scalar Functions and Operators

A *scalar function* in SQL is invoked within a SQL statement. Abstractly, it takes one or more single-value input parameters, performs an operation based on the input, and then produces a single value. As a concrete example, consider the SQL function in power(x, p). This power function returns x raised to the power of p:

```
SELECT power(2, 3);
 _col0
-------
   8.0
(1 row)
```

Of course, you could simply use the multiplication operators to achieve the same goal. Using our example, 2 × 2 × 2 also produces the value 8. But using functions allows the logic to be encapsulated, making it easier to reuse in SQL. Moreover, we achieve other benefits such as reducing room for mistakes and optimizing execution of the function.

Scalar functions can be used anywhere in a SQL statement where an expression can be used, provided it is semantically correct. For example, you can write a SQL query SELECT * FROM page_views WHERE power(2, 3). This passes the syntactic checks but fails during semantic analysis because the return type of the power function is a double value and not the required Boolean. Writing the SQL query as SELECT * FROM `page_views WHERE power(2, 3) = 8` works, even though it may not be a useful query.

Presto contains a set of built-in functions and operators that can be immediately used. In this section, you learn about common uses and highlights of some interesting ones. We do not fully enumerate every function and operator, since this chapter is not meant to be a reference. After learning the basics here, you can refer to the Presto documentation to learn more.

> Presto also supports user-defined functions (UDFs), which allow you to write your own function implementations in Java and deploy them in Presto to execute within SQL queries. This is, however, beyond the scope of this book.

Boolean Operators

Boolean operators are binary operators and used in SQL to compare the values of two operands producing a Boolean result of TRUE, FALSE, or NULL. These are most commonly used on conditional clauses such as WHERE, HAVING, or ON, and are listed in Table 9-1. They can be used anywhere in a query that an expression can be used.

Table 9-1. Boolean operators

Operator	Description
<	Less than
<=	Less than or equal
>	Greater than
>=	Greater than or equal
=	Equal
<>	Not equal
!=	Not equal

> The syntax != is not part of the SQL standard but is commonly used in various programming languages. It is implemented in other popular databases, and therefore also provided in Presto for convenience.

Here are some example usages of Boolean operators:

What are the best days of the week to fly out of Boston in the month of February?

```
SELECT dayofweek, avg(depdelayminutes) AS delay
FROM flights_orc
WHERE month = 2 AND origincityname LIKE '%Boston%'
GROUP BY dayofweek
ORDER BY dayofweek;
```

```
 dayofweek |        delay
-----------+--------------------
         1 | 10.613156692553677
         2 |  9.97405624214174
         3 |  9.548045977011494
         4 | 11.822725778003647
         5 | 15.875475113122173
         6 | 11.184173669467787
         7 | 10.788121285791464
(7 rows)
```

What is the average delay per carrier per year between the years 2010 and 2014?

```
SELECT avg(arrdelayminutes) AS avg_arrival_delay, carrier
FROM flights_orc
WHERE year > 2010 AND year < 2014
GROUP BY carrier, year;
```

```
 avg_arrival_delay  | carrier
--------------------+---------
 11.755326255888736 | 9E
 12.557365851045104 | AA
  13.39056266711295 | AA
 13.302276406082575 | AA
 6.4657695873247745 | AS
  7.048865559750841 | AS
  6.907012760530203 | AS
 17.008730526574663 | B6
  13.28933909176506 | B6
 16.242635221309246 | B6
...
```

Logical Operators

Three more operators you use in SQL and in Presto are the *logical operators* AND, OR, and NOT. The operators AND and OR are referred to as *binary operators* since they take two parameters as input. NOT is a unary operator that takes a single parameter as input.

These logical operators return a single Boolean variable of TRUE, FALSE, or NULL (UNKNOWN), based on Boolean type input data. Typically, these operators are used together to form a conditional clause, just like the Boolean operators.

The concept of these three operators are similar to programming languages but have different semantics because of the way the NULL value affects the semantics. For example, NULL AND NULL does not equate to TRUE but rather to NULL. If you think of NULL as the absence of a value, this becomes easier to comprehend. Table 9-2 displays how the operators handle the three values.

Table 9-2. Logical operator results for AND and OR

x	y	x AND y	x OR y
TRUE	TRUE	TRUE	TRUE
TRUE	FALSE	FALSE	TRUE
TRUE	NULL	NULL	TRUE
FALSE	TRUE	FALSE	TRUE
FALSE	FALSE	FALSE	FALSE
FALSE	NULL	FALSE	NULL
NULL	TRUE	NULL	TRUE
NULL	FALSE	FALSE	NULL
NULL	NULL	NULL	NULL

When it comes to the NOT operator, just keep in mind that NOT NULL evaluates to NULL, and not TRUE or FALSE.

Range Selection with the BETWEEN Statement

The *BETWEEN statement* can be considered a special case of a binary operator and defines a range. It's really two comparisons connected by an AND. The data types of the selected field and the two range values have to be identical. NOT BETWEEN is simply the negation. The following two queries are equivalent, as you can see from the result:

```
SELECT count(*) FROM flights_orc WHERE year BETWEEN 2010 AND 2012;
  _col0
----------
 18632160
(1 row)

SELECT count(*) FROM flights_orc WHERE year >= 2010 AND year <= 2012;
  _col0
----------
 18632160
(1 row)
```

Value Detection with IS (NOT) NULL

The IS NULL statement allows you to detect if a value exists. It can be considered a special type of unary operator. IS NOT NULL is the negation. You may want to count some rows, but not want to count rows without values. Perhaps the data is incomplete or does not make sense.

For example, to calculate the average delay of airplanes by year, you have to ensure that you are counting only flights that actually happened. This is reflected by the fact that airtime has a value, which this query takes into account:

```
SELECT avg(DepDelayMinutes) AS delay, year
FROM flights_orc
WHERE airtime IS NOT NULL and year >= 2015
GROUP BY year
ORDER BY year desc;
       delay          | year
----------------------+------
 12.041834908176538 | 2019
 13.178923805354275 | 2018
 12.373612267166829 | 2017
  10.51195619395339 | 2016
 11.047527214544516 | 2015
(5 rows)
```

Mathematical Functions and Operators

Mathematical functions and operators open up a wide range of use cases and are of critical importance for many of them. Table 9-3 lists mathematical operators, and Table 9-4 lists mathematical functions.

Table 9-3. Mathematical operators

Operator	Description	Example
+	Addition	SELECT 1+1
-	Subtraction	SELECT 2-1
*	Multiplication	SELECT 2*3
/	Division	SELECT 9/2
%	Modulus	SELECT 6 % 5

Table 9-4. Commonly used mathematical functions

Function	Return type	Description	Example
abs(x)	Same as input	Absolute value of x	SELECT abs(-1)
cbrt(x)	double	Cube root of x	SELECT cbrt(9)
ceiling(x)	Same as input	Round x up to nearest integer	SELECT ceiling(4.2)
degrees(x)	double	Convert the angle x from radians to degrees	SELECT degrees(1.047)
exp(x)	double	Euler's number raised to the power of x	SELECT exp(1)
floor(x)	Same as input	Round x down to the nearest integer	SELECT floor(4.2)
ln(x)	double	Natural logarithm of x	SELECT ln(exp(1))
log(b, x)	double	Base b logarithm of x	SELECT log(2, 64)
log2(x)	double	Base 2 logarithm of x	SELECT log2(64)
log10(x)	double	Base 10 logarithm of x	SELECT log10(140)
mod(n, m)	Same as input	Modulos. Equivalent to n % m	SELECT mod(3, 2)
power(x, p)	double	X raised to the power of p	SELECT pow(2, 6)
radians(x)	double	Convert the angle x from degrees to radians	SELECT radians(60)
round(x)	Same as input	Round x to the nearest integer	SELECT round(pi())
round(x, d)	Same as input	Round x to d decimal places	SELECT round(pi(), 2)
sqrt(x)	double	Square root of x	SELECT sqrt(64)
truncate(x)	double	Round x to integer by truncating the digits after the decimal point	SELECT truncate(e())

Trigonometric Functions

Presto provides a set of *trigonometric functions* that take the argument type radians. The return data type is double for all functions.

If you wish to convert between radians and degrees, Presto provides conversion functions degrees(x) and radians(x). Table 9-5 lists the trigonometric functions.

Table 9-5. Trigonometric functions

Function	Description
cos(x)	Cosine of x
acos(x)	Arc cosine of x
cosh(x)	Hyperbolic cosine of x
sin(x)	Sine of x
asin(x)	Arc sine of x
tan(x)	Tangent of x
atan(x)	Arc tangent of x
atan2(y, x)	Arc tangent of y / x
tanh(x)	Hyperbolic tangent of x

Constant and Random Functions

Presto provides functions that return *mathematical constants* and conceptual values as well as random values, as shown in Table 9-6.

Table 9-6. Miscellaneous mathematical constants and functions

Function	Return type	Description	Example
e()	double	Euler's number	2.718281828459045
pi()	double	Pi	3.141592653589793
infinity()	double	Presto constant used to represent infinity	Infinity
nan()	double	Presto constant use to represent not a number	NaN
random()	double	Random double >= 0.0 and < 1.0	SELECT random()
random(n)	Same as input	Random double >= 0.0 and < *n*	SELECT random(100)

String Functions and Operators

String manipulation is another common use case, and Presto includes rich support for it. The || operator is used to concatenate strings together:

```
SELECT 'Emily' || ' Grace';
    _col0
------------
  Emily Grace
(1 row)
```

Presto provides several useful string functions, shown in Table 9-7.

Table 9-7. String functions

Function	Return type	Description	Example
chr(*n*)	varchar	Unicode code point *n* as a character string.	SELECT chr(65)
codepoint(*string*)	integer	Unicode code point of character.	SELECT codepoint(*A*)
concat(*string1*, …, *stringN*)	varchar	Equivalent to the operator.	SELECT concat(*Emily*, ' , 'Grace*);
length(*string*)	bigint	Length of string.	SELECT length(*saippuakivikauppias*)
lower(*string*)	varchar	Convert string to lowercase.	SELECT lower(*UPPER*);
lpad(*string, size, padstring*)	varchar	Left pad the string with *size* number of characters. Truncates the string if the *size* is less than the actual length of the string.	SELECT lpad(*A*, 4, ' ')
ltrim(*string*)	varchar	Trim the leading whitespace.	SELECT ltrim(lpad(*A*, 4, ' '))
replace(*string, search, replace*)	varchar	Replace instances of *search* in string with *replace*.	SELECT replace(*555.555.5555*, ., -)
reverse(*string*)	varchar	Reverse the character string.	SELECT reverse(*saippuakivikauppias*)

Function	Return type	Description	Example
rpad(*string, size, padstring*)	varchar	Right pad the string with *size* number of character. Truncates the string if *size* is less than the actual length of the string.	SELECT rpad(*A*, 4, #)
rtrim(*string*)	varchar	Trim the trailing whitespace.	SELECT rtrim(rpad(*A*, 4, ' '))
split(*string, delimiter*)	array(varchar)	Splits string on delimiter and returns an array.	SELECT split(*2017,2018,2019,* ,)
strpos(*string, substring*)	bigint	Starting position at first instance of the substring in the string. Index starts at 1. 0 is returned if the substring is not found.	SELECT strpos(*prestosql.io, .io*);
substr(*string, start, length*)	varchar	Substring from *start* position of length. Index starts at 1. Negative index is backward from end.	SELECT substr(*prestosql.io*, 1, 9)
trim(*string*)	varchar	Remove leading and trailing whitespace. Same as applying both rtrim and ltrim.	SELECT trim(' A ')
upper(*string*)	varchar	Converts string to uppercase.	SELECT upper(*lower*)
word_stem(*word, lang*)	varchar	Returns the stem of the word using the specified language.	SELECT word_stem(*presto, it*)

Strings and Maps

Two string functions return maps that are interesting, given Presto's ability to further process map data:

```
split_to_map(string, entryDelimiter, keyValueDelimiter) → map<varchar, varchar>
```

This function splits the `string` argument by using the `entryDelimiter`, which splits the string into key-value pairs and then uses the `keyValueDelimiter` to split each pair into a key and value. The result is a map.

A useful example usage of this function is parsing of URL parameters:

```
SELECT split_to_map('userid=1234&reftype=email&device=mobile', '&', '=');
                   _col0
-------------------------------------------
 {device=mobile, userid=1234, reftype=email}
(1 row)
```

When there are multiple occurrences of the same key, the `split_to_map` function returns an error.

The similar function `split_to_multimap` can be used when there are multiple occurrences of the same key. In the preceding example, say there is a duplicate device:

```
SELECT
split_to_multimap(
  'userid=1234&reftype=email&device=mobile&device=desktop',
  '&',
  '=');
```

Unicode

Presto provides a set of *Unicode functions*, shown in Table 9-8. These functions work on valid UTF-8 encoded Unicode points. Functions consider each code point separately, even if multiple code points are used to represent a single character.

Table 9-8. Unicode-related functions

Function	Return type	Description
chr(*n*)	varchar	Returns the Unicode code point *n* as a single character string
codepoint(*string*)	integer	Returns the Unicode code point of the only character of *string*
normalize(*string*)	varchar	This function transforms string with NFC normalization form
normalize(*string, form*)	varchar	This function transforms with the specified normalization form

The form argument must be one of the keywords in Table 9-9:

Table 9-9. Normalization forms

Form	Description
NFD	Canonical decomposition
NFC	Canonical decomposition, followed by canonical composition
NFKD	Compatibility decomposition
NFKC	Compatibility decomposition, followed by canonical composition

The Unicode standard (*http://unicode.org/reports/tr15/#Norm_Forms*) describes these forms in detail.

> This SQL-standard function has special syntax and requires specifying form as a keyword, not as a string.

to_utf8(*string*) → varbinary
: The function encodes the string into an UTF-8 varbinary representation.

from_utf8(*binary*) → varchar
: The function decodes the UTF-8 encoded string from binary. Any invalid UTF-8 sequences are replaced with the Unicode replacement character U+FFFD.

from_utf8(*binary, replace*) → varchar
: This function decodes a UTF-8 encoded string from binary. Any invalid UTF-8 sequences are replaced with *replace*.

Let's use the chr function to return the Unicode code point as a string:

```
SELECT chr(241);
 _col0
-------
 ñ
(1 row)
```

In this example, we are using the function codepoint to return the Unicode code point of the string:

```
SELECT codepoint(u&'\00F1');
 _col0
-------
   241
(1 row)
```

Now we are demonstrating how the Spanish eñe character can be represented multiple ways in Unicode. It can be represented as either a single code point or by composing multiple code points. When compared to each other directly, they are not treated as equivalent. This is where the normalization function can be used to normalize them to a common form to be compared and treated as equivalent:

```
SELECT u&'\00F1',
u&'\006E\0303',
u&'\00F1' = u&'\006E\0303',
normalize(u&'\00F1') = normalize(u&'\006E\0303');

 _col0 | _col1 | _col2 | _col3
-------+-------+-------+-------
 ñ     | ñ     | false | true
(1 row)
```

In some instances, code points can be composed as a single code point. For example, the Roman number IX can be written with two code points for I and X. Or you can use a single code point for it. To compare the two for equivalence, you need to use the normalization function:

```
SELECT u&'\2168', 'IX', u&'\2168' = 'IX', normalize(u&'\2168', NFKC) = 'IX';
 _col0 | _col1 | _col2 | _col3
-------+-------+-------+-------
 IX    | IX    | false | true
(1 row)
```

Regular Expressions

Presto supports pattern matching by providing both the SQL LIKE operator and regular expression (regex) functions. LIKE returns a Boolean and uses the syntax *search* LIKE *pattern*.

LIKE is simple to use for basic patterns but may not be expressive enough for all situations. LIKE patterns support two symbols: _ denotes matching any single character, and % denotes matching zero or more characters.

For example, let's say you want to find flights originating from the Dallas area. You can write the following query:

```
SELECT origincityname, count(*)
FROM flights_orc
WHERE origincityname LIKE '%Dallas%'
GROUP BY origincityname;

    origincityname    | _col1
----------------------+---------
 Dallas/Fort Worth, TX | 7601863
 Dallas, TX            | 1297795
(2 rows)
```

Anything more complex requires using regular expression functions, which provide powerful pattern matching using the Java pattern syntax. These functions listed in Table 9-10 are used for more complex matching, replacing matching strings, extracting matching strings, and splitting strings based on the matched location. Table 9-10 lists regular expression functions.

Table 9-10. Regular expression functions

Function	Description
regexp_extract_all(*string, pattern,* [*group*]) → array(varchar)	Return an array of substrings matched by the pattern in *string*. A variant of the function takes a group argument for the capturing group.
regexp_extract(*string, pattern* [*group*]) → varchar	Return the substring matched by pattern in *string*. A variant of the function takes a group argument for the capturing group.
regexp_like(*string, pattern*) → boolean	Returns a Boolean whether or not the pattern is contained within the string. This differs from LIKE, as LIKE tries to match the entire string with the pattern.
regexp_replace(*string, pattern,* [*replacement*]) → varchar	Returns a string for which the substrings matched by *pattern* are replaced with *replacement*. There is a variant of the function without *replacement*. In this case, the strings are simply removed. Capturing groups can be used in the replacement string.
regexp_replace(*string, pattern, function*) → varchar	This is similar to regexp_replace(*string, pattern,* [*replacement*]) except that it takes a Lambda expression.
regexp_split(*string, pattern*) → array(varchar)	Returns an array of strings split by the pattern. The pattern is like a delimiter. Similar to split(*string, delimiter*) with a more expression delimiter as a pattern.

Table 9-11 shows common selected pattern examples you can use. The full range of supported patterns is extensively documented in the Java documentation about regular expressions.

Table 9-11. Regular expression examples

Pattern	Description	Examples
.	Any character	A
a	The single character a	regexp_like(*abc, a*) → true
[a-zA-Z]	Range of characters	regexp_like(*abc, [a-zA-Z]*), regexp_like(*123, [a-zA-Z]*)
1	The single digit 1	regexp_like(*123, 1*)
\d	Any digit	regexp_like(*123, \d*)
^	Match to beginning of line	regexp_like(*abc, ^ab^*), regexp_like(*abc, ^bc^*)
$	Match to end of line	regexp_like(*abc, bc$*), regexp_like(*abc, ab$*)
?	One or zero	regexp_like(*abc, d?*)
+	One or more	regexp_like(*abc, d+*)
*	Zero or more	

In this example, we want to extract the character b from the string. This results in an array where each entry is a match:

```
SELECT regexp_extract_all('abbbbcccb', 'b');
    _col0
--------------
 [b, b, b, b, b]
(1 row)
```

Let's extract the character b again. However, we wish to extract a sequence of them. The result is an array with only two entries this time, since one of the entries contains the contiguous sequence:

```
SELECT regexp_extract_all('abbbbcccb', 'b+');
 _col0
--------
 [bbbb, b]
(1 row)
```

In this example, we leverage the capturing groups in the replacement. We are searching for a sequence of bc and then swap the order:

```
SELECT regexp_replace('abc', '(b)(c)', '$2$1');
 _col0
-------
 acb
(1 row)
```

Unnesting Complex Data Types

The UNNEST operation allows you to expand the complex collection data types, discussed in "Collection Data Types" on page 149, into a relation. This is extremely powerful for using big data and nested structural data types. By unnesting the data into a relation, you can more easily access the values that are wrapped inside the structure for querying.

As an example, let's say you have stored some access control policies and wish to query them. First, we have a user that can be associated with one or more roles. And a role can be associated with one or more sets of permissions. And perhaps this logic is defined by a schema that looks like the following:

```
SELECT * FROM permissions;
  user  |                       roles
--------+-------------------------------------------------
 matt   | [[WebService_ReadWrite, Storage_ReadWrite],
            [Billing_Read]]
 martin | [[WebService_ReadWrite, Storage_ReadWrite],
            [Billing_ReadWrite, Audit_Read]]
(2 rows)
```

We can expand each role and associate to the user by using UNNEST:

```
SELECT user, t.roles
FROM permissions,
UNNEST(permissions.roles) AS t(roles);
  user  |              roles
--------+-----------------------------------------
 martin | [WebService_ReadWrite, Storage_ReadWrite]
 martin | [Billing_ReadWrite, Audit_Read]
 matt   | [WebService_ReadWrite, Storage_ReadWrite]
 matt   | [Billing_Read]
(4 rows)
```

Now let's say we want to filter the data, and find only the users with the Audit_Read permission. We can expand it further:

```
SELECT user, permission
FROM permissions,
UNNEST(permissions.roles) AS t1(roles),
UNNEST(t1.roles) AS t2(permission);
  user  |     permission
--------+----------------------
 martin | WebService_ReadWrite
 martin | Storage_ReadWrite
 martin | Billing_ReadWrite
 martin | Audit_Read
 matt   | WebService_ReadWrite
 matt   | Storage_ReadWrite
```

```
    matt  | Billing_Read
    (7 rows)
```

And finally, let's add our filter:

```
SELECT user, permission
FROM permissions,
UNNEST(permissions.roles) AS t1(roles),
UNNEST(t1.roles) AS t2(permission)
WHERE permission = 'Audit_Read';
   user  | permission
--------+-----------
  martin | Audit_Read
  (1 row)
```

JSON Functions

In modern applications and systems, JSON data is ubiquitous and has a variety of applications. *JavaScript Object Notation (JSON)* is a human readable and flexible data format. It is commonly used in web applications for transferring data between the browser and server. A lot of data that requires analysis originates from web traffic and is therefore commonly produced and stored using the JSON format. Dedicated document stores as well as many relational database systems now support JSON data.

As Presto is a SQL-on-Anything engine, it may retrieve data from data sources in JSON format. For example, the Kafka, Elasticsearch, and the MongoDB connectors return JSON or can expose the source JSON data. Presto can also use JSON files in HDFS or cloud object storage. Rather than force the connectors to transform data from JSON format into a strict relational data structure with columns and rows, Presto can operate on the JSON data with the functions in Table 9-12. This allows the user to perform the actions they would like with the original data.

Table 9-12. JSON-related functions

Function	Description	Example
is_json_scalar(*json*)	Returns Boolean if the values is a scalar	SELECT is_json_scalar(*abc*)
json_array_contains(*json, value*)	Returns Boolean true if the value is contained in the JSON array	SELECT json_array_contains([*1, 2, 3*], 1)
json_array_length(*json*)	Returns the length of the array in bigint	SELECT json_array_length([*1, 2, 3*])

Date and Time Functions and Operators

In "Temporal Data Types" on page 150, we discussed temporal data types in Presto. You learned about the varying types that exist, input and output formatting and representations, time zones and the nuances, and finally intervals. While that covered storing and representing the temporal types, it's often common and important to operate on the data using functions and operators.

Presto supports + and - operators for temporal types. These operators can be used when adding or subtracting a date time with an interval type, or with two interval types. However, it doesn't have any meaning to add together two timestamps. Additionally, YEAR TO MONTH and DAY TO SECOND interval types cannot be combined.

You can add one hour to the time 12:00 to get the value 13:00:

```
SELECT TIME '12:00' + INTERVAL '1' HOUR;
    _col0
--------------
 13:00:00.000
(1 row)
```

Next, you can add together one year and 15 months, and get the result of two years and three months:

```
SELECT INTERVAL '1' YEAR + INTERVAL '15' MONTH;
 _col0
-------
 2-3
(1 row)
```

Another useful operator AT TIME ZONE allows you to calculate the time in different time zones:

```
SELECT TIME '02:56:15 UTC' AT TIME ZONE '-08:00'
        _col0
--------------------
 18:56:15.000 -08:00
(1 row)
```

You can parse a literal string to a timestamp value as long as you use the correct format:

```
SELECT TIMESTAMP '1983-10-19 07:30:05.123';
          _col0
-------------------------
 1983-10-19 07:30:05.123
```

In many cases, it is more convenient to parse a date or timestamp from a string by using the ISO 8601 format and one of the functions in Table 9-13.

Table 9-13. ISO8061 parsing functions

Function	Return type	Description
from_iso8601_timestamp(*string*)	timestamp with time zone	Parses a ISO 8601 formatted string and returns a timestamp with time zone
from_iso8601_date(*string*)	date	Parses the ISO 8601 formatted string and returns a date

ISO 8061 is a well-documented standard in terms of how to format the time string. When specifying a string to one of the preceding functions, it must use one of the following formats:

- YYYY
- YYYY-MM
- YYYY-MM-DD
- HH
- HH:MM
- HH:MM:SS
- HH:MM:SS.SSS

In addition, you can combine the date and time by using the T delimiter. Let's look at a few examples.

Here, we are parsing the iso8601 date and time into a SQL timestamp:

```
SELECT from_iso8601_timestamp('2019-03-17T21:05:19Z');
            _col0
---------------------------
 2019-03-17 21:05:19.000 UTC
(1 row)
```

Next, we specify a time zone other than the default UTC:

```
SELECT from_iso8601_timestamp('2019-03-17T21:05:19-05:00');
            _col0
-------------------------------
 2019-03-17 21:05:19.000 -05:00
(1 row)
```

The standard also allows you to specify the weeks into the year. In this example, week 10 of 2019 equates to March 4, 2019:

```
SELECT from_iso8601_timestamp('2019-W10');
            _col0
---------------------------
 2019-03-04 00:00:00.000 UTC
(1 row)
```

In this example, we do not specify time and parse the `iso8601` string to a SQL `date` type:

```
SELECT from_iso8601_date('2019-03-17');
   _col0
------------
 2019-03-17
(1 row)
```

Presto provides a rich set of date- and time-related functions. These are crucial for any application involving time, where you may often want to convert, compare, or extract time elements. Table 9-14 shows a selection of available functions. Check out "Documentation" on page 13 for further useful functions and other tips and tricks.

Table 9-14. Miscellaneous temporal functions and values

Function	Return type	Description
current_timezone()	varchar	Return the current time zone
current_date	date	Return the current date
current_time	time with time zone	Return the current time and time zone
current_timestamp or now()	timestamp with time zone	Return the current date, time and time zone
localtime	time	Return the time only, based on the local time zone
localtimestamp	timestamp	Return the date and time, based on the local time zone
from_unixtime(unixtime)	timestamp	Convert a Unix time and produce the date and time
to_unixtime(timestamp)	double	Convert a date and time to a Unix time value
to_milliseconds(interval)	bigint	Convert interval to milliseconds

Histograms

Presto provides the `width_bucket` function that can be used to create *histograms* with consistent widths:

```
width_bucket(x, bound1, bound2, n) -> bigint
```

The expression *x* is the numeric expression for which to create the histogram. The consistent width histogram contains *n* buckets and is bounded between the values for *bound1* and *bound2*. The function returns the bucket number for each value of expression *x*.

Let's take our flight data set and compute a histogram over a 10-year period from 2010 to 2020:

```
SELECT count(*) count, year, width_bucket(year, 2010, 2020, 4) bucket
FROM flights_orc
WHERE year >= 2010
GROUP BY year;
```

```
  count  | year | bucket
---------+------+--------
 7129270 | 2010 |      0
 7140596 | 2011 |      1
 7141922 | 2012 |      1
 7455458 | 2013 |      1
 7009726 | 2014 |      2
 6450285 | 2015 |      2
 6450117 | 2016 |      3
 6085281 | 2017 |      3
 6096762 | 2018 |      3
 6369482 | 2019 |      4
(10 rows)
```

Note that in addition to the expected buckets 1, 2, 3, and 4, we have buckets 0 and 5. These buckets are used for the values outside the minimum and maximum bounds of the histogram—values for years 2010 and 2019, in this case.

Aggregate Functions

In SQL, *aggregate functions* operate and compute a value or a set of values. Unlike scalar functions that produce a single value for each input value, aggregate functions produce a single value for a set of input values. Presto supports the common general aggregate functions you find in most other database systems, as you can see in Table 9-15.

Aggregate functions can take an optional ORDER BY clause after the argument. Semantically, this means that the input set is ordered before performing the aggregation. For most aggregations the order doesn't matter.

Table 9-15. Aggregate functions

Function	Return type	Description
count(*)	bigint	Count the number of values returned
count(x)	bigint	Count the number of non-null values
sum(x)	Same as input	Compute the sum of the input values
min(x)	Same as input	Return the minimum value of all the input values
max(x)	Same as input	Return the maximum of all the input values
avg(x)	double	Return the arithmetic mean of the input values

Map Aggregate Functions

Presto supports several useful map-related functions, detailed in Table 9-16. For some of these functions, the optional ORDER BY clause is needed, depending on the desired results. We demonstrate this use by example with our iris data set (see "Iris Data Set" on page 15).

Table 9-16. Map aggregate functions

Function	Return type	Description
histogram(*x*)	map(*K, bigint*)	This function creates a histogram from the *x* item. It returns a map where the key is *x* and the value is the number of times *x* appears.
map_agg(*key, value*)	map(*K, V*)	Creates a map from a column of keys and values. Duplicates chosen at random. Use multimap_agg to retain all the values.
map_union(*x(K, V)*)	map(*K, V*)	The function performs the unions of multiple maps into a single map. The caveat is that if the same key is found in multiple maps, the value chosen has no guarantee. The function does not merge the two values.
multimap_agg(*key, value*)	map(*K, array(V)*)	This function is similar to map_agg in that it creates a map from the column and keys.

Let's create a histogram of `petal_length_cm`. Because the data is precise, you can use the `floor` function to create wider buckets for the histogram:

```
SELECT histogram(floor(petal_length_cm))
FROM memory.default.iris;
                    _col0
-------------------------------------------
 {1.0=50, 4.0=43, 5.0=35, 3.0=11, 6.0=11}
(1 row)
```

You may recognize that a histogram output is similar to what you see when doing a GROUP BY and COUNT. We can use the result as input to the `map_agg` function to create the histogram with the same results:

```
SELECT floor(petal_length_cm) k, count(*) v
FROM memory.default.iris
GROUP BY 1
ORDER BY 2 DESC;
  k  | v
-----+----
 1.0 | 50
 4.0 | 43
 5.0 | 35
 3.0 | 11
 6.0 | 11
(5 rows)

SELECT map_agg(k, v) FROM (
  SELECT floor(petal_length_cm) k,
    count(*) v
  FROM iris
  GROUP BY 1
);
                    _col0
-------------------------------------------
 {4.0=43, 1.0=50, 5.0=35, 3.0=11, 6.0=11}
(1 row)
```

```
SELECT multimap_agg(species, petal_length_cm)
FROM memory.default.iris;
--------------------------------------------------
 {versicolor=[4.7, 4.5, 4.9..], ,
 virginica=[6.0, 5.1, 5.9, ..],
 setosa=[1.4, 1.4, 1…] ..
(1 row)
```

The `map_union` function is useful for combining maps. Say you have multiple maps. We'll use the histogram function in this example to create them:

```
SELECT histogram(floor(petal_length_cm)) x
FROM memory.default.iris
GROUP BY species;
             x
-------------------------
 {4.0=6, 5.0=33, 6.0=11}
 {4.0=37, 5.0=2, 3.0=11}
 {1.0=50}
(3 rows)
```

We can use `map_union` to combine them. However, notice how keys 4.0 and 5.0 exist in different maps. In these cases, Presto arbitrarily picks one set of values. It does not perform any type of merging. While adding them is correct in this case, it does not always make sense. For example, the values could be strings, which make it less clear how to combine them:

```
SELECT map_union(m)
FROM (
  SELECT histogram(floor(petal_length_cm)) m
  FROM memory.default.iris
  GROUP BY species
  );
                   _col0
------------------------------------------
 {4.0=6, 1.0=50, 5.0=33, 6.0=11, 3.0=11}
(1 row)
```

Approximate Aggregate Functions

When working with large amounts of data and aggregations, data processing can be resource intensive, requiring more hardware to scale Presto out to provide interactivity. Sometimes scaling out becomes prohibitively expensive.

To help in this scenario, Presto provides a set of aggregation functions that return the approximation rather than the exact result. These *approximation aggregation functions* use much less memory and computation power at the expense of not providing the exact result.

In many cases when dealing with big data, this is acceptable since the data itself is often not completely exact. There may be a missing day of data, for example. But when considering aggregations over a year, the missing data doesn't matter for certain types of analysis.

Remember, Presto is not designed or meant to be used for OLTP-style queries. It is not suitable to produce reports for a company's ledger with absolute accuracy. However, for OLAP use cases—analytics requiring you to understand trends only but not to have completely accurate results—can be acceptable and satisfy the requirements.

Presto provides two main approximation functions: `approx_distinct` and `approx_percentile`.

Presto implements `approx_distinct` by using the HyperLogLog algorithm. Counting distinct rows is a very common query that you likely need in order to satisfy a data analysis requirement. For example, you may want to count the number of distinct user IDs or IP addresses in your logs to know how many users visited your website on a given day, month, or year. Because users may have visited your website multiple times, simply counting the number of entries in your log does not work. You need to find the distinct number of users, requiring you to count each user's representation only once. Doing so requires you to keep a structure in memory so you know not to double-count membership. For large amounts of data, this becomes impractical and certainly slow. HyperLogLog provides an alternative approach. The actual algorithm is not discussed in this book.

To implement the approximate distinct result, Presto provides a HyperLogLog (HLL) data type that you can also use as a user. Because Presto provides HyperLogLog as a data type, this means that it can be stored as a table. This becomes incredibly valuable because you can store computations to merge them back later. Say your data is partitioned by day. Each day, you can create a HyperLogLog structure for the users that day and store it. Then when you want to compute the approximate distinct, you can merge the HLLs together to get the cardinality for `approx-distinct`.

Window Functions

Presto supports the use of standard *window functions* from SQL, which allow you to define a set of records to use as input for a function.

For example, let's look at the sepal length from our iris flowers (see "Iris Data Set" on page 15).

Without the window function, you can get the average sepal length for all species:

```
SELECT avg(sepal_length_cm)
FROM memory.default.iris;
5.8433332
```

Alternatively you can calculate the average for a specific species:

```
SELECT avg(sepal_length_cm)
FROM memory.default.iris
WHERE species = 'setosa';
5.006
```

However, what if you want a list of all measurements and each compared to the overall average? The OVER() window function allows you to do just that:

```
SELECT species, sepal_length_cm,
  avg(sepal_length_cm) OVER() AS avgsepal
FROM memory.default.iris;
  species    | sepal_length_cm | avgsepal
-----------+----------------+----------
  setosa     |            5.1 | 5.8433332
  setosa     |            4.9 | 5.8433332
  ...
  versicolor |            7.0 | 5.8433332
  versicolor |            6.4 | 5.8433332
  versicolor |            6.9 | 5.8433332
  ...
```

The window function basically says to calculate the average overall values in the same table. You can also create multiple windows with the PARTITION BY statement:

```
SELECT species, sepal_length_cm,
  avg(sepal_length_cm) OVER(PARTITION BY species) AS avgsepal
FROM memory.default.iris;
  species    | sepal_length_cm | avgsepal
-----------+----------------+----------
  setosa     |            5.1 |    5.006
  setosa     |            4.9 |    5.006
  setosa     |            4.7 |    5.006
  ...
  virginica  |            6.3 |    6.588
  virginica  |            5.8 |    6.588
  virginica  |            7.1 |    6.588
  ...
```

Now the average length is specific to the species. With the help of DISTINCT and by omitting the individual length, you can get a list of the averages per species:

```
SELECT DISTINCT species,
  avg(sepal_length_cm) OVER(PARTITION BY species) AS avgsepal
FROM memory.default.iris;
  species    | avgsepal
-----------+----------
  setosa     |    5.006
  virginica  |    6.588
  versicolor |    5.936
(3 rows)
```

The window functions in Presto support all aggregate functions as well as numerous window-specific functions:

```
SELECT DISTINCT species,
    min(sepal_length_cm) OVER(PARTITION BY species) AS minsepal,
    avg(sepal_length_cm) OVER(PARTITION BY species) AS avgsepal,
    max(sepal_length_cm) OVER(PARTITION BY species) AS maxsepal
FROM memory.default.iris;
    species    | minsepal | avgsepal | maxsepal
 ------------+----------+----------+----------
    virginica  |     4.9 |   6.588 |     7.9
    setosa     |     4.3 |   5.006 |     5.8
    versicolor |     4.9 |   5.936 |     7.0
(3 rows)
```

Check out the Presto documentation for more details (see "Documentation" on page 13).

Lambda Expressions

An advanced concept for working with array elements is the use of *lambda expressions* in SQL statements. If you have a programming background, you might be familiar with them in terms of syntax, or you may know these expressions by other names such as lambda functions, anonymous functions, or closures.

A number of array functions, such as zip_with, support the use of lambda expressions. The expression simply defines a transformation from an input value to an output value separated by ->:

```
x -> x + 1
(x, y) -> x + y
x -> IF(x > 0, x, -x)
```

Other functions commonly used with lambda expressions are transform , filter, reduce , array_sort, none_match, any_match, and all_match.

Have a look at this example:

```
SELECT zip_with(ARRAY[1, 2, 6, 2, 5],
                ARRAY[3, 4, 2, 5, 7],
                (x, y) -> x + y);

[4, 6, 8, 7, 12]
```

As you can see, the lambda expression is simple yet powerful. It adds the *n*th elements from the two arrays, creating a new array with the sums. Basically, an iteration over both arrays takes place, and the function is called in each iteration, all without needing to write any code for looping through the array data structure.

Geospatial Functions

The SQL support of Presto expands beyond standard SQL, and includes a significant set of functionality in the realm of geospatial analysis. As with other SQL support, Presto aligns closely with relevant standard and common usage across other tools.

In the case of *geospatial functions*, Presto uses the ST_ prefix supporting the SQL/MM specifications and the Open Geospatial Consortium's (OGC) OpenGIS Specifications.

Because of the large scope of the geospatial support, you get only a glimpse in this section.

Presto supports numerous constructors to create geospatial objects from source, for example:

- ST_GeometryFromText(varchar) -> Geometry
- ST_GeomFromBinary(varbinary) -> Geometry
- ST_LineFromText(varchar) -> LineString
- ST_LineString(array(Point)) -> LineString
- ST_Point(double, double) -> Point
- ST_Polygon(varchar) -> Polygon

These objects can then be used in the many, many functions to compare locations and other aspects:

- ST_Contains(Geometry, Geometry) -> boolean
- ST_Touches(Geometry, Geometry) -> boolean
- ST_Within(Geometry, Geometry) -> boolean
- ST_Length(Geometry) -> double
- ST_Distance(Geometry, Geometry) -> double
- ST_Area(SphericalGeography) -> double

The geospatial support in Presto is detailed in the Presto documentation (see "Documentation" on page 13). We strongly suggest you check it out if you are dealing with geospatial data in your use of Presto.

Prepared Statements

Prepared statements are a useful approach to be able to run the same SQL statement with different input parameter values. This allows reuse, simplifies repeated usage for users, and creates cleaner, better maintainable code. Prepared statements are queries that are saved in the Presto session for the user.

Use and creation of prepared statements are separated into two steps. The PREPARE statement is used to create the statement and make it available for repeated use in the session:

```
PREPARE example
FROM SELECT count(*) FROM hive.ontime.flights_orc;
```

The EXECUTE command can be used to run the query one or multiple times:

```
EXECUTE example;
  _col0
-----------
 166628027
(1 row)
```

Prepared statements can support parameter values to be passed at execution time:

```
PREPARE delay_query FROM
SELECT dayofweek,
       avg(depdelayminutes) AS delay
FROM flights_orc
WHERE month = ?
AND origincityname LIKE ?
GROUP BY dayofweek
ORDER BY dayofweek;
```

Using the query with parameters requires you to pass them along for the execution in the correct order after the USING keyword:

```
EXECUTE delay_query USING 2, '%Boston%';
 dayofweek |        delay
-----------+--------------------
         1 | 10.613156692553677
         2 |   9.97405624214174
         3 |  9.548045977011494
         4 | 11.822725778003647
         5 | 15.875475113122173
         6 | 11.184173669467787
         7 | 10.788121285791464
(7 rows)
```

Difference Between PREPARE Statement in RDBMSs and Presto

Using PREPARE in other relational database systems has a purpose more than just convenience of executing similar queries with different parameter values. Many systems may actually parse and plan the SQL during the PREPARE statement. Then during the EXECUTE command, the values are passed to the system and bound to the execution plan operators. For transaction systems, this is often an important optimization since it has to parse and plan the query only once for many executions, even with different values. This is the original purpose behind prepared statements.

Another common example of this is INSERT queries, where you want to insert a lot of new values as quickly as possible. PREPARE eliminates the overhead of planning for each insert.

Currently, Presto does not implement this optimization, and the query and parse are planned for each EXECUTE. Given the nature of Presto's main use case, it's not as important of an optimization to be concerned about. Prepared statements were originally introduced into Presto for the JDBC and ODBC drivers, since tools may rely on the functionality.

The DESCRIBE command can be useful for understanding prepared statements with the DESCRIBE INPUT and DESCRIBE OUTPUT commands. These commands are used internally by the JDBC and ODBC drivers for metadata information and error-handling purposes:

```
DESCRIBE INPUT delay_query;
 Position |  Type
----------+---------
        0 | integer
        1 | varchar
(2 rows)

DESCRIBE OUTPUT delay_query;
 Column Name | Catalog | Schema |    Table    |  Type   | Type Size | Aliased
-------------+---------+--------+-------------+---------+-----------+--------
 dayofweek   | hive    | ontime | flights_orc | integer |         4 | false
 delay       |         |        |             | double  |         8 | true
(2 rows)
```

When you exit the Presto session, the prepared statements are automatically deallocated. You can manually remove the prepared statement with DEALLOCATE PREPARE:

```
DEALLOCATE PREPARE delay_query;
DEALLOCATE
```

Conclusion

Congratulations, you made it! This chapter is certainly pretty deep in terms of documenting the SQL support and processing in Presto. This is a central feature of Presto and, as such, very important. And you did not even learn all the details. Make sure you refer to the official documentation described in "Documentation" on page 13 for the latest and greatest information, including a full list of all functions and operators and lots more details about all of them.

Understanding the depth of SQL support hopefully really gets you into the idea of running Presto in production to bring the benefits to your users. In the next part of the book, you learn more about what is involved in terms of security, monitoring, and more. And you get to find out examples of applications to use with Presto and some information about real-world use in other organizations and companies.

With the knowledge from the last two chapters about the SQL support in Presto, you can now go back to Chapter 4 and learn more about query planning and optimizations. Or you can advance to the next part of this book to learn more about Presto use in production, integrations with Presto, and other users.

Presto in Real-World Uses

So far you've gotten an introduction to Presto, learned how to install it for production use, learned how to hook up data sources with different connectors, and saw how powerful the SQL support is.

In this third part, you learn other aspects of using Presto in production, such as security and monitoring, and you get to explore applications that can be used together with Presto to provide tremendous value for your users.

Last but not least, you hear about other organizations and their use of Presto.

Security

Deploying Presto at scale, discussed in Chapter 5, is an important step toward production usage. In this chapter, you learn more about securing Presto itself as well as the underlying data.

In a typical Presto cluster deployment and use, you can consider securing several aspects:

- Transport from user client to the Presto coordinator
- Transport within the Presto cluster, between coordinator and workers
- Transport between the Presto cluster and each data source, configured per catalog
- Access to specific data within each data source

In Figure 10-1, you can see how the different network connections of Presto need to be secured. The connection to your client—for example, Presto CLI or an application using the JDBC driver—needs to be secured. The traffic within the cluster needs to be secured. And the connections with all the different data sources need to be secured.

Let's explore these needs in more detail in the following sections, starting with authenticating to Presto as a user.

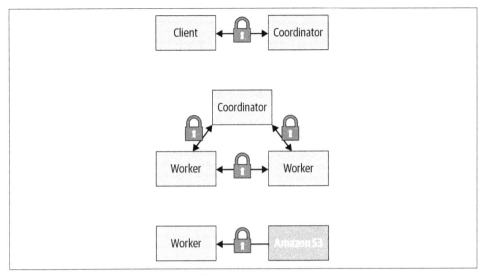

Figure 10-1. Network connections of Presto usage to secure

Authentication

Authentication is the process of proving an identity to a system. Authentication is essential to any secure system. A variety of authentication methods are supported by computer systems, including Kerberos, password with Lightweight Directory Access Protocol (LDAP), and certificate authentication. It is up to each system to support the particular authentication method. In Presto, clients commonly authenticate to the Presto cluster via one of following methods:

- Password via LDAP—see details that follow
- Certificates—see "Certificate Authentication" on page 219
- Kerberos—see "Kerberos" on page 222

By default, no authentication is configured in Presto. Anyone who can access the coordinator can connect and therefore issue queries and perform other operations. In this chapter, you learn details about LDAP and certificate authentication mechanisms, since they are the most commonly used.

However, authentication is just one piece. Once the principal is authenticated, they are assigned the privileges that determine what the user is able to do. What you can do is referred to as *authorization* and is governed by the SystemAccessControl and ConnectorAccessControl. We describe this in more detail in "Authorization" on page 203. For now, let's assume that once authenticated, the user can perform any action. By default, this is true for accessing anything at the system level, such as querying the system catalog.

Password and LDAP Authentication

Password authentication is an authentication method you probably use every day. By providing a username and password to the system, you are proving who you say you are by providing something you know. Presto supports this basic form of authentication by using its password authenticator. The *password authenticator* receives the username and password credentials from the client, validates them, and creates a principal. The password authenticator is designed to support custom password authenticators deployed as a plug-in in Presto.

Currently, password authentication supported by Presto uses the LDAP authenticator, and therefore an LDAP service.

> Password file authentication is a less commonly used, simple, and supported authentication mechanism.

LDAP stands for *Lightweight Directory Access Protocol*, an industry-standard application protocol for accessing and managing information in a directory server. The data model in the directory server is a hierarchical data structure that stores identity information. We won't elaborate on too many more details about what LDAP is or how it works. If you are interested in learning more, there is plenty of information available in books or on the web (*https://ldap.com*).

When using the LDAP authenticator, a user passes a username and password to the Presto coordinator. This can be done from the CLI, JDBC driver, or any other client that supports passing the username and password. The coordinator then validates these credentials with an external LDAP service and creates the principal from the username. You can see a visualization of this flow in Figure 10-2. To enable LDAP authentication with Presto, you need to add to the *config.properties* file on the Presto coordinator:

```
http-server.authentication.type=PASSWORD
```

By setting the authentication type to `PASSWORD`, we are telling the Presto coordinator to use the password authenticator to authenticate.

In addition, you need to configure the LDAP service with the additional file *password-authenticator.properties* in the *etc* directory:

```
password-authenticator.name=ldap
ldap.url=ldaps://ldap-server:636
ldap.user-bind-pattern=${USER}@example.com
```

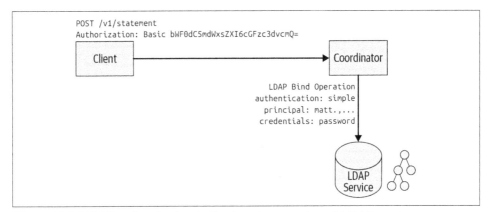

```
POST /v1/statement
Authorization: Basic bWF0dC5mdWxsZXI6cGFzc3dvcmQ=
```

Client ──────────────────────────▶ Coordinator

```
LDAP Bind Operation
authentication: simple
   principal: matt.,...
credentials: password
```

LDAP Service

Figure 10-2. LDAP authentication to Presto using an external LDAP service

The `password-authenticator.name` specifies to use the LDAP plug-in for the password authenticator. The following lines configure the LDAP server URL and the pattern to locate the user record. The preceding bind pattern is an example usage with Active Directory. Other LDAP servers or configurations define a user ID (UID):

```
ldap.user-bind-pattern=uid=${USER},OU=people,DC=example,DC=com
```

In LDAP, several operation types interact with the LDAP directory, such as add, delete, modify, search, and bind. *Bind* is the operation used to authenticate clients to the directory server and is what Presto uses for supporting LDAP authentication. In order to bind, you need to supply identification and proof of identity such as a password. LDAP allows for different types of authentication, but user identity, also known as the *distinguished name*, and password is the main supported method by Presto for LDAP authentication.

A secondary method, which was recently added, is to authenticate and authorize with a LDAP service user. Check the Presto documentation for configuration tips.

Presto requires using *secure LDAP*, which is referred to as *LDAPS*. Therefore, you need to make sure you have TLS enabled on your LDAP server. In addition, ensure that the URL for the `ldap-url` property uses `ldaps://` and not `ldap://`. Because this communication occurs over TLS, you need to import the LDAP server TLS certificate to the truststore used by the Presto coordinator. Or if the LDAP server is using a certificate signed by a certificate authority (CA), you need to make sure that the CA chain is in the truststore.

To securely use the LDAP authenticator, you also need to configure HTTPS access to the Presto coordinator. This ensures that the password sent from the client is not in clear text over an unsecure network. We discuss this setup in "Encryption" on page 209.

Once the LDAP configuration is in place, you can test it with the Presto CLI:

```
presto --user matt --password
```

Specifying `--password` causes the CLI to prompt you to enter the password. When you configure the LDAP password authenticator, you have set the user bind pattern.

When the username and password are passed to the Presto coordinator from the client, the CLI in our example, Presto replaces this username in the bind pattern and sends this as a security principal, and the password as the security credentials, as part of the bind request for LDAP. In our example, the principal used to match the distinguished name in the directory structure is `uid=matt,OU=people,DC=exam ple,DC=com`. Each entry in the LDAP directory may consist of multiple attributes. One such attribute is `userPassword`, which the bind operation uses to match the password sent.

Presto can further restrict access based on group memberships. You learn more about the importance of groups in the following authorization sections. By using groups, you can assign privileges to a group, so the users in that group inherit all the privileges of that group rather than having to manage privileges individually. Say, for example, you want to allow only people in the `engineering` group to authenticate with Presto. In our example, we want users `matt` and `maria` to be able to authenticate to Presto, but not user `jane`.

To further restrict users based on group membership, Presto allows you to specify additional properties in the *password-authenticator.properties* file.

```
ldap.user-base-dn=OU=people,DC=example,DC=com

ldap.group-auth-pattern=(&(objectClass=inetOrgPerson)(uid=${USER})(memberof=
CN=developers,OU=groups,DC=example,DC=com))
```

In our example, the preceding filter restricts users from the base distinguished name and allows only users who belong to the `developers` group in LDAP. If user `jane` tries to authenticate, the bind operation succeeds since `jane` is a valid user, but the user is filtered out of the results because she does not belong to the `developers` group.

Authorization

In the previous section you learned about authentication, or proving to Presto who you are. However, in an environment with many users and sensitive data, you do not want any user who can authenticate to access any data.

To restrict access, you need to configure *authorization* of what a user can do. Let's first examine the SQL model in Presto in terms of what access controls exist. Then you learn how to control access to Presto at the system and connector level.

System Access Control

System access control enforces authorization at the global Presto level and allows you to configure access for catalogs and rules for the principals used.

Lower-level rights and restrictions within a catalog have to be configured with connector access control; see "Connector Access Control" on page 207.

As you learned in the authentication section, security principals are the entity used to authenticate to Presto. The principal may be an individual user or a service account. Presto also separates the principal for authentication from the user who is running queries. For example, multiple users may share a principal for authenticating, but run queries as themselves. By default, Presto allows any principal who can authenticate to run queries as anyone else:

```
$ presto --krb5-principal alice@example.com --user bob
```

This is generally not what you would want to run in a real environment, since it potentially elevates the access granted to one user, bob, beyond his authorization. Changing this default behavior requires additional configuration. Presto supports a set of built-in system access control configurations.

By default, Presto allows any authenticated user to do anything. This is the least secure and not recommended when deploying in a production environment. While it is the default, you can set it explicitly by creating *access-control.properties* within the *etc* directory.

```
access-control.name=allow-all
```

Read-only authorization is slightly more secure in that it allows only any operation that is reading data or metadata. This includes SELECT queries, but not CREATE, INSERT, or DELETE queries:

```
access-control.name=read-only
```

> Using this method to set access control to read-only is a very fast, simple, and effective way to reduce risk from Presto usage to the underlying data. At the same time, read access is completely suitable to analysis usage, and you can easily create a dedicated Presto cluster with read-only access to allow anybody in your company access to a large amount of data for analysis, troubleshooting, or simply exploration or learning more about Presto.

To configure system access control beyond simple allow-all or read-only, you can use a file-based approach. This allows you to specify access control rules for catalog access by users and what users a principal can identify as. These rules are specified in a file that you maintain.

When using file-based system access control, all access to catalogs is denied unless there is a matching rule for a user that explicitly gives them permission. You can enable this in the *access-control.properties* file in the *etc* configuration directory:

```
access-control.name=file
security.config-file=etc/rules.json
```

The `security.config-file` property specifies the location of the file containing the rules. It must be a JSON file using the format detailed in the following code. Best practice is to keep it in the same directory as all other configuration files:

```
{
  "catalogs": [
    {
      "user": "admin",
      "catalog": "system",
      "allow": true
    },
    {
      "catalog": "hive",
      "allow": true
    },
    {
      "user": "alice",
      "catalog": "postgresql",
      "allow": true
    }
    {
      "catalog": "system",
      "allow": false
    }
  ]
}
```

Rules are examined in order, and the first rule that matches is used. In this example, the `admin` user is allowed access to the `system` catalog, whereas all other users are denied because of the last rule. We mentioned earlier that all catalog access is denied by default unless there is a matching rule. The exception is that all users have access to the `system` catalog by default.

The example file also grants access to the `hive` catalog for all users, but only the user `alice` is granted access to the `postgresql` catalog.

System access controls are very useful for restricting access. However, they can be used to configure access only at the catalog level. More fine-grained access cannot be configured with it.

As we mentioned earlier, authenticated principal can run queries as any user by default. This is generally not desirable, as it allows users to potentially access data as someone else. If the connector has implemented a connector access control, it means that a user can authenticate with a principal and pretend to be another user to access data they should not have access to. Therefore, it is important to enforce an appropriate matching between the principal and the user running the queries.

Let's say we want to set the username to that of the LDAP principal:

```
{
  "catalogs": [
    {
      "allow": "all"
    }
  ],
  "principals": [
    {
      "principal": "(.*)",
      "principal_to_user": "$1",
      "allow": "all"
    }
  ]
}
```

This can be further extended to enforce the user to use exactly their Kerberos principal name. In addition, we can match the username to a group principal that may be shared:

```
"principals": [
  {
    "principal": "([^/]+)/?.*@example.com",
    "principal_to_user": "$1",
    "allow": "all"
  },
  {
    "principal": "group@example.com",
    "user": "alice|bob",
    "allow": "all"
  }
]
```

Therefore, if you want a different behavior, you must override the rule; in this case, the users bob and alice can use the principal group@example.com as well as their own principals, bob@example.com and alice@example.com.

Connector Access Control

Recall the set of objects Presto exposes in order to query data. A *catalog* is the configured instance of a connector. A catalog may consist of a set of namespaces called *schemas*. And, finally, the schemas contain a collection of tables with columns using specific data types and rows of data. With connector access control, Presto allows you to configure fine-grained rights within a catalog.

Presto supports the SQL standard GRANT to grant privileges on tables and views to a user or role, and also to grant user membership to a role. Today, Presto supports a subset of privileges defined by the SQL standard. In Presto, you can grant the following privileges to a table or view:

SELECT
> Equivalent to read access

INSERT
> Equivalent to create access, or write access for new rows

DELETE
> Equivalent to delete access, or removal of rows

 As of this writing, only the Hive connector supports roles and grants. Because this depends on the connector implementation, each connector needs to implement the ConnectorAccessControl to support this SQL standard functionality.

Let's look at an example:

```
GRANT SELECT on hive.ontime.flights TO matt;
```

The user running this query is granting to user matt the SELECT privilege on table flights that is in the ontime schema of the hive catalog.

Optionally, you can specify the WITH GRANT OPTION that allows the grantee matt to grant the same privileges to others. You can also specify more than one privilege by separating commas or by specifying ALL PRIVILEGES to grant SELECT, INSERT, and DELETE to the object:

```
GRANT SELECT, DELETE on hive.ontime.flights TO matt WITH GRANT OPTION;
```

To grant privileges, you must possess the same privileges and the GRANT OPTION. Or you must be an owner of the table or view, or member of the role that owns the table or view. At the time of this writing, there is no way in Presto to alter the owner of the object, so that must be done by the underlying data source. For example, you can run the following SQL statement:

```
ALTER SCHEMA ontime SET OWNER USER matt;
```

A *role* consists of a collection of privileges that can be assigned to a user or another role. This makes administering privileges for many users easier. By using roles, you avoid the need to assign privileges directly to users. Instead, you assign the privileges to a role, and then users are assigned to that role and inherit those privileges. Users can also be assigned multiple roles. Using roles to manage privileges is generally the best practice.

Let's reuse our example of the flights table and use roles:

```
CREATE ROLE admin;
GRANT SELECT, DELETE on hive.ontime.flights TO admin;
GRANT admin TO USER matt, martin;
```

Now let's say you wish to remove privileges from a user. Instead of having to remove all the privileges on an object granted to a user, you can simply remove the role assignment from the user:

```
REVOKE admin FROM USER matt;
```

In addition to removing users from a role, you can also remove privileges from a role so that all users with the role no longer have that privilege:

```
REVOKE DELETE on hive.ontime.flights FROM admin;
```

In this example, we revoked the DELETE privileges on the flights table from the admin role. However, the admin role and its members still have the SELECT privilege.

Users may belong to multiple roles, and those roles may have distinct or an intersection of privileges. When a user runs a query, Presto examines the privileges that the user has either assigned directly or through the roles. If you wish to use only the privileges of a single role you belong to, you can use the SET ROLE command. For example, say you belong to both an admin role and the developer role, but you want to be using only the privileges assigned to the developer role:

```
SET ROLE developer;
```

You can also set the role to ALL so that Presto examines your privileges for every role you belong to. Or you can set it to NONE.

Encryption

Encryption is a process of transforming data from a readable form to an unreadable form, which is then used in transport or for storage, also called *at rest*. At the receiver end, only authorized users are able to transform data back to a readable form. This prevents any malicious attacker who intercepts the data from being able to read it. Presto uses standard cryptographic techniques to encrypt data in motion and at rest, and you can see a comparison between the plain text and the encrypted version in Table 10-1.

Table 10-1. Comparison of an equivalent text in plain and encrypted format

Plain text	Encrypted text
SSN: 123-45-6789	5oMgKBe38tSsOpI/Rg7lITExIWtCITEzIfSVydAHF8Gux1cpnCg=

Encrypted data in motion includes the following data transfers and is displayed in Figure 10-3:

- Between the client, such as a JDBC client or the Presto CLI, and the Presto coordinator (at left in the figure)
- Within the Presto cluster, between the coordinator and workers (center)
- From the data sources, configured in the catalogs, to the workers and the coordinator in the cluster (at right)

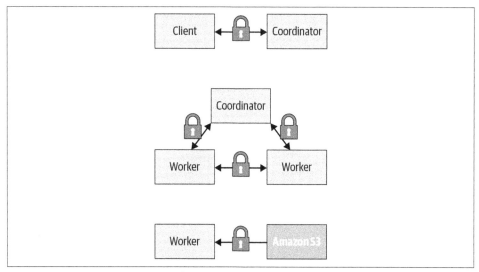

Figure 10-3. Encryption options for data in transit

Encryption of data at rest includes the following locations and is displayed in Figure 10-4:

- Data sources, so outside the Presto cluster (right)
- Storage on the workers and/or coordinator used for the spilling to disk functionality, so inside the Presto cluster (left)

Figure 10-4. Encryption options for data at rest

Each of these can be configured in Presto independently. S3 is used as an example for a connected data source.

These different encryption usages can be combined. For example, you can configure Presto to encrypt client-to-coordinator communication and intercluster communication, but leave data at rest unencrypted and therefore not secured. Or you may choose to configure Presto only for encrypted client-to-coordinator communication.

While each combination is possible to configure, some combinations do not make much sense. For example, configuring only intercluster communication but leaving client-to-coordinator communication unencrypted does not make sense because it leaves any data accessed by queries from a Presto client open to attacks.

As you've learned, external and internal communication in Presto happens exclusively over HTTP. To secure communication between the client and coordinator and intercluster communication, Presto can be configured to use Transport Layer Security (TLS) on top of HTTP, referred to as *HTTPS*. TLS is a cryptographic protocol for encrypting data over a network, and HTTPS uses TLS to secure the HTTP protocol.

TLS is the successor to Secure Sockets Layer (SSL), and sometimes the terms are used interchangeably. SSL is an older protocol with known vulnerabilities and is considered insecure. Because of the prominence and name recognition of SSL, when someone refers to SSL, they often are referring to TLS.

You are probably familiar with HTTPS from visiting websites because most sites use HTTPS now. For example, if you are logged into your online bank account, HTTPS is used to encrypt data between the web server and your web browser. On modern web browsers, you typically see the padlock icon in the address line, indicating the data transfer is secured and the server you are connected to is identical to the one identified in the certificate.

How Does HTTPS Work?

While this chapter is not intended to give a deep dive on the technical details of TLS, you should understand the basic concepts in order to understand how HTTPS works with Presto. We have discussed how Presto uses HTTPS to use TLS to encrypt the data in motion. Any malicious user eavesdropping on the network and intercepting data being processed in Presto won't be able to view the original unencrypted data.

The process of setting up this secured communication occurs when a user connects to a web page from their browser, and the server where the web page is hosted sends a TLS certificate to start the TLS handshake process. The TLS certificate relies on public-key (asymmetric) cryptography and is used during the handshake process to establish a secret key used for symmetric encryption during the session. During the handshake, both sides agree on the encryption algorithms to use and verify that the TLS certificate is authentic and the server is who they say they are. They generate session secret keys to be used for encrypting data after the handshake. Once the handshake is completed, data remains encrypted between the two, and the secure communication channel, displayed in Figure 10-5, is established for the duration of the session.

Figure 10-5. Secured communication between a client web browser and web server using TLS

Encrypting Presto Client-to-Coordinator Communication

It's important to secure the traffic between the client and Presto for two reasons. First, if you are using LDAP authentication, the password is in clear text. And with Kerberos authentication, the SPNEGO token can be intercepted as well. Additionally, any data returned from queries is in plain text.

Understanding the lower-level details of the TLS handshake for encryption algorithms is not crucial to understanding how Presto encrypts network traffic. But it is important to understand more about certificates, since you need to create and configure certificates for use by Presto. Figure 10-5 depicts communications between a client web browser and web server secured over HTTPS. This is exactly how HTTPS communication is used between the Presto coordinator and a Presto client such as the Presto Web UI, the Presto CLI, or the JDBC driver, displayed in Figure 10-6.

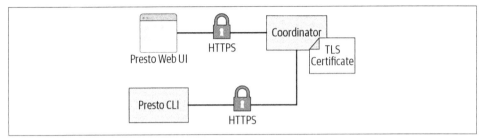

Figure 10-6. Secured communication over HTTP between Presto clients and the Presto coordinator

A TLS certificate relies on public-key (asymmetric) cryptography using key pairs:

- A public key, which is available to anyone
- A private key, which is kept private by the owner

Anyone can use the public key to encrypt messages that can be decrypted only by those who have the private key. Therefore, any message encrypted with the public key should be secret, as long as only the owner of the key pair does not share or have its private key stolen. A TLS certificate contains information such as the domain the certificate was issued for, the person or company it was issued to, the public key, and several other items. This information is then hashed and encrypted using a private key. The process of signing the certificate creates the signature to include in the certificate.

These certificates are often signed by a trusted certificate authority such as DigiCert or GlobalSign. These authorities verify that the person requesting a certificate to be issued is who they say they are and that they own the domain as stated in the certificate. The certificate is signed by the authority's private key, for which their public keys are made widely available and typically installed by default on most operating systems and web browsers.

The process of signing the certificate is important during the TLS handshake to verify authenticity. The client uses the public key of the pair to decrypt the signature and compare to the content in the certificate to make sure it was not tampered with.

Now that you understand the basics of TLS, let's look at how we can encrypt data between the Presto clients and coordinator. To enable HTTPS on the Presto coordinator, you need to set additional properties in the *config.properties* file (see Table 10-2).

Table 10-2. Configuration properties for HTTPS communication

Property	Description
http-server.https.enabled	Set this to true to enable HTTPS for Presto. Defaults to false.
http-server.http.enabled	Set this to false to disable HTTP for Presto. Defaults to true.
http-server.https.port	Specify the HTTPS port to use. 8443 is a common default port for HTTPS for Java application servers.
http-server.https.keystore.path	Specify the path to the Java keystore file that stores the private key and certificate used by Presto for TLS.
http-server.https.keystore.key	Specify the Java keystore password Presto needs to access the keystore.

 Even though you are configuring Presto to use HTTPS, by default HTTP is still enabled as well. Enabling HTTPS does not disable HTTP. If you wish to disable HTTP access, this needs to be configured. However, you may want to keep HTTP enabled until you have completed configuring the secured Presto environment. Testing how or if something works over HTTP may be a good way to debug an issue if you run into complications during configurations.

Take, for example, the following lines to add to your *config.properties*:

```
http-server.https.enabled=true
http-server.https.port=8443
http-server.https.keystore.path=/etc/presto/presto_keystore.jks
http-server.https.keystore.key=slickpassword
```

Remember to restart the Presto coordinator after you update the properties file.

Java Keystores and Truststores

While configuring encryption, you need to work with Java keystores. A *keystore* is a repository used to store cryptographic keys, X.509 certificate chains, and trusted certificates. In Presto, the keystore can be used as either a keystore or truststore. There is no difference in the implementation or tools using these stores. The major difference is what is stored in the keystore and truststore and how each is used. A keystore is used when you need to prove your identity, while the truststore is used when you need to confirm another identity.

For Presto, the Presto coordinator needs a keystore that contains the private key and signed certificate. When the Presto client connects, Presto presents this certificate to the client as part of the TLS handshake.

The Presto client, such as the CLI, uses a truststore that contains the certificates needed to verify the authenticity of the certificate presented by the server. If the Presto coordinator certificate is signed by a certificate authority (CA), then the truststore contains the root and intermediate certificates. If you are not using a CA, the truststore contains the same Presto TLS certificate. Self-signed certificates simply mean that the certificate is signed by the private key of the public key in the certificate. These are far less secure, as an attack can spoof a self-signed certificate as part of a man-in-the-middle attack. You must be sure of the security of the network and machine the client is connecting to when using self-signed certificates. Using self-signed certificates is more acceptable for securing the intercluster communication since the whole cluster is typically located within a secured network.

What Is an X.509 Certificate?

X.509 is the standard that defines the format of a public-key certificate such as the ones we want to generate to secure Presto. The certificate includes the domain name it is issued for, the person of organization it is issued to, the issue date and expiration, the public key, and the signature. The certificate is signed by a CA, or is self-signed. You can learn more from the official standard (*https://www.itu.int/rec/T-REC-X.509*).

Creating Java Keystores and Java Truststores

The Java `keytool`, a command-line tool for creating and managing keystores and truststores, is available as part of any Java Development Kit (JDK) installation. Let's go over a simple example for creating a Java keystore and truststore. For simplicity, we use self-signed certificates.

Let's first create the keystore to be used by the Presto coordinator. The following `key tool` command creates a public/private key pair and wraps the public key in a certificate that is self-signed:

```
$ keytool -genkeypair \
    -alias presto_server \
    -dname CN=*.example.com \
    -validity 10000 -keyalg RSA -keysize 2048 \
    -keystore keystore.jks \
    -keypass password
    -storepass password
```

The generated *keystore.jks* file needs to be used on the server and specified in the `http-server.https.keystore.path` property. Similar usage applies for the `store pass` password in the `http-server.https.keystore.key` property.

In this example, you are using a *wildcard certificate*. We specify the common name (CN) to be `*.example.com`. This certificate can be shared by all the nodes on the Presto cluster, assuming they use the same domain; this certificate works with `coordi nator.example.com`, `worker1.example.com`, `worker2.example.com`, and so on. The disadvantage to this approach is that any node under the *example.com* domain can use the certificate.

You can limit the subdomains by using a subject alternative name (`SubjectAltName`), where you list the subdomains. This allows you to create a single certificate to be shared by a limited, specific list of hosts. An alternative approach is to create a certificate for each node, requiring you to explicitly define the full domain for each. This adds an administrative burden and makes it challenging when scaling a Presto cluster, as the new nodes require certificates bound to the full domain.

When connecting a client to the coordinator, the coordinator sends its certificate to the client to verify its authenticity. A truststore is used to verify the authenticity by containing the coordinator certificate if self-signed, or a certificate chain if signed by a CA. Later, we discuss how to use a certificate chain of a CA. Because the keystore also contains the certificate, you could simply copy the keystore to the client machine and use that as the truststore. However, that is not secure, as the keystore also contains the private key that we want to keep secret. To create a custom truststore, you need to export the certificate from the keystore and import it into a truststore.

First, on the coordinator where your keystore was created, you export the certificate:

```
$ keytool --exportcert \
    -alias presto_server \
    -file presto_server.cer \
    -keystore keystore.jks \
    -storepass password
```

This command creates a *presto_server.cer* certificate file. As a next step, you use that file to create the truststore:

```
$ keytool --importcert \
    -alias presto_server \
    -file presto_server.cer \
    -keystore truststore.jks \
    -storepass password
```

Since the certificate is self-signed, this `keytool` command prompts you to confirm that you want to trust this certificate. Simply type **yes** and the *truststore.jks* is created. Now you can safely distribute this truststore to any machine from which you use a client to connect the coordinator.

Now that we have the coordinator enabled with HTTPS using a keystore and we've created a truststore for the clients, we can securely connect to Presto such that the communication between the client and coordinator is encrypted. Here is an example using the Presto CLI:

```
$ presto --server https://presto-coordinator.example.com:8443 \
    --truststore-path ~/truststore.jks \
    --truststore-password password
```

Encrypting Communication Within the Presto Cluster

Next let's look at how to secure the communication between the workers, and the workers and the coordinator, all within the Presto cluster, by using HTTP over TLS again as shown in Figure 10-7.

While the client-to-coordinator communication may be over an untrusted network, the Presto cluster is generally deployed on a more secure network, making secured intercluster communication more optional. However, if you're concerned about a malicious attacker being able to get onto the network of the cluster, communication can be encrypted.

As with securing client-to-coordinator communication, cluster internal communication also relies on the same keystore. This keystore you created on the coordinator must be distributed to all worker nodes.

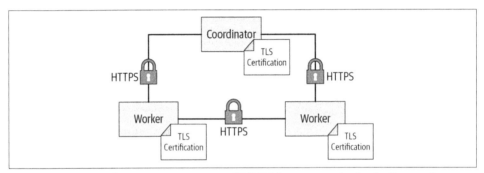

Figure 10-7. Secured communication over HTTPS between nodes in the Presto cluster

The same method of performing the TLS handshake to establish trust between the client and server, and create an encrypted channel, works for the intercluster communication. Communication in the cluster is bidirectional, meaning a node may act as a client sending the HTTPS request to another node, or a node can act as a server when it receives the request and presents the certificate to the client for verification. Because each node can act as both client and server for different connections, it needs a keystore that contains both the private key and the public key wrapped in the certificate.

All nodes need to enable HTTPS in *config.properties*, including for internal communication:

```
http-server.https.enabled=true
http-server.https.port=8443

internal-communication.https.required=true
discovery.uri=https://coordinator.example.com:8443
```

```
internal-communication.https.keystore.path=/etc/presto/presto_keystore.jks
internal-communication.https.keystore.key=slickpassword
```

Remember to restart the workers after you update the properties file. Now you have entirely secured the internal and external communication and secured it against eavesdroppers on the network trying to intercept data from Presto.

 Once you have everything working, it's important to disable HTTP by setting `http-server.http.enabled=false` in *config.properties*; otherwise, a user can still connect to the cluster using HTTP.

Certificate Authority Versus Self-Signed Certificates

When you try out Presto for the first time and work to get it configured securely, it's easiest to use a self-signed certificate. In practice, however, it may not be allowed in your organization as they are much less secure and susceptible to attacks in certain situations. Therefore, you may use a certificate that was digitally signed by a CA.

Once you have created the keystore, you need to create a certificate signing request (CSR) to send to the CA to get the keystore signed. The CA verifies you are who you say you are and issues you a certificate signed by them. The certificate is then imported into your keystore. This CA signed certificate is presented to the client instead of the original self-signed one.

An interesting aspect is related to the use of the Java truststore. Java provides a default truststore that may contain the CA already. In this case, the certificate presented to the client can be verified by the default truststore. Using the Java default truststore can be cumbersome because it may not contain the CA. Or perhaps your organization has its own internal CA for issuing organizational certifications to employees and services. So if you're using a CA, it is still recommended that you create your own truststore for Presto to use. However, you can import the CA certificate chain instead of the actual certificates being used for Presto. A *certificate chain* is a list of two or more TLS certificates, where each certificate in the chain is signed by the next one in the chain. At the top of the chain is the root certificate, and this is always self-signed by the CA itself. It is used to sign the downstream certificates known as *intermediate certificates*. When you are issued a certificate for Presto, it is signed by an intermediate certificate, which is the first one in the chain. The advantage to this is that, if there are multiple certificates for multiple Presto clusters or if certificates are reissued, you don't need to reimport them into your truststore each time. This reduces the need for the CA to reissue an intermediate or root certificate.

The scenario in Figure 10-8 shows the use of a certificate issued by a CA. The truststore contains only the intermediate and root certificates of the CA. The TLS certificate from the Presto coordinator is verified using this certificate chain in the client truststore.

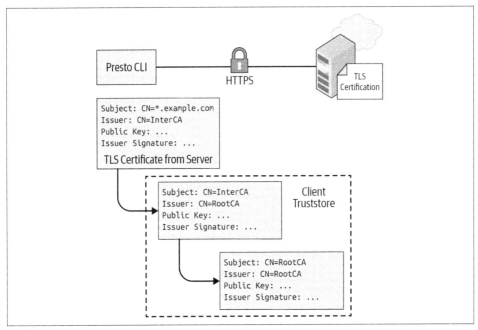

Figure 10-8. Presto using a certificate issued by a CA

Let's say you had your Presto certificate signed by a CA. In order for the client to trust it, we need to create a truststore containing the intermediate and root certificates. As in the earlier example in which we imported the Presto self-signed certificate, you perform the same import of the CA certificate chain:

```
$ keytool --importcert \
    -alias presto_server \
    -file root-ca.cer \
    -keystore truststore.jks \
    -storepass password
```

After the root CA certificate is imported, you continue to import all necessary intermediate certificate from the chain:

```
$ keytool --importcert \
    -alias presto_server \
    -file intermediate-ca.cer \
    -keystore truststore.jks \
    -storepass password
```

Note that there may be more than a single intermediate certificate and that we're using a single one here for simplicity.

Certificate Authentication

Now that you've learned about TLS, certificates, and the related usage of the Java key tool, you can have a look at using these tools for authenticating clients connecting to Presto with TLS. This certificate authentication is displayed in Figure 10-9.

As part of the TLS handshake, the server provides the client a certificate so that the client can authenticate the server. *Mutual TLS* means that the client, as a part of the handshake, provides a certificate to the server to be authenticated. The server verifies the certificate in the same way you have seen the client verify the certificate. The server requires a truststore that contains the CA chain, or the self-signed certificate for verification.

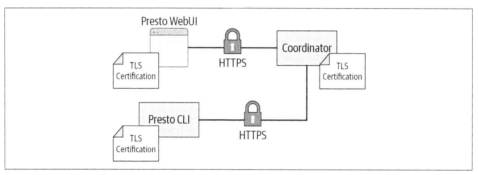

Figure 10-9. Certificate authentication for Presto clients

To configure the Presto coordinator for mutual TLS authentication, you need to add some properties to the *config.properties* file on the coordinator. Let's look at a complete configuration:

```
http-server.http.enabled=false
http-server.https.enabled=true
http-server.https.port=8443

http-server.https.keystore.path=/etc/presto/presto_keystore.jks
http-server.https.keystore.key=slickpassword

http-server.https.truststore.path=/etc/presto/presto_truststore.jks
http-server.https.truststore.key=slickpassword

node.internal-address-source=FQDN
internal-communication.https.required=true
internal-communication.https.keystore.path=/etc/presto/presto_keystore.jks
internal-communication.https.keystore.key=slickpassword

http-server.authentication.type=CERTIFICATE
```

The property `http-server.authentication` indicates the type of authentication to use. In this case, Presto is using `CERTIFICATE` authentication. This causes the Presto coordinator to use the full TLS handshake for mutual authentication. In particular, the server-side coordinator sends a certificate request message as part of the full TLS handshake to the client to provide the signed certificate for verification. In addition, you need to configure the truststore on the coordinator in order to verify the certificate presented by the client.

Let's use our command to connect with the CLI to Presto:

```
$ presto --server https://presto-coordinator.example.com:8443 \
      --truststore-path ~/truststore.jks \
      --truststore-password password \
      --user matt
presto> SELECT * FROM system.runtime.nodes;
Error running command: Authentication failed: Unauthorized
```

You'll find that authentication failed, because the client does not use the keystore that has the certificate to provide the client certificate to the coordinator for mutual authentication.

You need to modify your command to include a keystore. Note that this keystore is different from the keystore on the cluster. This keystore specifically contains the key pair for the client. Let's first create our keystore on the client side:

```
$ keytool -genkeypair \
    -alias presto_server \
    -dname CN=matt \
    -validity 10000 -keyalg RSA -keysize 2048 \
    -keystore client-keystore.jks \
    -keypass password
    -storepass password
```

In this example, you see that we set the CN to user `matt`. In this case, it's more than likely that this is a self-signed certificate or that an organization has its own internal CA. Let's specify the client keystore in the CLI command:

```
$ presto --server https://presto-coordinator.example.com:8443 \
      --truststore-path ~/truststore.jks \
      --truststore-password password \
      --keystore-path ~/client-keystore.jks \
      --keystore-password password \
      --user matt

presto> SELECT * FROM system.runtime.nodes;
Query failed: Access Denied:
Authenticated user AuthenticatedUser[username=CN=matt,principal=CN=matt]
cannot become user matt
```

Now that we have authenticated, authorization is failing. Recall that authentication proves who you are, and authorization controls what you can do.

In the case of certificate authentication, Presto extracts the subject distinguished name from the X.509 certificate. This value is used as the principal to compare to the username. The username defaults to the operating system username unless it is specified explicitly using the `--user` option in the CLI. In this case, the user `matt` is compared to the distinguished common name in the certificate `CN=matt`. One workaround is to simply pass the option to the CLI as `--user CN=matt`. Alternatively, you can leverage the built-in file-based system access control you learned about earlier for some customization.

First, you need to create a file in the Presto installation directory *etc/access-control.properties*, on the Presto coordinator.

```
access-control.name=file
security.config-file=/etc/presto/rules.json
```

Next we need to create the *rules.json* file on the coordinator as the path location specified in the *access-control.properties* file and define the mapping from principal to user to include `CN=`:

```
{
  "catalogs": [
    {
      "allow": true
    }
  ],
  "principals": [
    {
      "principal": "CN=(.*)",
      "principal_to_user": "$1",
      "allow": true
    }
  ]
}
```

We are matching a principal regex with a capturing group. We then use that capturing group to map the principal to the user. In our example, the regex matches `CN=matt`, where `matt` is part of the capturing group to map to the user. Once you create these files and restart the coordinator, both the certificate authentication and authorization of that subject principal to the user work:

```
SELECT * FROM system.runtime.nodes;
-[ RECORD 1 ]+----------------------------------------------------------
node_id      | i-0779df73d79748087
http_uri     | https://coordinator.example.com:8443
node_version | 312
coordinator  | true
state        | active
-[ RECORD 2 ]+----------------------------------------------------------
node_id      | i-0d3fba6fcba08ddfe
http_uri     | https://worker-1.example.com:8443
```

```
node_version | 312
coordinator  | false
state        | active
```

Kerberos

The network authentication protocol *Kerberos* (*http://web.mit.edu/kerberos*) is widely used. Support for Kerberos in Presto is especially critical for users of Presto, who are using the Hive connector (see "Hive Connector for Distributed Storage Data Sources" on page 93), since Kerberos is a commonly used authentication mechanism with HDFS and Hive.

 The Kerberos (*http://web.mit.edu/kerberos*) documentation can be a useful resource for learning about the protocol and the related concepts and terms. In this section, we assume that you are sufficiently familiar with these aspects or that you have gone off and read some of the documentation and other resources available.

Presto supports clients to authenticate to the coordinator by using the Kerberos authentication mechanism. The Hive connector can authenticate with a Hadoop cluster that uses Kerberos authentication.

Similar to LDAP, Kerberos is an authentication protocol, and a principal can be authenticated using a username and password or a *keytab* file.

Prerequisites

Kerberos needs to be configured on the Presto coordinator, which needs to be able to connect to the Kerberos key distribution center (KDC). The *KDC* is responsible for authenticating principals and issues session keys that can be used with Kerberos-enabled services. KDCs typically use TCP/IP port 88.

Using MIT Kerberos, you need to have a [realms] section in the */etc/krb5.conf* configuration file.

Kerberos Client Authentication

To enable Kerberos authentication with Presto, you need to add details to the *config.properties* file on the Presto coordinator. You need to change the authentication type, configure the location of the *keytab* file, and specify the user name of the Kerberos service account to use:

```
http-server.authentication.type=KERBEROS
http.server.authentication.krb5.service-name=presto
http.server.authentication.krb5.keytab=/etc/presto/presto.keytab
```

No changes to the worker configuration are required. The worker nodes continue to connect to the coordinator over unauthenticated HTTP.

To connect to this kerberized Presto cluster, a user needs to set up their *keytab* file, their principal, and their *krb5.conf* configuration file on the client and then use the relevant parameters for the Presto CLI or the properties for a JDBC connection. You can find all the details including a small wrapper script in the Presto documentation.

Cluster Internal Kerberos

If you want to secure the cluster internal communication, the Kerberos authentication must be enabled on workers, and internal communication needs to be changed to use SSL/TLS; see "Encrypting Communication Within the Presto Cluster" on page 216. This requires specifying valid Kerberos credentials for the internal communication.

Presto itself, as well as any users connecting to Presto with Kerberos, need a Kerberos principal. You need to create these users in Kerberos by using `kadmin`. In addition, the Presto coordinator needs a *keytab* file.

When using Kerberos authentication, client access to the Presto coordinator should use HTTPS; see "Encrypting Presto Client-to-Coordinator Communication" on page 211.

You can optionally set the Kerberos hostname for the coordinator, if you want Presto to use this value in the host part of the Kerberos principal instead of the machine's hostname. You can also specify an alternate location of the Kerberos configuration file *krb5.conf*, different from the default */etc/krb5.conf*:

```
http.server.authentication.krb5.principal-hostname=presto.example.com
http.authentication.krb5.config=/etc/presto/krb5.conf
```

For securing cluster internal communication with Kerberos, you need to specify valid Kerberos credentials for the internal communication and enable it:

```
internal-communication.kerberos.enabled=true
```

Make sure that you've also set up Kerberos on the worker nodes. The Kerberos principal for internal communication is built from `http.server.authentication` `.krb5.service-name` after appending it with the host name of the node where Presto is running and the default realm from the Kerberos configuration.

Data Source Access and Configuration for Security

Another aspect of securing the data available to Presto users is visible in Figure 10-10. Each catalog configured in Presto includes the connection string as well as the user credentials used to connect to the data source. Different connectors and target data source systems allow different access configurations.

A user first authenticates to the coordinator. The Presto connector issues requests to the data sources, which typically require authentication as well.

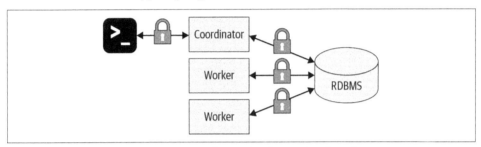

Figure 10-10. Data source security configuration impacting data for users

Authentication from the connectors to the data sources are dependent on the connector implementation. In many connector implementations, Presto authenticates as a service user. Therefore, for any user who runs a query using such a connector, the query is executed in the underlying system as that service user.

For example, if the user credentials to the target data source do not include the rights to perform any write operations, you effectively restrict all Presto users to read-only operations and queries. Similarly, if the user does not have access rights to a specific schema, database, or even table, Presto usage has the same restrictions.

To provide a more fine-grained access control, you can create several service users with different permissions. You can then have multiple catalog configurations with the same connector to the same data source, but using different service users.

Similar to using different service users, you can also create catalogs with different connections strings. For example, the PostgreSQL connection string includes a database name, which means you can create different catalogs to separate access to these databases running on the same PostgreSQL server. The MS SQL Server connections string allows an optional configuration of a database.

Details such as connection strings, user credentials, and other aspects are discussed in Chapter 6.

Beyond the schema and database level, you can even push access rights and data content configuration all the way down to the database itself. For example, if you want to limit access to certain columns in a table or certain rows in a table, you can limit access to the source tables and instead create views with the desired content. These are then available in Presto like traditional tables and therefore implement your security. The extreme case of this scenario is the creation of a separate database or data warehouse using ETL tools, including even Presto itself. These target databases with the desired data can then be configured for access in Presto with separate catalogs as well.

If you end up having multiple catalogs defined on your Presto deployment using some of the preceding logic, and you want to allow access to these catalogs to specific users, you can take advantage of the system access control discussed in "System Access Control" on page 204.

A relatively new feature available in some connectors from Presto, as well as some commercially available connectors, is end-user impersonation. This allows the end-user credentials in the Presto CLI or other tools to be passed through all the way to the data source. The access rights in Presto then reflect the configured access rights in the database.

One common example of data source security configuration is the use of Kerberos with HDFS and therefore with the Hive connector; see "Hive Connector for Distributed Storage Data Sources" on page 93. Let's look at the details now.

Kerberos Authentication with the Hive Connector

After learning about Kerberos configuration and data source security in general earlier, let's now look at the combination of Kerberos, HDFS/Hive, and the Hive connector.

By default, no authentication is enabled for Hive connector use. However, the connector does support Kerberos authentication. All you need to do is configure the connector to work with two services on the Hadoop cluster:

- The Hive metastore Thrift service
- The Hadoop Distributed File System (HDFS)

> If your *krb5.conf* location is different from */etc/krb5.conf*, you must set it explicitly using the `java.security.krb5.conf` JVM property in the *jvm.config* file:
>
> ```
> -Djava.security.krb5.conf=/example/path/krb5.conf
> ```

Hive Metastore Thrift Service Authentication

In a kerberized Hadoop cluster, Presto connects to the Hive metastore Thrift service by using Simple Authentication and Security Layer (SASL) and authenticates by using Kerberos. You can easily enable Kerberos authentication for the metastore service in your catalog properties file:

```
hive.metastore.authentication.type=KERBEROS
hive.metastore.service.principal=hive/hive-metastore-host.example.com@EXAMPLE.COM
hive.metastore.client.principal=presto@EXAMPLE.COM
hive.metastore.client.keytab=/etc/presto/hive.keytab
```

This setting activates the use of Kerberos for the authentication to HMS. It also configures the Kerberos principal and *keytab* file location that Presto uses when connecting to the metastore service. The *keytab* file must be distributed to every node in the cluster.

> `hive.metastore.service.principal` can use the `_HOST` placeholder in the value. When connecting to the HMS, the Hive connector substitutes this with the hostname of the metastore server it is connecting to. This is useful if the metastore runs on multiple hosts. Similarly, `hive.metastore.client.principal` can have the `_HOST` placeholder in its value. When connecting to the HMS, the Hive connector substitutes this with the hostname of the worker node Presto is running on. This is useful if each worker node has its own Kerberos principal.

Presto connects as the Kerberos principal specified by the property `hive.meta store.client.principal` and authenticates this principal by using the *keytab* specified by the `hive.metastore.client.keytab` property. It verifies that the identity of the metastore matches `hive.metastore.service.principal`.

> The principal specified by `hive.metastore.client.principal` must have sufficient privileges to remove files and directories within the *hive/warehouse* directory. Without this access, only the metadata is removed, and the data itself continues to consume disk space. This occurs because the HMS is responsible for deleting the internal table data. When the metastore is configured to use Kerberos authentication, all HDFS operations performed by the metastore are impersonated. Errors deleting data are silently ignored.

HDFS Authentication

Enabling Kerberos authentication to HDFS is similar to metastore authentication, with the following properties in your connectors properties file. When the authentication type is KERBEROS, Presto accesses HDFS as the principal specified by the `hive.hdfs.presto.principal` property. Presto authenticates this principal by using the *keytab* specified by the `hive.hdfs.presto.keytab` property:

```
hive.hdfs.authentication.type=KERBEROS
hive.hdfs.presto.principal=hdfs@EXAMPLE.COM
hive.hdfs.presto.keytab=/etc/presto/hdfs.keytab
```

Cluster Separation

Another large-scale security option is the complete separation of the data sources and configured catalogs by using them on separate Presto clusters. This separation can make sense in various scenarios:

- Isolating read-only operations from ETL and other write operation use cases
- Hosting clusters on completely different infrastructure because of regulatory requirements for the data; for example, web traffic data as compared to heavily regulated data such as medical or financial or personal data

This separation of clusters can allow you to optimize the cluster configuration for the different use cases and data, or locate the clusters closer to the data. Both situations can achieve considerable performance as well as cost advantages, while at the same time satisfying security needs.

Conclusion

Now you can feel safe about your data and the access Presto provides to it. You know about the many options you have to secure Presto access and the exposed data. This is a critical part of running Presto and has to be augmented by other activities such as monitoring, discussed in Chapter 12.

But first you need to learn about numerous tools to use with Presto to achieve some amazingly powerful results. Check it out in our next chapter, Chapter 11.

Integrating Presto with Other Tools

As you learned in Chapter 1, Presto unlocks a wide array of choices on how to use Presto. By now you've learned a lot about running a Presto cluster, connecting with JDBC, and writing queries running against one or multiple catalogs.

It is time to look at some applications that are successfully used with Presto in numerous organizations. The following sections cover various scenarios representing a small subset of the possibilities.

Queries, Visualizations, and More with Apache Superset

Apache Superset (*https://superset.apache.org*) can be described as a modern, enterprise-ready business intelligence web application. But this short and concise description really does not do justice to Superset.

Superset runs as a web application in your infrastructure and therefore does not require your business analysts and other users to install or manage their tools on their workstations. It supports Presto as a data source and so can be used as a front-end for your users accessing Presto, and all the configured data sources.

Once connected to Superset, users can start writing their queries in the included rich SQL query editor called *SQL Lab*. SQL Lab allows you to write queries in multiple tabs, browse the metadata of the database for assistance, run the queries, and receive the results in the user interface in a table. Even long-running queries are supported. SQL Lab also has numerous UI features that help you write the queries, or reduce that effort to a button click or two. For users, SQL Lab alone is already valuable and powerful. However, it is only the first step of benefiting from Superset. SQL Lab allows you a smooth transition to the real power of Superset: visualizing your data.

The visualizations supported by Superset are rich. You can get a first glance by looking at the visualizations gallery (*https://superset.apache.org/gallery.html*). You can create all the typical visualizations including data point plots, line charts, bar charts, or pie charts. Superset, however, is much more powerful and supports 3D visualizations, map-based data analysis, and more.

Once you have created the necessary queries and visualizations, you can assemble them into a dashboard and share them with the rest of your organization. This allows business analysts and other specialists to create useful aggregations of data and visualizations and expose them to other users conveniently.

Using Presto with Superset is simple. Once both systems are up and running, you just need to configure Presto as a database in Superset.

After Presto and Superset are connected, it can be useful to slowly expose it to your users. The simplicity of Superset allows users to create powerful, but also computationally heavy, queries with large data sets that can have a significant impact on the sizing and configuration of your Presto cluster. Scaling usage step-by-step in terms of users and use cases allows you to keep track of the cluster utilization and ensure that you scale the cluster based on the new demands.

Performance Improvements with RubiX

When you scale Presto to access large distributed storage systems and expose it to many users and tools, demands on your infrastructure increase tremendously. Compute performance needs can be handled by scaling the Presto cluster itself. The queried data source can be tuned as well. Even having those optimizations all in place and tuned, however, leaves you with a gap—the connection between Presto and the data.

The lightweight data-caching framework *RubiX* (*https://github.com/qubole/rubix*) from Qubole (*http://www.qubole.com*) can be located between the Presto compute resources and the data sources and act as a caching layer. It supports disk and in-memory caching. The performance gains from using this open source platform when querying distributed storage systems can result in significant performance improvements and cost reductions because of avoided data transfers and repeated queries on the underlying source.

RubiX introduces support for a new protocol `rubix://` for the URL scheme of a table location in the Hive metastore. It therefore acts as a transparent enhancement to the Hive connector, and from the view of a Presto user, nothing really changes. Metadata about the storage as well as actual data is cached in RubiX. The RubiX storage is distributed and can be collocated with the Presto cluster for maximum performance improvements.

Using RubiX and Presto together is an established practice, since the benefits are very complementary when querying distributed object storage.

Workflows with Apache Airflow

Apache Airflow (https://airflow.apache.org) is a widely used system to programmatically author, schedule, and monitor workflows. It has a strong focus on data pipeline processing and is widely used in the data science community. It is implemented in Python and capable of orchestrating the executions of complex workflows written in Python, calling out to many supported systems and including the execution of shell scripts.

To integrate Presto with Airflow, you can take advantage of Presto hooks in Airflow, or run the Presto CLI from the command line. Airflow supports many data sources beyond Presto and can therefore be used outside Presto to prepare data for later consumption via Presto as well as by accessing and working with the data via Presto to take advantage of its performance, scalability, and integration with many data sources.

The goal with Airflow and Presto is often to get the source data processed to end up with a high-quality data set that supports use in applications and machine learning models alike. Once the workflows, orchestrated by Airflow and run by Presto, and potentially other integrations, have produced the desired data sets, Presto can be used to access it and expose it to users with reports and dashboard, potentially using Apache Superset; see "Queries, Visualizations, and More with Apache Superset" on page 229.

Embedded Presto Example: Amazon Athena

Amazon Athena (https://aws.amazon.com/athena) is a query service that can be used to run SQL queries directly on data in files of any size stored in Amazon S3. Athena is a great example of an application that wraps Presto and uses it as a query engine to provide significant power and features. Athena is offered as a service and essentially uses Presto and the Hive connector to query S3. The Hive metastore used with the storage is another service, AWS Glue (*https://aws.amazon.com/glue*).

Figure 11-1 shows a high-level overview of the Amazon Athena architecture. Clients access Athena via the Athena/Presto REST API. Queries are run on the deployment of Presto with Athena by interacting with the Glue Data Catalog for the metadata of the data stored in S3 and queried by Presto.

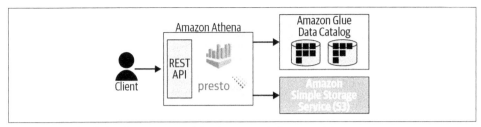

Figure 11-1. High-level overview of the Amazon Athena architecture

Athena is a *serverless architecture*, which means you do not have to manage any infrastructure such as Amazon Elastic Compute Cloud (EC2) instances or manage, install, or upgrade any database software to process the SQL statements. Athena takes care of all that for you. With no setup time, Athena instantly provides you the endpoint to submit your SQL queries. Serverless is a key design of Athena, providing high availability and fault tolerance as built-in benefits. Amazon provides the guarantees of uptime and availability of its services as well as resilience to failures or data loss.

Because Athena is serverless, it uses a different pricing model compared to when you're managing the infrastructure yourself. For example, when you run Presto on EC2, you pay an EC2 instance cost per hour regardless of how much you use Presto. With Athena, you pay only for the queries by paying for the amount of data read from S3 per query.

Amazon provides several clients to interact with and submit queries to, Athena and therefore Presto. You can use the AWS command-line interface, the REST API, the AWS Web Console, and applications using the JDBC driver, ODBC driver, or the Athena SDK.

Now, after all these benefits, it is important to understand that from a user's perspective Athena is *not a managed Presto deployment* at all. Here are a few important aspects that distinguish it from a Presto deployment:

- No use of other data sources within AWS or outside possible
- No access to the Presto Web UI for query details and other aspects
- No control of Presto itself, including version, configuration, or infrastructure

Let's look at a short example of using Athena with the iris data set: see "Iris Data Set" on page 15. After creating a database and table and importing the data into Athena, you are ready to use it.

You can run a query with Athena by using the AWS CLI with the `start-query-execution` Athena command. You need to use two arguments:

`--query-string`

    This is the query you want to execute in Athena.

`--cli-input-json`

    This is a JSON structure that provides additional context to Athena. In this case we specify the database in the Glue Data Catalog where the `iris` table exists and we specify where to write the query results.

 All queries run in Athena write the results to a location in S3. This is configurable in the AWS Web Console and can be specified when using the client tools for Athena.

We are using this JSON structure, stored in *athena-input.json*, for running this query:

```
{
    "QueryExecutionContext": {
        "Database": "iris"
    },
    "ResultConfiguration": {
        "OutputLocation": "s3://presto-book-examples/results/"
    }
}
```

Let's run the Athena query with the AWS CLI:

```
$ aws athena start-query-execution \
--cli-input-json file://athena-input.json \
--query-string 'SELECT species, AVG(petal_length_cm), MAX(petal_length_cm), \
  MIN(petal_length_cm) FROM iris GROUP BY species'

{
    "QueryExecutionId": "7e2a9640-04aa-4ae4-8e88-bd6fe4d9c289"
}
```

Because Athena executes the query asynchronously, the call to `start-query-execution` returns a query execution ID. It can be used to get the status of the query execution, or the results, when it is complete. The results are stored in S3 in CSV format:

```
$ aws athena get-query-execution \
  --query-execution-id 7e2a9640-04aa-4ae4-8e88-bd6fe4d9c289

{
    "QueryExecution": {
    ...
        "ResultConfiguration": {
            "OutputLocation":
                "s3://...7e2a9640-04aa-4ae4-8e88-bd6fe4d9c289.csv"
        },
```

```
    ...
}
$ aws s3 cp --quiet
s3://.../7e2a9640-04aa-4ae4-8e88-bd6fe4d9c289.csv
/dev/stdout


"species","_col1","_col2","_col3"
"virginica","5.552","6.9","4.5"
"versicolor","4.26","5.1","3.0"
"setosa","1.464","1.9","1.0"
```

You can also use the `aws athena get-query-results` command to retrieve the results in a JSON structure format. Another choice is the open source AthenaCLI (*https://github.com/dbcli/athenacli*).

Stop and think about this. Without *any* infrastructure to manage, you can simply point a command-line interface and run SQL queries on data files stored in S3. Without Athena and Glue, you have to deploy and manage the infrastructure and software to execute SQL queries on the data.

And without Presto, you have to somehow ingest and format the data into a database for SQL processing.

The combination of Athena and Glue make for an incredible, powerful tool to use. And the feature allowing you to use standard SQL against the S3 data is all powered by Presto.

This quick introduction does not provide a comprehensive look at Athena, but it gives you a glimpse at how Presto is being used in the industry and how much other offerings can differ from Presto.

Using Athena satisfies various needs and comes with specific restrictions and characteristics. For example, Athena imposes limits for larger, longer-running queries.

Since you are paying for the processed data volume rather than the infrastructure to run the software, costing is also very different. Each time you run a query, you pay for the data processed. Depending on your usage patterns, this can be cheaper or more expensive. Specifically, you can preprocess the data in S3 to use formats such as Parquet and ORC as well as compression to reduce query cost. Of course, the preprocessing comes at a price as well, so you have to try to optimize for overall cost.

Many other platforms use Presto in a similar, hidden fashion that can provide tremendous power to the user and the provider of these platforms. If you are looking for control and flexibility, running your own Presto deployment remains a powerful option.

Starburst Enterprise Presto

Starburst (http://starburstdata.com) is the enterprise company behind the Presto open source project and a major sponsor of the project and the Presto Software Foundation. The founding team members at Starburst were early contributors to Presto at Teradata, and they started Starburst to focus on continuing the success of Presto in the enterprise. The founders of the Presto open source project from Facebook joined Starburst in 2019, and Starburst has become one of the largest contributors and committers to the Presto project.

Starburst offers commercial support for an enhanced distribution of Presto, with additional enterprise features such as more connectors, performance and other improvements to existing connectors, a management console for clusters and catalogs, and enhanced security features.

Starburst Enterprise Presto includes support for deployments anywhere. Bare-metal servers, virtual machines, and containers on Kubernetes are all supported. You can run Presto on all major cloud providers and cloud platforms, on-premises systems, and hybrid cloud infrastructure.

Other Integration Examples

You've only scratched the surface of tools and platforms that can be used with Presto or that integrate Presto. Just the list of business intelligence and reporting tools known to be used with Presto is extensive. It at least includes the following:

- Apache Superset
- DBeaver
- HeidiSQL
- Hue
- Information Builders
- Jupyter Notebook
- Looker
- MicroStrategy
- Microsoft Power BI
- Mode
- Redash
- SAP Business Objects
- SQuirreL SQL Client

- Tableau
- Toad

Data platforms, hosting platforms, and other systems using or supporting Presto include the following:

- AWS and Amazon Elastic Kubernetes Service
- Amazon EMR
- Google Kubernetes Engine
- Microsoft Azure Kubernetes Service
- Microsoft Azure HDInsight
- Qlik
- Qubole
- Red Hat OpenShift

Many of these users and vendors, such as Qubole, contribute to the project.

Custom Integrations

Presto is an open platform for integrating your own tools. The open source community around Presto is actively creating and improving integrations.

Simple integrations use the Presto CLI or the Presto JDBC driver. More advanced integrations use the HTTP-based protocol exposed by the Presto coordinator for executing queries and more. The JDBC driver simply wraps this protocol; other wrappers for platforms including R and Python are available and linked on the Presto website.

Many organizations take it to the next level by implementing new plug-ins for Presto. These plug-ins can add features such as connectors to other data sources, event listeners, access controls, custom types, and user-defined functions to use in query statements. The Presto documentation contains a useful developer guide that can be your first resource. And don't forget to reach out to the community for help and feedback; see "Community Chat" on page 13.

Conclusion

Isn't it amazing how widely used Presto is, and how many different tools you can integrate with Presto to create some very powerful solutions? We only scratched the surface in our tour here.

Lots of other tools are available and are used regularly, thanks to the availability of the JDBC driver, ODBC drivers, the Presto CLI, and integrations built on top of these and other extensions.

Whatever commercial or open source business intelligence reporting tool, or data analytics platform, you prefer to use, be sure to investigate the availability of Presto support or integration. Similarly, it is often worth understanding if Presto is used under the hood in your toolchain. This might give you a better view of potential improvements or expansions to your usage, or even a migration to first-class, direct usage of Presto.

Depending on the level of ownership of the Presto deployment, you have access to customizations, updates, and expansions as desired, or you can lean back and let your provider manage Presto for you as part of the integration. Find your own ideal fit and enjoy the benefits of Presto. And if you manage your own Presto deployment, make sure to learn more about it in Chapter 12.

Presto in Production

After learning about and installing Presto, first as a simple exploratory setup in Chapter 2 and then as a deployment in Chapter 5, you now get to dive into further details. After all, simply installing and configuring a cluster is a very different task from keeping it up and running day and night, with different users and changing data sources and entirely separate usage.

In this chapter you are therefore getting to explore other aspects you need to learn about in order to be a successful operator of your Presto clusters.

Monitoring with the Presto Web UI

As discussed in "Presto Web UI" on page 35, the Presto Web UI is accessible on every Presto cluster coordinator and can be used to inspect and monitor the Presto cluster and processed queries. The detailed information provided can be used to better understand and tune the Presto system overall as well as individual queries.

> The Presto Web UI exposes information from the Presto system tables, discussed in "Presto System Tables" on page 134.

When you first navigate to the Presto Web UI address, you see the main dashboard shown in Figure 12-1. It displays Presto cluster information in the top section and a list of queries in the bottom section.

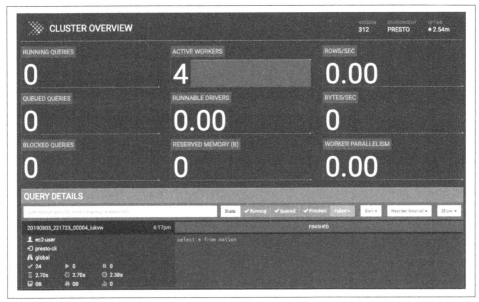

Figure 12-1. Presto Web UI main dashboard

Cluster-Level Details

Let's first discuss the Presto cluster information:

Running Queries

The total number of queries currently running in the Presto cluster. This accounts for all users. For example, if Alice is running two queries and Bob is running five queries, the total number in this box shows seven queries.

Queued Queries

The total number of queued queries for the Presto cluster for all users. Queued queries are waiting for the coordinator to schedule them, based on the resource group configuration.

Blocked Queries

The number of blocked queries in the cluster. A blocked query is unable to be processed due to missing available splits or other resources. You learn more about query states in the next sections.

Active Workers

The number of active worker nodes in the cluster. Any worker nodes added or removed, manually or by auto scaling, are registered in the discovery service, and the displayed number is updated accordingly.

Runnable Drivers

The average number of runnable drivers in the cluster, as described in Chapter 4.

Reserved Memory

The total amount of reserved memory in bytes in Presto.

Rows/Sec

The total number of rows processed per second across all queries running in the cluster.

Bytes/Sec

The total number of bytes processed per second across all queries running in the cluster.

Worker Parallelism

The total amount of worker parallelism, which is the total amount of thread CPU time across all workers, across all queries running in the cluster.

Query List

The bottom section of the Presto Web UI dashboard lists the recently run queries. An example screenshot is displayed in Figure 12-2. The number of available queries in this history list depends on the Presto cluster configuration.

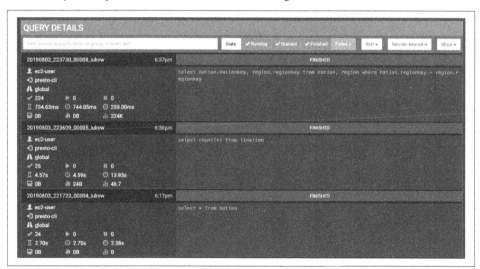

Figure 12-2. List of queries in the Presto Web UI

Above the list itself, controls are available to select the criteria that determine which queries are listed. This allows you to locate specific queries even when a cluster is very busy and runs dozens or hundreds of queries.

The input field allows you to type criteria text to use in order to search for a specific query. The criteria include the username of the query initiator, the query source, the query ID, a resource group, or even the SQL text of the query and the query state.

The *State* filter beside the text input field allows you to include or exclude queries based on the state of the query—running, queued, finished, and failed queries. Failed queries can be further detailed to include or exclude for specific failure reasons—internal, external, resource, and user errors.

Controls on the left allow you to determine the sort order of the displayed queries, the timing of the reordering when the data changed, and the maximum number of queries to show.

Each row underneath the query criteria represents a single query. The left column in the row displays information about the query. The right column displays the SQL text and the state of the query. An example of the query summary is available in Figure 12-3.

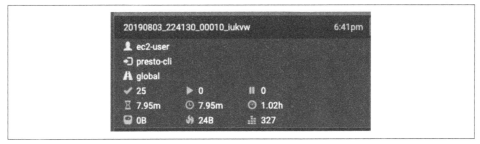

Figure 12-3. Information for a specific query in the Presto Web UI

Let's take a closer look at the query details. Each query has the same information for each query run. The text at the top left is the query ID. In this example, the value is 20190803_224130_00010_iukvw. Looking closer, you may notice that the date and time (UTC) make up the beginning of the ID using the format YYYYMMDD_HHMMSS. The latter half is an incremental counter for the query. Counter value 00010 simply means it was the 10th query run since the coordinator started. The final piece, iukvw, is a random identifier for the coordinator. Both this random identifier and the counter value are reset if the coordinator is restarted. The time on the top right is the local time when the query was run.

The next three values in the example—ec2-user, presto-cli, and global—represent the end user running the query, the source of the query, and the resource group used to run the query. In this example, the user is the default ec2-user, and we were using the presto-cli to submit the query. If you specify the --user flag when running the Presto CLI, the value changes to what you specified. The source may also be something other than presto-cli; for example, it may display presto-jdbc when an application connects to Presto with the JDBC driver. The client can also set it to any desired value with the `--source` flag for the Presto CLI, or JDBC connection string property.

The grid of values below is not well labeled in the Presto Web UI, but it contains some important information about the query, as explained in Table 12-1.

Table 12-1. Grid of values for a specific query

Completed Splits: The number of completed splits for the query. The example shows 25 completed splits. At the beginning of query execution, this value is 0. It increases during query execution as splits complete.	**Running Splits:** The number of running splits for the query. When the query is completed, this value is always 0. However, during execution, this number changes as splits run and complete.	**Queued Splits:** The number of queued splits for the query. When the query is completed, this value is always 0. However, during execution, this number changes as splits move between queued and run states.
Wall Time: The total wall time spent executing the query. This value continues to grow even if you're paging results.	**Total Wall Time:** This value is the same as the wall time except that it includes queued time as well. The wall time excludes any time for which the query is queued. This is the total time you'd observe, from when you submit to query to when you finish receiving results.	**CPU Time:** The total CPU time spent processing the query. This value is often larger than the wall time because parallel execution between workers and threads on workers all count separately and add up. For example, if four CPUs spend 1 second to process a query, the resulting total CPU time is 4 seconds.
Current Total Reserved Memory: The current total reserved memory used for the time of query execution. For completed queries, this value is 0.	**Peak Total Memory:** The peak total memory usage during the query execution. Certain operations during the query execution may require a lot of memory, and it is useful to know what the peak was.	**Cumulative User Memory:** The cumulative user memory used throughout the query processing. This does not mean all the memory was used at the same time. It's the cumulative amount of memory.

 Many of the icons and values in the Presto Web UI have pop-up tooltips that are visible if you hover your mouse cursor over the image. This is helpful if you are unsure of what a particular value represents.

Next you need to learn more about the different states of query processing, displayed above the query text itself. The most common states are RUNNING, FINISHED, USER CANCELLED, or USER ERROR. The states RUNNING and FINISHED are self-explanatory and exactly what they say. USER CANCELLED means that the query was killed by the user. USER ERROR, on the other hand, signifies that the SQL query statement submitted by the user contained a syntactic or semantic error.

The BLOCKED state occurs when a query that is running becomes blocked while waiting on something such as resources or additional splits to process. Seeing a query go to and from this state is normal. However, if a query gets stuck in this state, there are many potential reasons, and this may indicate a problem with the query or the Presto cluster. If you find a query that appears to be stuck in this state, first check the memory use and configuration of the system. It may be that this query requires an unusually high amount of memory or is computationally expensive. Additionally, if the client is not retrieving the results or cannot read the results fast enough, this back pressure can put the query into a BLOCKED state.

The QUEUED state occurs when a query is started, or stopped from processing, and put into a waiting stage as part of the rules defined for resource groups. The query is simply waiting to be executed.

You may also see a query in the PLANNING state. This typically occurs for larger, complex queries that require a lot of planning and optimizations for running the query. If you see this often, and planning seems to take a noticeable amount of time for queries, you should investigate possible reasons, such as insufficient memory availability or processing power of the coordinator.

Query Details View

So far you have seen information about the Presto cluster overall and higher-level information about the queries. The Web UI offers even more details about each query. Simply click the name of the specific query, as shown in Figure 12-3, to access the Query Details view.

The Query Details view contains a lot of information about a specific query. Let's explore enough for you to feel comfortable using it.

The Query Details view is often used by Presto developers and users with in-depth knowledge of Presto. This level of sophistication requires you to be very familiar with the Presto code and internals. Checking out this view may still be useful for normal users. Over time, you learn more and acquire more expertise.

The Query Details view uses several tabs for viewing more detailed information about the Presto query. Apart from the tabs, the query ID and the state are always visible. You can see an example header of the view with the tabs in Figure 12-4.

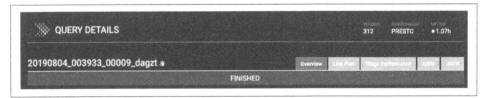

Figure 12-4. Query Details header and tabs

Overview

The Overview page includes the information visible in the Query Details section of the query list and much more detail in numerous sections:

- Session
- Execution
- Resource Utilizations Summary
- Timeline
- Query
- Prepare Query
- Stages
- Tasks

The Stages section, shown in Figure 12-5, displays information on the query stages.

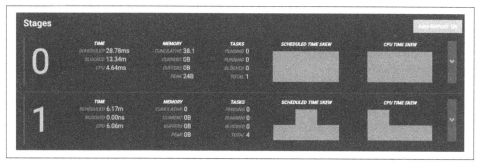

Figure 12-5. Stages section in the Overview tab of the Query Details page

This particular query was the SELECT count(*) FROM lineitem query. Because it is a simpler query, it consists of only two stages. Stage 0 is the single-task stage that runs on the coordinator and is responsible for combining the results from the tasks in stage 1 and performing the final aggregation. Stage 1 is a distributed stage that runs tasks on each of the workers. This stage is responsible for reading the data and computing the partial aggregation.

The following list explains the numerical values from the Stages section, available for each stage:

TIME—SCHEDULED
> The amount of time the stage remained scheduled before all tasks for the stage were completed.

TIME—BLOCKED
> The amount of time the stage was blocked while waiting for data.

TIME—CPU

The total amount of CPU time of the tasks in the stage.

MEMORY-CUMULATIVE

The cumulative memory used throughout the stage. This does not mean all the memory was used at the same time. It is the cumulative amount of memory used over the time of processing.

MEMORY—CURRENT

The current total reserved memory used for the stage. For completed queries, this value is 0.

MEMORY—BUFFERS

The current amout of memory consumed by data, waiting for processing.

MEMORY—PEAK

The peak total memory during the stage. Certain operations during the query execution may require a lot of memory, and it is useful to know what the peak was.

TASKS—PENDING

The number of pending tasks for the stage. When the query is completed, this value is always 0.

TASKS—RUNNING

The number of running tasks for the stage. When the query is completed, this value is always 0. During execution, the value changes as tasks run and complete.

TASKS—BLOCKED

The number of blocked tasks for the stage. When the query is completed, this value is always 0. However, during execution this number will change as tasks move between blocked and running states.

TASKS—TOTAL

The number of completed tasks for the query.

SCHEDULED TIME SKEW, CPU TIME SKEW, TASK SCHEDULED TIME, and TASK CPU TIME

These histogram charts show the distribution and changes of scheduled time, CPU time, task scheduled time, and task CPU time for multiple tasks across workers. This allows you to diagnose utilization of the workers during the execution of a longer-running, distributed query.

The section below the Stages section describes more details of the tasks, displayed in Figure 12-6.

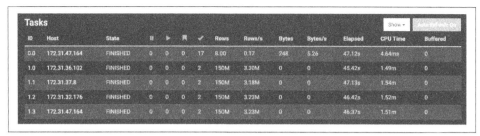

Figure 12-6. Tasks information in the Query Details page

Let's examine the values in the tasks list; take a look at Table 12-2.

Table 12-2. Description of the columns in the tasks list in Figure 12-6

Column	Description
ID	The task identifier in the format *stage-id.task-id*. For example, ID 0.0 indicates Task 0 of Stage 0, and 1.2 indicates Task 2 of Stage 1.
Host	The IP address of the worker node where the task is run.
State	The state of the task, which can be PENDING, RUNNING, or BLOCKED.
Pending Splits	The number of pending splits for the task. This value changes as the task is running and shows 0 when the task is finished.
Running Splits	The number of running splits for the task. This value changes as the task is running and shows 0 when the task is finished.
Blocked Splits	The number of blocked splits for the task. The value changes as the task is running and shows 0 when the task is finished.
Completed Splits	The number of completed splits for the task. The value changes as the task is running and equals the total number of splits run when the task is finished.
Rows	The number of rows processed in the task. This value increases as the task runs.
Rows/s	The number of rows processed per second in the task.
Bytes	The number of bytes processed in the task. This value increases as the task runs.
Bytes/s	The number of bytes processed per second in the task.
Elapsed	The total amount of elapsed wall time for the task scheduled.
CPU Time	The total amount of CPU time for the task scheduled.
Buffered	Current amount of buffered data, waiting for processing.

If you examine some of these values carefully, you'll notice how they roll up. For example, the total CPU time for all tasks in a stage equals the CPU time listed in the stage for which they belong. The total CPU time for the stages equals the amount of CPU time listed on the query CPU time.

Live Plan

The Live Plan tab allows you to view query processing performed by the Presto cluster, in real time, while it is executing. You can see an example in Figure 12-7.

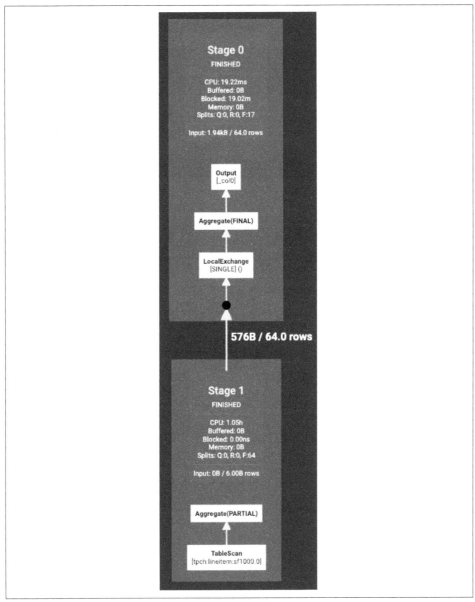

Figure 12-7. Live plan example for the count(*) query on lineitem

During query execution, the counters in the plan are updated while the query execution progresses. The values in the plan are the same as described for the Overview tab, but they are overlaid in real time on the query execution plan. Looking at this view is useful to visualize where a query is stuck or spending a lot of time, in order to diagnose or improve a performance issue.

Stage Performance

The Stage Performance view provides a detailed visualization of the stage performance after query processing is finished. An example is displayed in Figure 12-8.

The view can be thought of as a drill-down from the Live Plan view, where you can see the operator pipeline of the task within the stage. The values in the plan are the same as described for the Overview tab. Looking at this view is useful to see where a query is stuck or spending a lot of time, in order to diagnose or fix a performance issue. You can click on each individual operator to access detailed information.

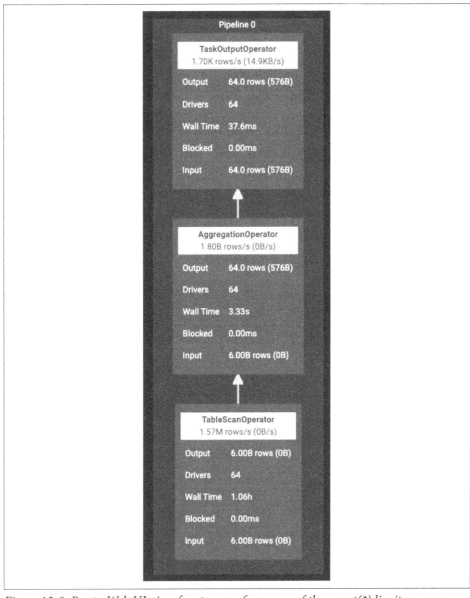

Figure 12-8. Presto Web UI view for stage performance of the count(*) lineitem query

Splits

The Splits view shows a timeline for the creation and processing of splits during the query execution.

JSON

The JSON tab provides all query detail information in JSON format. The information is updated based on the snapshot for which it is retrieved.

> Parts of the Web UI are helpful for copying lengthy strings to the system clipboard. Keep a look out for the clipboard icon. By clicking it, the associated string is copied to the system clipboard for you to paste somewhere else.

Tuning Presto SQL Queries

In "Query Planning" on page 53, you learned about the cost-based optimizer in Presto. Recall that SQL is a declarative language in which the user writes a SQL query to specify the data they want. This is unlike an imperative program. With SQL, the user does not specify how to process the data to get the result. It is left to the query planner and optimizer to determine the sequence of steps to process the data for the desired result. The sequence of steps is referred to as the *query plan*.

In most cases, the end user submitting the SQL queries can rely on Presto to plan, optimize, and execute a SQL query efficiently to get the results fast. As an end user, you should not have to worry about the details.

However, sometimes you are not getting the performance you expect, so you need to be able to tune Presto queries. You need to identify whether a specific execution is an outlier single query that is not performing well, or whether multiple queries of similar properties are not performing well.

Let's start with tuning an individual query, assuming the rest of the queries you run are fine on the system. When examining a poorly performing query, you should first look to see if the tables that the query references have data statistics. At the time of this writing, the only tables that provide data statistics to Presto are those used with the Hive connector. It is expected that additional connectors will start to provide data statistics.

```
presto:ontime> SHOW STATS FOR flights;
```

Joins in SQL are one of the most expensive operations. You need to focus on joins when tuning the performance of your query, and determine the join order by running an EXPLAIN on the query:

```
presto:ontime> EXPLAIN
               SELECT f.uniquecarrier, c.description, count(*) AS ct
               FROM postgresql.airline.carrier c,
                   hive.ontime.flights_orc f
               WHERE c.code = f.uniquecarrier
               GROUP BY f.uniquecarrier, c.description
               ORDER BY count(*) DESC
               LIMIT 10;
```

As a general rule, you want the smaller input to a join to be on the build side. This is the input to the hash join for which a hash table is built. Because the build side requires reading in the entire input and building a hash table in memory, you want this to be the smaller of the inputs. Being able to determine whether Presto got the join order correct requires some domain knowledge of the data to further investigate. For example, if you know nothing about the data, you may have to run some experimental queries to obtain additional information.

If you have determined that the join order is nonoptimal, you can override the join reordering strategy by setting a toggle to use the syntactic order of the tables listed in the SQL query. This can be configured in the *config.properties* file as the property `optimizer.join-reordering-strategy`. However, if you want to override a single query, you often want to just see the session property `join_reordering_strategy` (see "Session Information and Configuration" on page 146). The allowed values for this property are AUTOMATIC, ELIMINATE_CROSS_JOINS and NONE. Setting the value to ELIMINATE_CROSS_JOINS or NONE performs an override of the cost-based optimizer. ELIMINATE_CROSS_JOINS is a good compromise since it reorders joins only to eliminate cross joins, which is good practice, and otherwise stays with the lexical order suggested by the query author:

```
...
FROM postgresql.airline.carrier c,
hive.ontime.flights_orc f
...

...
FROM hive.ontime.flights_orc f,
postgresql.airline.carrier c
...
```

Besides join optimizations, Presto includes some heuristic-based optimizations. These optimizers are not costed and do not always result in best results. Optimizations can take advantage of the fact that Presto is a distributed query engine; aggregations are performed in parallel. This means that an aggregation can be split into multiple smaller parts that can then be distributed to multiple workers, run in parallel, and be aggregated in a final step from the partial results.

A common optimization in Presto and other SQL engines is to push partial aggregations before the join to reduce the amount of data going into the join. Using it can be configured with the `push_aggregation_through_join` property. Because the aggregation produces partial results, a final aggregation is still performed after the join. The benefit of using this optimization depends on the actual data, and the optimization can even result in a slower query. For example, if the join is highly selective, then it may be more performant to run the aggregation after the join completes. To experiment, you can simply turn this optimization off by setting the property to `false` for the current session.

Another common heuristic is to compute a partial aggregation before the final aggregation:

```
presto:ontime> EXPLAIN SELECT count(*) FROM flights_orc;
                         Query Plan
-------------------------------------------------------------------
 - Output[_col0]
        Layout: [count:bigint]
        _col0 := count
     - Aggregate(FINAL)
           Layout: [count:bigint]
           count := "count"("count_3")
        - LocalExchange[SINGLE] ()
              Layout: [count_3:bigint]
           - RemoteExchange[GATHER]
                  Layout: [count_3:bigint]
```

```
          - Aggregate(PARTIAL)
                Layout: [count_3:bigint]
                count_3 := "count"(*)
              - TableScan[hive:ontime:flights_orc]
                    Layout: []
    (1 row)
```

When this is a generally a good heuristic, the amount of memory to keep for the hash table can be tuned. For example, if the table has a lot of rows with few distinct values in the grouping keys, this optimization works well and reduces the amount of data early before being distributed over the network. However, if there are a higher number of distinct values, the size of the hash tables needs to be larger in order to reduce the amount of data. By default, the memory used for the hash table is 16 MB, but this can be adjusted by setting `task.max-partial-aggregation-memory` in the *config.properties* file. However, with too high a count of distinct group keys, the aggregation does nothing to reduce the network transfer, and it may even slow down the query.

Memory Management

Getting the memory configuration and management for your Presto cluster right is not an easy task. Many constantly changing factors influence the memory needs:

- Number of workers
- Memory of coordinator and worker
- Number and type of data sources
- Characteristics of running queries
- Number of users

For Presto, a multiuser system using a cluster of workers, resource management is a fairly challenging problem to solve. Ultimately, you have to pick a starting point and then monitor the system and adjust to the current and upcoming needs. Let's look at some details and talk about recommendations and guidelines around memory management and monitoring in Presto.

All memory management discussed applies to the JVM running the Presto server. The values are allocations within the JVMs on the workers, and the JVM configuration needs to consider the size of these values to allow allocation.

Depending on the number of concurrent queries, the JVM needs to be adjusted to a much larger value. The next example provides some insight.

All of the preceding factors combine into what we call the *workload*. Tuning the cluster's memory relies heavily on the workload being run.

For example, most query shapes contain multiple joins, aggregations, and window functions. If the query size of the workload is small, you can set lower memory limits per query and increase the concurrency—and the other way around for larger query sizes. For context, query size is a product of query shape and amount of input data. Presto provides a way to manage memory utilization across the cluster by setting certain properties at the time of deployment in *config.properties*:

- `query.max-memory-per-node`
- `query.max-total-memory-per-node`
- `query.max-memory`
- `query.max-total-memory`

Memory management in Presto is separated into two kinds of memory allocations:

User memory
  User queries such as aggregations and sorting control the user memory allocation.

System memory
  System memory allocation is based on the execution implementation by the query engine itself and includes read, write, and shuffle on buffers, table scans, and other operations.

With this separation in mind, you can examine the memory properties some more:

`query.max-memory-per-node`
  The maximum *user* memory a query can utilize on a specific worker for processing aggregations, input data allocation, etc.

`query.max-total-memory-per-node`
  The maximum allowed total of user and system memory, required to be larger than `query.max-memory-per-node`. When the memory consumed by a query in user and system allocations exceeds this limit, it is killed.

`query.max-memory`
  The maximum *user* memory a query can utilize across all workers in the cluster.

`query.max-total-memory`
  The maximum utilization of memory by a query for user and system allocations for the entire cluster, as a result necessarily greater than `query.max-memory`.

If a query ends up exceeding these limits and as a result is killed, error codes expose the reason:

- `EXCEEDED_LOCAL_MEMORY_LIMIT` means that `query.max-memory-per-node` or `query.max-total-memory-per-node` was exceeded.
- `EXCEEDED_GLOBAL_MEMORY_LIMIT` means that `query.max-memory` or `query.max-total-memory` was exceeded.

Let's look at a real-world example for a small cluster of one coordinator and ten workers and their characteristics:

- One coordinator
- Ten workers; typically workers are all identical system specifications
- Physical memory per worker: 50 GB
- Max JVM heap size configured in `-Xmx` in `jvm.config` to 38 GB
- `query.max-memory-per-node`: 13 GB
- `query.max-total-memory-per-node`: 16 GB
- `memory.heap-headroom-per-node`: 9 GB
- `query.max-memory`: 50 GB
- `query.max-total-memory`: 60 GB

Let's break these numbers down a bit more.

The total available memory on each worker is ~50 GB and we leave ~12 GB for the operating system, agents/daemons, and components running outside the JVM on the system. These systems include monitoring and other systems that allow you to manage the machine and keep it functioning well. As a result, we determine to set the JVM max heap size to 38 GB.

When query size and shape is small, concurrency can be set higher. In the preceding example, we are assuming query size and shape to be medium to large and are also accounting for data skew. `query.max-memory` is set to 50 GB, which is at the overall cluster level. While looking at `max-memory`, we also consider initial-hash-partitions; this should ideally be a number less than or equal to the number of workers.

If we set that to 8 with `max-memory` 50 GB, we get 50/8, so about 6.25 GB per worker. Looking at the local limit `max-memory-per-node` set to 13 GB, we keep some headroom for data skew by allowing two times the memory consumption per node. These numbers vary significantly based on how the data is organized and what type of queries are typically run—basically, the workload for the cluster. In addition, the infrastructure used for the cluster, such as the available machine sizes and numbers, has a big impact on the selection of the ideal configuration.

A configuration can be set to help avoid a deadlock situation: `query.low-memory-killer.policy`. This can be set to `total-reservation` or `total-reservation-on-blocked-nodes`. When set to `total-reservation`, Presto kills the largest running query on the cluster to free up resources. On the other hand, `total-reservation-on-blocked-nodes` kills the query that is utilizing the most memory on the nodes that are blocked.

As you can see from the example, you just end up making some assumptions to get started. And then you adjust based on what happens with your actual workloads.

For example, running a cluster for interactive ad hoc queries from users with a visualization tool can create many small queries. An increase of users then ends up increasing the number of queries and the concurrency of them. This typically does not require a change of the memory configuration, but just a scaling up of the number of workers in the cluster.

On the other hand, if that same cluster gets a new data source added that exposes massive amounts of data for complex queries that most likely blow the limits, you have to adjust memory.

This gets us to another point that is worth mentioning. Following the best practice recommendation, in a typical Presto cluster infrastructure setup, all workers are the same. All use the same virtual machine (VM) image or container size with identical hardware specifications. As a result, changing the memory on these workers typically means that the new value is either too large for the physical available memory, or too small to make good use of the overall system. Adjusting the memory therefore creates the need to replace all worker nodes in the cluster. Depending on your cluster infrastructure using, for example, virtual machines in a private cloud or containers in a Kubernetes cluster from a public cloud provider, this process can be more or less laborious and fast to implement.

This leads us to one last point worth mentioning here. Your assessment of the workloads can reveal that they are widely different: lots of queries are small, fast, ad hoc queries with little memory footprint, and others are massive, long-running processes with a bunch of analysis in there, maybe even using very different data sources. These workload differences indicate very different memory configuration, and even very different worker configuration and maybe even monitoring needs. In this scenario, you really should take the next step and separate the workloads by using different Presto clusters.

Task Concurrency

To improve performance for your Presto cluster, certain task-related properties may need to be adjusted from the default settings. In this section, we discuss two common properties you may have to tune. However, you can find several others in the Presto documentation. All these properties are set in the *config.properties* file:

Task worker threads

The default value is set to the number of CPUs of the machine multiplied by 2. For example, a dual hex core machine uses 2 × 6 × 2, so 24 worker threads. If you observe that all threads are being used and the CPU utilization in the machine is still low, you can try to improve CPU utilization and thus performance by increasing this number via the `task.max-worker-threads` setting. The recommendation is to slowly increment this number, as setting it too high can have a diminishing return or adverse effects due to increased memory usage and additional context switching.

Task operator concurrency

Operators such as joins and aggregations are processed in parallel by partitioning the data locally and executing the operators in parallel. For example, the data is locally partitioned on the `GROUP BY` columns, and then multiple aggregation operators are performed in parallel. The default concurrency for these parallel operations is `16`. This value can be adjusted by setting the `task.concurrency` property. If you are running many concurrent queries, the default value may result in reduced performance due to the overhead of context switching. For clusters that run only a smaller number of concurrent queries, a higher value can help increase parallelism and therefore performance.

Worker Scheduling

To improve performance of your Presto cluster, certain scheduling related properties may need to be adjusted from the default settings. You can tune three common configurations:

- Splits per task
- Splits per node
- Local scheduling

Several others are explained in the Presto documentation.

Scheduling Splits per Task and per Node

Each worker node processes a maximum number of splits. By default, the maximum number of splits processed per worker node is 100. This value can be adjusted with the `node-scheduler.max-splits-per-node` property. You may want to adjust this if you're finding that the workers have maxed out this value and are still underutilized. Increasing the value improves performance, particularly when a lot of splits exist. In addition, you can consider increasing the `node-scheduler.max-pending-splits-per-task` property. This value should not exceed `node-scheduler.max-splits-per-node`. It ensures that work is queued up when the workers finish the tasks in process.

Local Scheduling

When scheduling splits on worker nodes, the Presto scheduler uses two methods. The method to use depends on the deployment of Presto. For example, if workers run on the same machines as distributed storage, it is optimal to schedule splits on the worker nodes where the data is located. Scheduling splits where the data is not located requires the data to be transferred over the network to the worker node for processing. Therefore, you see an increase in performance when scheduling splits on the same node where the data is stored.

The default method `legacy` does not account for the data location when scheduling splits. The improved `flat` method does account for the data location when scheduling splits, and it can be used by setting `node-scheduler.network-topology`. The Presto scheduler uses 50% of the queue for scheduling local splits.

The common use case for using the flat method occurs when Presto is installed and collocated on HDFS data nodes or when using RubiX for caching (see "Performance Improvements with RubiX" on page 230). RubiX caches data from the distributed storage on the worker nodes. Therefore, scheduling local splits is advantageous.

Network Data Exchange

Another important factor affecting the performance of your Presto cluster is the network configuration and setup within the cluster and the closeness to the data sources. Presto supports network-specific properties that can be adjusted from the defaults to adopt to your specific scenario.

In addition to improving performance, sometimes other network-related issues require tuning in order for queries to perform well. Let's discuss some of the common properties you may have to tune.

Concurrency

Presto exchange clients make requests to the upstream tasks producing data. The default number of threads used by the exchange clients is 25. This value can be adjusted by setting the property `exchange.client-threads`.

Setting a larger number of threads can improve performance for larger clusters or clusters configured for high concurrency. The reason is that when more data is produced, additional concurrency to consume the data can decrease latency. Keep in mind that these additional threads increase the amount of memory needed.

Buffer Sizes

Data sent and received during the exchange is kept in buffers on the target and source sides of the exchange. The buffer sizes for each side can be adjusted independently.

On the source side, data is written by the tasks to a buffer waiting to be requested from the downstream exchange client. The default buffer size is 32 MB. It can be adjusted by setting the `sink.max-buffer-size` property. Increasing the value may increase throughput for a larger cluster.

On the target side, data is written to a buffer before it is processed by the downstream task. The default buffer size is 32 MB. It can be adjusted by setting the property `exchange.max-buffer-size`. Setting a higher value can improve query performance by allowing retrieval of more data over the network before back pressure is applied. This is especially true for larger clusters.

Tuning Java Virtual Machine

In Chapter 2, you used the configuration file *etc/jvm.config*, which contains command-line options for the JVM. The Presto launcher uses this file when starting the JVM running Presto. Compared to the earlier mentioned configuration, a more suitable configuration for production usage uses higher memory values:

```
-server
-XX:+UseG1GC
-XX:+ExplicitGCInvokesConcurrent
-XX:+ExitOnOutOfMemoryError
-XX:+UseGCOverheadLimit
-XX:+HeapDumpOnOutOfMemoryError
-XX:-UseBiasedLocking
-Djdk.attach.allowAttachSelf=true
-Xms16G
-Xmx16G
-XX:G1HeapRegionSize=32M
-XX:ReservedCodeCacheSize=512M
-Djdk.nio.maxCachedBufferSize=2000000
```

Typically you need to increase the maximum memory allocation pool for the JVM with the Xmx value, in this case, upped to 16 GB. The Xms parameter sets the initial, minimal memory allocation. The general recommendation is to set both Xmx and Xms to the same value.

In the preceding configuration example memory allocation is set to 16 GB. The actual value you use depends on the machines used by your cluster. The general recommendation is to set both the Xmx and Xms to 80% of the total memory of the system. This allows for plenty of headroom for other system processes running. Further details about the memory management of Presto and related configuration can be found in "Memory Management" on page 254.

For large Presto deployments, memory allocations of 200 GB and beyond are not uncommon.

While small processes such as monitoring can run on the same machine as Presto, it's highly discouraged to share the system with other resource-intensive software. For example, Apache Spark and Presto should not be run on the same set of hardware.

If you suspect Java garbage collection (GC) issues, you can set additional parameters to help you with debugging:

```
-XX:+PrintGCApplicationConcurrentTime
-XX:+PrintGCApplicationStoppedTime
-XX:+PrintGCCause
-XX:+PrintGCDateStamps
-XX:+PrintGCTimeStamps
-XX:+PrintGCDetails
-XX:+PrintReferenceGC
-XX:+PrintClassHistogramAfterFullGC
-XX:+PrintClassHistogramBeforeFullGC
-XX:PrintFLSStatistics=2
-XX:+PrintAdaptiveSizePolicy
-XX:+PrintSafepointStatistics
-XX:PrintSafepointStatisticsCount=1
```

These options can be helpful when troubleshooting a full GC pause. In combination with the advancements of JVM and the engineering of the Presto query engine, a GC pause should be a very rare event. If it does happen, it should be investigated. First steps to fix these issues are often an upgrade of the JVM version and the Presto version used, since both receive performance improvements regularly.

JVM and garbage collection algorithms and configuration are complex topics. Documentation on GC tuning is available from Oracle and other JVM vendors. We strongly recommend adjusting these settings in small changes in test environments, before attempting to roll them out to production systems. Also keep in mind that Presto currently requires Java 11. Older or newer JVM versions, as well as JVM versions from different vendors, can have different behavior.

Resource Groups

Resource groups are a powerful concept in Presto used to limit resource utilization on the system. The resource group configuration consists of two main pieces: the resource group properties and the selector rules.

A resource group is a named collection of properties that define available cluster resources. You can think of a resource group as a separate section in the cluster that is isolated from other resource groups. The group is defined by CPU and memory limits, concurrency limits, queuing priorities, and priority weights for selecting queued queries to run.

The selector rules, on the other hand, allow Presto to assign an incoming query request to a specific resource group.

The default resource group manager uses a file-based configuration and needs to be configured in *etc/resource-groups.properties*:

```
resource-groups.configuration-manager=file
resource-groups.config-file=etc/resource-groups.json
```

As you can see, the actual configuration uses a JSON file. The content of the file defines the resource groups as well as the selector rules. Note that the JSON file can be any path that is accessible to Presto and that resource groups need to be configured only on the coordinator:

```
{
  "rootGroups": [],
  "selectors": [],
  "cpuQuotaPeriod": ""
}
```

cpuQuotaPeriod is optional.

Let's look at the definition of two resource groups to get started:

```
"rootGroups": [
  {
    "name": "ddl",
    "maxQueued": 100,
    "hardConcurrencyLimit": 10,
    "softMemoryLimit": "10%",
```

```
    },
    {
      "name": "ad-hoc",
      "maxQueued": 50,
      "hardConcurrencyLimit": 1,
      "softMemoryLimit": "100%",
        }
]
```

The example defines two resource groups named ddl and ad-hoc. Each group has a set maximum number of concurrent queries and total amount of distributed memory limits. For the given group, if the limits are met for concurrency or memory limits, then any new query is placed in the queue. Once the total memory usage goes down or a query completes, the resource group chooses a query from the queue to schedule to run. Each group also has a maximum number of queries to queue. If this limit is reached, any new queries are rejected and the client receives an error indicating that.

In our example, the ad hoc group is designed for all queries that are not DDL queries. This group allows only one query to run concurrently, with up to 50 queries to be queued. The group has a memory limit of up to 100%, meaning it could use all the available memory to run it.

DDL queries have their own group, with the idea that these types of queries are relatively short and lightweight and should not be starved by longer-running ad hoc SQL queries. In this group, you specify that there should be no more than 10 DDL queries running concurrently, and the total amount of distributed memory used by all queries running should be no more than 10% of the Presto clusters memory. This allows a DDL query to be executed without having to wait in the ad hoc query line.

Now that the two groups are defined, you need to define the selector rules. When a new query arrives in the coordinator, it is assigned to a particular group. Let's take a look at the example:

```
"selectors": [
    {
      "queryType": "DATA_DEFINITION",
      "group": "ddl"

    },
    {
      "group": "ad-hoc"
    }
]
```

The first selector matches any query type of DATA_DEFINITION and assigns it to the ddl resource group. The second selector matches all other queries and places those queries in the ad-hoc resource group.

The order of the selectors is important because they are processed sequentially, and the first match assigns the query to the group. And in order to match, all properties specified must match. For example, if we switch the order of the selectors, then all queries including DDL are to be assigned to the ad-hoc resource group. No queries are ever assigned to the ddl resource group.

Resource Group Definition

Let's take a closer look at the following configuration properties for resource groups:

name
> The required name of the resource group, referenced by the selector rule for assignment.

maxQueued
> The required maximum number of queries queued for the group.

hardConcurrencyLimit
> The required maximum number of concurrent queries that can be running in the group.

softMemoryLimit
> The required maximum amount of distributed memory that can be used by concurrent running queries. Once this limit is reached, new queries are queued until the memory reduces. Both absolute values (GB) and percentages (%) can be used.

softCpuLimit
> The optional soft limit on the amount of CPU time that can be used within a time period as defined by the cpuQuotaPeriod property. Once this limit is reached, a penalty is applied to the running queries.

hardCpuLimit
> The optional hard limit on the amount of CPU time that can be used within a time period as defined by the cpuQuotaPeriod property. Once this limit is reached, queries are rejected until the next quota period.

schedulingPolicy
> The policy used to schedule new queries to select a query from the queue in the resource group and process it. Details are provided in the following section.

schedulingWeight
> This optional property is to be used in conjunction with schedulingPolicy.

jmxExport
> Flag to cause resource groups to be exposed via JMX. Defaults to false.

subGroups

A container for additional nested resource groups.

Scheduling Policy

The schedulingPolicy value noted in the preceding list can be configured to various values to be run in the following modes:

Fair

Setting schedulingPolicy to fair schedules queries in a first-in, first-out (FIFO) queue. If the resource group has subgroups, the subgroups with queued queries alternate.

Priority

Setting schedulingPolicy to query_priority schedules queued queries based on a managed priority queue. The priority of the query is specified by the client by using the query_priority session property (see "Session Information and Configuration" on page 146). If the resource group has subgroups, the subgroups must also specify query_priority.

Weighted

Setting schedulingPolicy to weighted_fair is used to choose the resource group subgroup to start the next query. The schedulingWeight property is used in conjunction with this: queries are chosen in proportion to the scheduling Weight of the subgroups.

Selector Rules Definition

Selector rules are required to define the group property, since it determines the resource group to which a query is assigned. It is a good practice to have the last selector in the file set to define only a group. It then acts as an explicit catchall group.

Optional properties and regular expressions can be used to refine the selector rules:

user

Matches against a username value. Regular expressions may be used to match against multiple names.

source

Matches against the source value. For example, this may be presto-cli or presto-jdbc. Regular expressions may be used.

queryType

Matches against the type of query. The available options are DATA_DEFINITION, DELETE, DESCRIBE, EXPLAIN, INSERT, and SELECT.

clientTags

Matches against the client tags specified by the client submitting the query.

To set the source or client tags from the Presto CLI, you can use the `--source` and `--client-tags` options:

```
$ presto --user mfuller --source mfuller-cli
$ presto --user mfuller --client-tags adhoc-queries
```

Conclusion

Well done! You have come a long way with Presto. In this chapter, you immersed yourself in the details of monitoring, tuning, and adjusting Presto. Of course, there is always more to learn, and typically these skills are improved with practice. Be sure to connect with other users to exchange ideas and learn from their experience and join the Presto community (see "Community Chat" on page 13).

And in Chapter 13, you get to find out what others have achieved with Presto already.

Real-World Examples

As you know from "A Brief History of Presto" on page 16, development of Presto started at Facebook. Ever since it was open sourced in 2013, its use has picked up and spread widely across a large variety of industries and companies.

In this chapter, you'll see a few key numbers and characteristics that will give you a better idea about the potential for your own use of Presto. Keep in mind that all these companies started with a smaller cluster and learned on the go. Of course, many smaller and larger companies are using Presto. The data you find here should just give you a glimpse of how your Presto use can grow.

Also keep in mind that many platforms embed Presto. These platforms don't even necessarily expose the fact that Presto is under the hood. And these platforms do not typically expose user numbers, architecture, and other characteristics.

 The cited numbers and stats in this chapter are all based on publicly available information. The book repository contains links to sources such as blog posts, presentations from conferences, slide decks, and videos (see "Book Repository" on page 15). As you read this book, the data may have become outdated or inaccurate. However, growing use of Presto and the general content gives you a good understanding of what is possible with Presto and how other users successfully deploy, run, and use it.

Deployment and Runtime Platforms

Where and how you run your Presto deployment is an important factor. It impacts everything from low-level technical requirements to high-level user-facing aspects. The technical aspects include the level of direct involvement necessary to run Presto, the tooling used, and the required operations know-how. From a user perspective, the platform influences aspects such as overall performance, speed of change, and adaptation to different requirements.

Last but not least, other aspects might influence your choice, such as use of a specific platform in your company and the expected costs. Let's see what common practices are out there.

Where does Presto run? Here are some points to consider:

- Clusters of bare-metal servers are becoming rather rare.
- Virtual machines are most commonly used now.
- Container use is moving to be the standard and is posed to overtake VMs.

As a modern, horizontally scaling application, Presto can be found running in all the common deployment platforms:

- Private on-premises clouds such as OpenStack
- Various public cloud providers including AWS, GCP, and Azure
- Mixed deployments

Here are some examples:

- Lyft runs Presto on AWS.
- Pinterest runs Presto on AWS.
- Twitter runs Presto on a mix of on-premises cloud and GCP.

The industry trend of moving to containers and Kubernetes has made an impact on Presto deployments. An increasing number of Presto clusters run in that environment and in the related public offerings for Kubernetes use.

Cluster Sizing

The size of some Presto clusters running at some of the larger users is truly astounding, even in this age of big data everywhere. Presto has proven to handle scale in production for many years now.

So far, we've mostly talked about running a Presto cluster and have hinted at the fact that you can run multiple clusters.

When you look at real-world use of Presto at scale, you find that most large deployments use multiple clusters. Various approaches to using multiple clusters are available in terms of Presto configuration, data sources, and user access:

- Identical
- Different
- Mixed

Here are some advantages you can gain from identical clusters:

- Using a load-balancer enables you to upgrade the cluster without visible downtime for your users.
- Coordinator failures do not take the system offline.
- Horizontal scaling for higher cluster performance can include use of multiple runtime platforms; for example, you might use an internal Kubernetes cluster at all times and an additional cluster running in a Kubernetes offering from a public cloud provider for peak usage.

Separate clusters, on the other hand, allow you to clearly separate different use cases and tune the cluster in various aspects:

- Available data sources
- Location of cluster near data sources
- Different users and access rights
- Tuning of worker and coordinator configuration for different use cases—for example, adhoc interactive queries compared to long-running batch jobs

The following companies are known to run several Presto clusters:

- Comcast
- Facebook
- Lyft
- Pinterest
- Twitter

Most other organizations mentioned in this chapter probably also use multiple clusters. We just did not find a public reference to that fact.

After having a look at the number of clusters, let's look at the number of nodes. There are some truly massive deployments and others at a scale you might end up reaching yourself in the future:

- Facebook: more than 10,000 nodes across multiple clusters
- FINRA: more than 120 nodes
- LinkedIn: more than 500 nodes
- Lyft: more than 400 nodes, 100–150 nodes per cluster
- Netflix: more than 300 nodes
- Twitter: more than 2,000 nodes
- Wayfair: 300 nodes
- Yahoo! Japan: more than 600 nodes

Hadoop/Hive Migration Use Case

Probably still the most common use case to adopt Presto is the migration from Hive to allow compliant and performant SQL access to the data in HDFS. This includes the desire to query not just HDFS, but also Amazon S3, S3-compatible systems, and many other distributed storage systems.

This first use case for Presto is often the springboard to wide adoption of Presto for other uses.

Companies using Presto to expose data in these systems include Comcast, Facebook, LinkedIn, Twitter, Netflix, and Pinterest. And here is a small selection of numbers:

- Facebook: 300 PB
- FINRA: more than 4 PB
- Lyft: more than 20 PB
- Netflix: more than 100 PB

Other Data Sources

Beyond the typical Hadoop/Hive/distributed storage use case, Presto adoption is gaining ground for many other data sources. These include use of the connectors available from the Presto project but also have significant use of other data sources with third-party connectors from other open source projects, internal development, and commercial vendors:

Here are some examples:

- Comcast: Apache Cassandra, Microsoft SQL Server, MongoDB, Oracle, Teradata
- Facebook: MySQL
- Insight: Elasticsearch, Apache Kafka, Snowflake
- Wayfair: MemSQL, Microsoft SQL Server, Vertica

Users and Traffic

Last but not least, you can learn a bit more about the users of these Presto deployments and the number of queries they typically cause. Users include business analysts working on dashboards and ad hoc queries, developers mining log files and test results, and many others.

Here is a small selection of user counts:

- Arm Treasure Data: approximately 3,500 users
- Facebook: more than 1,000 employees daily
- FINRA: more than 200 users
- LinkedIn: approximately 1,000 users
- Lyft: approximately 1,500 users
- Pinterest: more than 1,000 monthly active users
- Wayfair: more than 200 users

Queries often range from very small, simple queries to large, complex analysis queries or even ETL-type workloads. As such, the number of queries tells only part of the story, although you nevertheless learn about the scale Presto operates:

- Arm Treasure Data: approximately 600,000 queries per day
- Facebook: more than 30,000 queries per day
- LinkedIn: more than 200,000 queries per day
- Lyft: more than 100,000 queries per day and more than 1.5 million queries per month
- Pinterest: more than 400,000 queries per month
- Slack: more than 20,000 queries per day
- Twitter: more than 20,000 queries per day
- Wayfair: up to 180,000 queries per month

Conclusion

What a wide range of scale and usage! As you can see, Presto is widely used across various industries. As a beginning user, you can feel confident that Presto scales with your demands and is ready to take on the load and the work that you expect it to process.

We encourage you to learn more about Presto from the various resources, and especially to also join the Presto community and any community events.

Conclusion

Whatever your motivation for learning more about Presto, you've truly made great progress. Congratulations!

We covered everything from an overview of Presto and its use cases, to installing and running a Presto cluster. You've gained an understanding of the architecture of Presto and how it plans and runs queries.

You learned about various connectors that allow you to hook up distributed storage systems, RDBMSs, and many other data sources. The standard SQL support of Presto then allows you to query them all, and even to combine the data from different sources in one query, a federated query.

And you found out more about the next steps required to run Presto in production at scale as well as about some real-world Presto use in other organizations.

We hope you are excited to put your knowledge into practice, and we look forward to hearing from you on the community chat; remember to look up the details in "Community Chat" on page 13.

Thanks for reading, and welcome to the Presto community!

Matt, Manfred, and Martin

Index

clusters
    coordinators and workers structure, 43-44
    creating, 73-76, 82
    encrypting communication within, 216-217,
      223
    installing Presto, 79-80
    K8s, 82, 268
    kerberized Hadoop cluster authentication,
      226
    Presto Web UI to view details, 240
    separation for security, 227
    sizing of, 83, 268-270
    Web UI cluster-level details, 240
codepoint() function, 176, 179
collection data types, 149
column family (Accumulo), 114
columns
    identifying those used in query, 54
    indexing on, 117
    JMX connector, 105
    modifying a table, 144
    SHOW COLUMNS statement, 132
    statistics, 65
    subquery restrictions, 166
column_mapping table property, 114
command-line interface (see CLI)
community chat, Presto resource, 13
complex data types
    collections as, 149
    unnesting, 182-182
concat() function, 176
concatenating operator (||), 176
concurrency, adjusting, 260
config.properties file
    access control, 201, 212, 216, 222
    cluster installation, 79, 219
    deployment configuration, 73
    installing Presto, 22
    session, 146
configuration
    connectors, 86
    initial configuration file setup, 22
    JVM, 77
    logging, 75-76
    node, 76, 80
    RPM, 82
    for security, 224-225
    server, 73-76
    session, 146

workers, 79
connecting to Presto, 32
connector.name property, 23, 24, 86
connectors, 85-108
    access control, 207-208
    Apache Cassandra, 117
    authentication, 92, 224
    black hole connector, 106
    catalogs and, 136
    configuration, 86
    data type support variations, 147
    defined, 37
    document store, 104, 120-122
    ETL, 129
    examples, 109-129
    federated queries, 122-129
    Hbase with Phoenix, 109
    Hive (see Hive connector)
    in Presto architecture, 47-48
    JMX connector, 104-106
    key-value store, 110-117
    mapping tables, 139
    memory connector, 107
    non-relational data sources, 104
    parallel, 90
    Phoenix, 109
    PostgreSQL RDBMS example, 87-92
    purpose, 85
    sources for other, 107
    specific command support differences, 132
    streaming system, 118-120
    table limitations with, 144
    TPC-H and TPC-DS connectors, 92
constant functions, 176
containers, as Presto deployment platforms, 19,
    268
coordinator property, 74, 79
coordinators, 45
    client-to-coordinator security, 211-215,
      219-221, 222
    configuration of, 79
    data source access control, 224-225
    defined, 44
    HTTPS access to, 202, 210-213, 216
    query execution role of, 49
correlated subquery, 165
cos() function, 175
cosh() function, 175
cost-based optimizer (see CBO)

count() function, 187
CQL (Cassandra Query Language), 117
CREATE SCHEMA statement, 137
CREATE TABLE AS (CTAS) query, 100, 119,
   143
CREATE TABLE AS SELECT, 100
CREATE TABLE AS statement, 118
CREATE TABLE statement, 103, 140
cross join elimination, 58
CrossJoin operation, 55, 58, 160
CSR (certificate signing request), 217
CTAS (CREATE TABLE AS) query, 100, 119,
   143
CUBE operation, 162
current_date function, 186
current_time function, 186
current_timetimestamp or now() function, 186
current_timezone() function, 186
custom Presto integrations, 236

D

dashboard, Presto Web UI, 240-242
data definition language (see DDL)
data lake, Presto as query engine for, 11
data location SPI, 50
data sources, 23
   (see also connectors)
   access control, 224-225
   adding, 23
   catalogs as applicable to all, 86
   non-relational, 104
   Presto as single access point for, 8
data storage (see storage)
data types, 147-154
   Boolean, 147
   collection, 149
   fixed-precision, 147
   floating point, 147
   integer, 147
   string, 148
   temporal, 150-153
   type casting, 154
   unnesting, 182-182
data warehouse
   access point use case, 8
   overview, 4
   Presto as virtual, 10
data, moving with Presto, 11
databases

access control for individual, 224
   distributed, 104, 110, 117
   Elasticsearch document store, 120-122
   memory connectors as, 107
   RDBMS, 87-92, 123-129, 145, 195
date and time functions and operators, 184-186
DATE data type, 150
DAY TO SECOND interval, 153, 184
DBeaver, 30, 31
DDL (data definition language), 97
DEBUG log level, 75
--debug option, 28
DECIMAL data type, 147
degrees() function, 174
DELETE privilege, 207
DELETE statement, 167
deleting data from a table, 167
deleting tables, 144
deployment considerations, 73-84
   cloud installation, 82
   cluster installation, 79-80
   configuration details, 73
   JVM configuration, 77
   launcher, 77-78
   logging, 75-76
   node configuration, 76, 79
   platforms for, 19, 267
   RPM installation, 80-82
   server configuration, 73-76
   sizing the cluster, 83, 268-270
DESCRIBE command, 121, 195
different separated clusters, 269
directory structure, installing, 81
discovery service, 44, 46, 74
discovery-server.enabled property, 74
discovery-uri property, 79
discovery.uri property, 75
DISTINCT keyword, 162, 191
distinguished name, 202
distributed join strategy, 69
distributed query plan, 50-52
distributed storage systems, 104
   (see also HDFS)
   Cassandra, 104, 110, 117
   federated queries, 123-129
division operator (/), 174
Docker container, 19
document stores, 104, 120-122
DOUBLE data type, 147

is_json_scalar() function, 183

J

Java keystores and truststores, 213-215
Java pattern syntax, 180
Java Virtual Machine (see JVM)
java.security.krb5.conf JVM property, 225
JavaScript Object Notation (see JSON)
JDBC (Java Database Connectivity) driver,
    30-34, 91, 110
JDK (Java Development Kit), 214
JMX (Java Management Extensions), 104-106
jmxExport property, resource groups, 264
JOIN statement, 160
joins
    broadcast vs. distributed, 68
    cost of, 64
    CrossJoin operation, 55, 57, 58, 160
    enumeration of, 68
    hash join, 64, 68
    lateral join decorrelation, 60
    performance tuning queries, 252-253
    semi-join (IN) decorrelation, 61
JSON (JavaScript Object Notation), 119, 183,
    251, 262
JSON data type, 149
json_array_contains() function, 183
json_array_length() function, 183
JVM (Java Virtual Machine)
    configuration with/in, 77
    installing Presto, 20
    JDBC in, 30
    memory management, 254
    performance tuning, 260-262
jvm.config file, 23, 77, 225, 260

K

K8s (Kubernetes), 82, 268
kadmin command, 223
Kafka, 118-120
KDC (Kerberos key distribution center), 222
Kerberos authentication protocol, 222, 226
Kerberos principal, 206, 223
key-value data stores, connector to, 110-117
keyspaces, Cassandra, 118
keystore.jks file, 214
keystores, Java, 213-215, 216, 220
keytab file, Kerberos, 222, 223
keytool command, 214

krb5.conf file, 225
Kubernetes (see K8s)

L

lambda expressions, 192
lateral join decorrelation, 60
LateralJoin operation, 56
launcher script, 77-78, 81
launcher.log file, 75
LDAP (Lightweight Directory Access Protocol),
    200-203
LDAPS (secure LDAP), 202
length() function, 176
less than (<) operator, 171
less than or equal operator (<=), 171
lib directory, installing Presto, 21
licensing, Presto, 14
LIKE clause, 132, 142
LIKE operator (SQL), 179
LIMIT clause, 58, 159
Linux, Presto installation on, 80-82
Live Plan tab, Query Details section, 248
ln() function, 174
loading data
    Accumulo, 115
    Hive connector, 100
local worker scheduling, 259
localtime function, 186
localtimestamp function, 186
log() function, 174
log.properties file, 75
log10() function, 174
log2() function, 174
logging, 75-76
logical operators, 172
logical query plan, 50
lower() function, 176
lpad() function, 176
ltrim() function, 176

M

machine learning (use case), 12
managed tables, Hive, 97-98
map aggregate functions, 187-189
MAP data type, 149
mapping tables, 114, 139
MapReduce programs, 94
maps and strings, 177
map_agg() function, 187, 188

OR operator, 172
ORDER BY clause, 53, 58, 159, 187
ordering tables with cost-based optimizer, 65
OutOfMemoryError, node.jvm.config file, 77
output formats, 30
OVER() window function, 191

P

pages, relationship to stages, 51
pagination of queries, 28
parallel connectors, 90
parsing
    data and time data types, 150
    queries, 54
partial aggregations, 59, 253
PARTITION BY statement, 191
_partition_id (Kafka), 119
_partition_offset (Kafka), 119
partitioned_by clause, 99
partitions
    creating, 101
    for nested arrays in ANALYZE, 71
    Hive connector, 98-100
    table statistics, 67
--password, 203
password authentication, 201-203
password property, JDBC driver, 33
password-authenticator.name property, 202
password-authenticator.properties file, 201, 203
performance
    cluster, 83
    Presto's design for, 5
    RubiX for improvements in, 230
performance tuning, 251-266
    JVM, 260-262
    memory management, 254-257
    network data exchange, 259
    query, 85, 251-254
    query tuning, 134
    resource groups, 262-266
    task concurrency, 258
    worker scheduling, 258
Phoenix, 109
pi() constant, 176
pipeline, 51
plugins directory, installing Presto, 21
plugins, function in Presto, 48
PostgreSQL, 70, 87-92, 123-128
power() function, 174

pre-aggregation, 59
predicate pushdown, 57, 115-117, 128
PREPARE statement, 194
prepared statements, 194
Presto
    advantages of, 4-12
    architecture, 43-72
    big data approach of, 3
    CLI, 19, 25-30, 80
    client libraries, 35
    configuration, 22
    connectors, 85-108
    history, 16
    installation, 19-22, 80-82
    integrations, 229-236
    JDBC driver, 30-34, 91, 110
    ODBC and, 35
    performance tuning, 251-266
    production-ready deployment, 73-84
    resources, 12-16
    running, 24, 80
    security, 199-227
    SQL in, 36-40, 131-167, 169-195
    uninstall for, 82
    use cases, 7-12
    Web UI, 35, 134, 239-251
Presto ANALYZE command, 70
Presto CLI (see CLI)
Presto Software Foundation, 12, 17
prestosql organization, 14
privileges, access, 203, 207-208
probe side of joined table, 64
Programming Hive (O'Reilly), 94
protocols
    Kerberos authentication, 222, 226
    LDAP, 201-203
    rubix://, 230
public-private key pairs, encryption, 212
publish-subscribe (pub/sub) systems, 118
push_aggregation_through_join property, 253
push_partial_aggregation_through_join session
    toggle, 59
Python, 21, 77

Q

quantified subquery, 166
queries
    analysis of, 54
    Apache Superset, 229

X

X.509 certificate, 214

Y

YARN, 94

YEAR TO MONTH interval, 152, 184

Z

ZooKeeper, 110, 111, 113

About the Authors

Matt Fuller is a cofounder at Starburst, the Presto Company. Prior to founding Starburst, Matt was a director of engineering at Teradata, where he worked to build the new Center for Hadoop division within the company. As a major part of this, Matt worked to bring Presto to the enterprise market. Matt has managed a team contributing to the open source Presto project since 2015 and led the internal Presto product roadmap. Starburst was later formed from this team at Teradata.

Before Teradata, Matt was an early engineer at Vertica, where he co-built the query optimizer. Matt is also a Very Large Databases (VLDB) published author and has US patents in the database management systems space.

Manfred Moser is a community advocate, writer, trainer, and software engineer at Starburst. Manfred has a long history of developing and advocating open source software. He is an Apache Maven committer, wrote the Hudson book and others, and continues to be active in the open source community and his projects. He is a seasoned trainer and conference presenter for CI/CD, Cloud Native, Agile, and other software development tools and processes, having trained well over 20,000 developers for companies including Walmart Labs, Sonatype, and Telus.

His database background includes designing databases and related applications in the RDBMS space and working as business intelligence consultant wrangling thousands of lines of SQL by hand. He is glad he can use Presto now, and is spreading the word about how great Presto is.

Martin Traverso is the cofounder of the Presto Software Foundation and CTO at Starburst. Prior to Starburst, Martin worked as a software engineer at Facebook where he saw the need for fast interactive SQL analytics. Martin and three other engineers worked to create what became Presto. Martin led the Presto development team, and in the spring of 2013 Presto was rolled out into production, later made open source in the fall of 2013. Since then, Presto has gained wide adoption both internal and external to Facebook.

Prior to Facebook, Martin was an architect at Proofpoint and Ning, where he led development and architecture design of numerous complex enterprise and social network applications.

Colophon

The animal on the cover of *Presto: The Definitive Guide* is a southern leopard frog (*Lithobates sphenocephalus*). These true frogs are native to eastern North America. They range from New York south to Florida, and as far west as eastern Oklahoma, and can be found near freshwater habitats and moist vegetation in the summer months.

The southern leopard frog is known for its distinctive round spots all along its green and brown body. It has a pointed head and notably long legs, as well as prominent ridges of raised skin that extend from behind its eyes to its hips. The female southern leopard frog tends to be larger than the male frog, though both lack digital pads on their toes.

These nocturnal frogs primarily eat small, invertebrate insects and spiders, though larger southern leopard frogs will occasionally eat small vertebrates as well. During the day, they hide in vegetation near bodies of fresh water. They often hop in sequences of three, and jump notably high. They congregate in large colonies during breeding season, but are otherwise solitary animals. They have paired vocal sacs, which are spherical when inflated, and have a short, guttural trill, often compared to the clucks of a chicken. The call of the southern leopard frog travels farther than that of many of its related species.

The southern leopard frog is prey to birds, river otters, some fish, and many snake species, and is collected in large numbers for use as bait, scientific research, and teaching. Though their conservation status is "Least Concern" at the time of writing, many of the animals on O'Reilly covers are endangered; all of them are important to the world.

The cover illustration is by Jose Marzan, based on a black and white engraving from *Wood's Natural History*. The cover fonts are Gilroy Semibold and Guardian Sans. The text font is Adobe Minion Pro; the heading font is Adobe Myriad Condensed; and the code font is Dalton Maag's Ubuntu Mono.

CPSIA information can be obtained
at www.ICGtesting.com
Printed in the USA
BVHW022335280420
R10777700001B/R107777PG578151BVX1B/1

9 781492 044277